THE GREAT BIG
COOKIE BOOK

THE GREAT BIG COOKIE BOOK

Over 200 Scrumptious
Recipes for Cookie Lovers

Barbara Grunes

and

Virgina Van Vynckt

PRIMA PUBLISHING

PRIMA PUBLISHING and colophon are registered trademarks of Prima Communications, Inc.

Library of Congress Cataloging-in-Publication Data

Grunes, Barbara.
The great big cookie book : over 200 scrumptious recipes for cookie lovers / Barbara Grunes and Virginia Van Vynckt.
    p. cm.
Includes index.
ISBN 0-7615-0674-8
1. Cookies. I. Van Vynckt, Virginia. II. Title.
TX772.V28 1996
641.8'654—dc20   96-29089
                                                                 CIP

96 97 98 99 00 01 AA 10 9 8 7 6 5 4 3 2 1
Printed in the United States of America

How to Order

Single copies may be ordered from Prima Publishing, P.O. Box 1260BK, Rocklin, CA 95677; telephone (916) 632-4400. Quantity discounts are also available. On your letterhead, include information concerning the intended use of the books and the number of books you wish to purchase.

Visit us online at http://www.primapublishing.com

To our favorite cookie eaters,

Lian and Steven, and Avi, Evelyn, Natalie,

Suzie, Marissa, Claire and Noah

Contents

Acknowledgments

We would be utterly lost without our patient and knowledgeable testers: Alan Magiera, Vicki Cave, Richard and Michele Chroman, Christine Feldman, and Cathy Hogan. An extra thank you goes to Vicki for finding the time and energy to make a Christmas barn scene in the middle of spring.

We are indebted to Claire Smith, a wonderful baker and cook and a generous soul, for sharing some marvelous cookie ideas with us.

We would also like to thank our agent, Martha Casselman, for sticking with this idea, and our editors, Jennifer Basye Sander and Dallas Middaugh, for seeing this project through.

Thanks also to Ginny Thiersch of the Sugar Association for clarifying the differences among sugars, and to Linda Braun and Elisa D'Amico-Maloberti of the American Egg Board for teaching us a new way to make royal icing.

Introduction

Cookies conjure memories of the best moments of childhood—just think of a chewy oatmeal cookie with a glass of cold milk. They also can play the sophisticate at adult gatherings—think of biscotti dipped into a good Italian dessert wine.

The word *cookie* comes from the Dutch *koekje*, but these sweet finger foods have traveled into cultures around the world. By their nature and numbers (nobody makes just one), cookies are sociable, the ideal partners to coffee, tea, milk, and friendly chatter.

When we decided to write *The Great Big Cookie Book*, we hoped to provide cookie lovers everywhere with the ultimate cookbook. We asked ourselves, "If we could have only one cookie book on our shelves, what would be in it?"

First, we decided, we would want plenty of recipes for great-tasting cookies—both basic and new—in various shapes, forms ,and textures, but always with plenty of flavor. We would want crisp chocolate cookies that taste like chocolate. Chewy spice cookies that taste spicy. Tender pecan cookies that burst with the flavor of sweet pecans. Shortbread that tastes like the freshest butter.

Second, we would want the book to answer the questions we might have about one cookie in particular or about cookie baking in general. How soft should the butter be? Is the brown sugar dark or light? Is there anything unusual about the texture of the dough? Do you grease the pans or leave them ungreased? Can this cookie be mailed across the country, or stored in the freezer?

Third, we would want some recipes that depart a bit from the usual—cookies made with whole grain flours, cookies with a tropical accent or with more offbeat spices, cookies made with herbs, and savory cookies (or crackers, if you prefer) that make good companions to a dessert of fruit and cheese. On the other hand, some cookies have become classics for good reason, which is why you will find a substantial number of variations on such old favorites as chocolate chip cookies, brownies, oatmeal cookies, peanut butter cookies, and basic butter cookies.

Fourth, we would want the book to emphasize the fun things you can do with cookies. Those of you with an artsy-craftsy bent will find plenty to keep you busy, from an elaborate Barnyard at Christmas (pages 269–279) gingerbread project to cookies shaped or painted in unique ways.

Whether you have been baking for thirty years or thirty days, you are bound to find plenty of favorites among the two hundred thoroughly tested recipes that follow. In addition to the basic drop, rolled, and bar cookies, we've included ethnic and international favorites, and cookies for special occasions year-round. Sprinkled throughout the chapters, you will also encounter signature cookies—the treats that are or were the specialties of some of our favorite bakers.

Occasionally we've stretched the definition of cookies to include tidbits that some might consider pastries or fritters or even cakes. We have included a chapter on bars, which, in the Midwest at least, are considered a whole different category from cookies. Indeed, bars often walk that line between cookies and cakes or pastries.

To make your cookie-baking journey more pleasant, we have also included plenty of basic information: baking tips and techniques, a guide to choosing equipment, a glossary of ingredients, and mail-order sources for harder-to-find provisions.

We hope you enjoy our creations as much as we do. Happy baking!

Barbara Grunes
Virginia Van Vynckt

HOW TO MAKE GREAT COOKIES

*M*uffins are forgiving. Cakes are fussy. Cookies lie somewhere between. The factors that affect cake baking—temperature of the butter and eggs, accuracy in measuring ingredients, amounts and types of leavening, oven temperature, altitude, humidity—affect cookies as well, but to a lesser extent.

With a little attention to detail, anybody can make great cookies.

Basic Techniques

How you mix up a cookie dough affects its texture, flavor, and baking qualities. In general, we divide preparation of cookie doughs into five methods.

Creaming method

The *creaming* method, common to most of the cookies in this book, calls for beating the fat and sugar together thoroughly, then adding eggs (if any) and flavorings, then dry ingredients. Thanks to electric mixers, which make the task easy, most modern cookie recipes call for this method. For most cookies, you'll want to cream the fat, alone or with the sugar, for a good two minutes or so, scraping down the sides of the bowl as necessary. The thorough beating works air into the dough and results in a lighter cookie.

For thin, crisp, fragile cookies, cream the butter and sugar for a shorter time—about a minute.

One-Stage method

You'll see the *one-stage* method in older American recipes and in many recipes from other countries. Basically, it means you combine all the ingredients at once, rather than in distinctly separate stages. The one-stage method dates to when most home bakers stirred or kneaded doughs by hand. After all, who has the patience to cream butter by hand for two minutes? We rarely use it because adding ingredients in stages makes it easier to incorporate them completely.

If you're in a hurry, the one-stage method works fine for chewy cookies such as oatmeal or chocolate chips, and for thin, rich cookies with few ingredients.

Pastry method

When you make cookies by the *pastry* method, you start by combining the dry ingredients, then work in the fat and liquid. This method, familiar to anyone who has made a pie crust, produces flaky, melt-in-the-mouth cookies. It's important to use a light touch; overworking the dough will produce leathery cookies.

For best results, use the food processor to make pastry. It cuts in the fat uniformly and quickly, without overheating the dough. If you don't have a food processor, use a pastry blender or two knives to cut in the fat. (For more on equipment, see chapter 9.)

Some experienced pastry makers also use their fingertips to quickly rub the fat into the flour. Rub the fat and flour together in short, quick motions and try to avoid overheating and overworking the dough.

Sponge method

To make cookies by the *sponge method,* you begin by beating the eggs and sugar together on medium to high speed until the mixture is thick and pale lemon–colored. You then add the fat, if any, and the dry ingredients. As the name implies, cookies made this way—madeleines are a classic example—resemble miniature sponge cakes.

The secret to making good sponge cookies is to thoroughly beat the eggs and sugar until the mixture falls off the beater in sheets. This will take a good two to five minutes, depending on your mixer. The rest of the ingredients are then gently folded in so that you do not deflate the beaten eggs.

Meringue method

The *meringue method* resembles the sponge method, except that you beat only the egg whites. For egg whites to beat properly, the bowl and beaters must be completely clean, free of even traces of grease. (To make sure, we wash the bowl and beaters in hot soapy water, rinse them in hot water mixed with a little white vinegar, then dry them off with a fresh towel.)

Meringue recipes often call for the addition of an acid, usually cream of tartar; this is optional, but helps change the proteins in the egg whites so that they whip more easily. Beat the egg whites on high speed just until they begin to go from being foamy to having soft peaks, then gradually beat in the sugar and flavorings. Never overbeat meringue; it should stand in stiff peaks, but look very glossy. If it looks dry, you have overbeaten it and it's best to start over.

No matter which method of mixing a cookie calls for, there's a step-by-step way to ensure success:

1. Make sure ingredients are at the proper temperature. For some cookies, the butter should be cold; for others it should be soft. The temperature of the eggs can also affect how cookies turn out. Eggs whip to a greater volume when they are at room temperature.

2. Preheat the oven at least 15 minutes before you're ready to bake the cookies.

    By the way, you should check your oven periodically with an oven thermometer to make sure it's keeping the proper temperature. If it runs too hot or too cool, you may want to call for repairs—or at least adjust for the difference in recipes.

3. Prepare the pans properly. Recipes call for using greased or ungreased cookie sheets, depending on the type of cookie. Greasing the sheet makes the cookies spread slightly more, and is essential for stickier cookies. Cookies with a large proportion of butter or those that are meant to hold a more rounded shape often are baked on ungreased sheets.

    Sticky cookies such as meringues may require lining the pan with foil or parchment, or spraying it, then dusting lightly with flour.

4. Have all the ingredients ready and measured before you start the recipe. For a guide to measuring individual ingredients, see chapter 9. Unless the dough requires standing or chilling, you should also turn the oven on and prepare the pans before you start to mix the dough.

    If the recipe calls for butter at room temperature, cut it into chunks so it is easier to cream. Now is also the time to separate eggs into yolks and whites.

If the cookie requires that you beat egg whites to make a meringue, make sure the bowl and beaters are scrupulously clean and that the egg whites are at room temperature.

5. If you're mixing the dough by hand or with a portable mixer, combine the dry ingredients before proceeding with the recipe. Usually you don't have to sift dry ingredients for cookies, which are not intended to be as light as cakes. You do need to incorporate the leavenings throughout the dry ingredients, however, so that you don't end up with the baking soda clumped up in one part of the dough. We usually put the dry ingredients in a bowl, whisk them together thoroughly with a fork or a balloon whisk (do not use a regular stirring whisk, which will send flour flying), then stir them into the batter. If the baking soda is lumpy, rub it through your fingers first.

   If flour and salt are the only dry ingredients, you can add the salt to the dough with the sugar, egg, or flavorings, then stir in the flour.

   If you have a stand mixer that leaves your hands free for other tasks, you can measure and whisk together the dry ingredients while the mixer creams the butter and sugar (or beats the eggs).

6. Unless otherwise stated, beat in any eggs one at a time, on medium speed. Beat just for about 30 seconds, until well combined, scraping down the sides of the bowl. The batter will often look curdled at this stage. This is the point at which you add extracts and other flavorings, such as grated orange zest.

7. Do not overbeat the dough after adding the dry ingredients; overworking the gluten (proteins) in the flour results in a tougher, chewier cookie. In most recipes, you stir in the flour and other dry ingredients just enough to make sure they're well incorporated. Stir in the dry ingredients with a wooden spoon. If you have a heavy-duty mixer, you can stir them in on the lowest speed. (Many hand mixers will labor mightily under the stress of mixing heavy doughs.) For really stiff doughs, it's easiest to knead in flour, raisins, and nuts briefly by hand.

   To fold ingredients such as chopped nuts into meringue or sponge-based batters, use a rubber spatula, cutting down the sides of the bowl to the bottom, then lifting the batter in a folding motion. We've also found that a balloon whisk works fairly well for folding. Whichever utensil you use, be gentle.

8. Here's where the bad news comes in: If you're tempted to taste a bit of the dough at this point, don't—at least not if it has eggs in it.

Because of a very small but real risk of salmonella, eating any-thing that contains raw eggs is a bad idea. This is especially true for young children, pregnant women, and people with illnesses that have compromised the immune system.

The good news is, there's no reason not to filch a taste of non-egg doughs. (You may, however, want to keep those from your children as well, so that they do not get in the habit of tast-ing raw doughs.)

9. Always put the cookie dough on cool cookie sheets. If the cookie sheet you want to use is still hot or warm, pick it up with potholders and run it under cold water in the sink until it cools down, then dry off completely.

10. Make the cookies an even size and thickness, and leave enough space between them. If you don't, some of them will burn be-fore others are baked through. Unless otherwise noted in the recipe, cookies should be placed at least 1½ inches apart on the cookie sheets.

11. Bake cookies one panful at a time (unless you have a larger-than-normal oven) on the center rack, and rotate sheets from front to back about halfway through the baking time. Cookies on one side of the pan invariably brown faster. Rotating the pans helps them bake evenly.

12. Set the stove timer and stick around while the cookies bake. Be-cause most cookies require such short baking times, only a cou-ple of minutes stands between a cookie that's half raw and one that's burnt to a crisp.

13. Remember that cookies continue to bake after they're removed from the oven. Soft or fragile cookies benefit from sitting on the cookie sheets a minute or two after they come out of the oven, so that they firm up. Other cookies will brown too much if they are not removed quickly to wire racks. Use a thin, metal, flex-ible spatula (a pancake turner) to transfer cookies.

14. Store cookies properly. Some cookies should be kept in airtight tins; others will get soggy if kept that way. For information on freezing cookies, see page 7.

Altitude and Humidity

The terrain may not be flat on Colorado's Front Range, where Virginia lives, but the cookies are. It was not possible for us to test every recipe at various altitudes, but we did discover some general "rules" about cookies and altitude. For example, leavened drop cookies and cakelike bars are most vulnerable to the low atmospheric pressure at high altitudes. Although they may spread a little more than they do at sea level, rolled and refrigerator cookies are little affected by altitude. Chewy cookies such as chocolate chips may need a bit more liquid and flour at altitudes above 5,000 feet or so.

In the introductions to several of the chapters, we provide general guidelines on producing good cookies of a given type at a given altitude. And on several of the cookies that seemed especially affected by altitude when we tested them, we give tips for adjusting the recipes.

Humidity also affects cookies, drying them out or making them chewier than usual. Meringue-based cookies will not work properly on a humid day—they absorb wetness from the air and turn gummy, rather than crisp.

If you live in a desert-dry climate, on the other hand, the atmosphere will suck moisture from cookies. That's good news for crisp meringues, bad news for chocolate chip cookies. In fact, all but the most buttery cookies will dry out in a day or two, even in airtight tins. If you won't be eating them quickly, it's best to wrap them well and pop them into the freezer.

Chilling and Freezing Dough

One of the joys of cookies is that you rarely have to bake them all at once. You can cover the bowl tightly and keep many cookie doughs in the refrigerator for several hours, or even a day or two. In fact, many doughs require chilling before they can be molded or rolled. Softer doughs (such as chocolate chip cookies) should be removed from the refrigerator about 30 minutes before you plan to use them, so they have time to soften up.

Butter-rich doughs that contain little or no leavening and no eggs (such as many rolled or refrigerator cookies) will hold even longer in the refrigerator if tightly wrapped. We've held such doughs for as long as a week.

Doughs that are rich in butter (or other fat) and that do not contain a lot of leavening also can be wrapped tightly and frozen for up to two weeks. Thaw in the refrigerator, then let stand at room temperature until pliable.

Egg-based cookie doughs, such as meringues or sponges, should be treated like cake batter and baked immediately. Doughs that contain a fairly large amount of leavening, especially baking soda, can be refrigerated briefly, but are best used within a couple of hours.

Storing Cookies

How you store cookies depends on whether they're soft, crisp, or in between. Most cookies keep well in either airtight containers or cookie jars; our recipes give storing instructions.

There are two storage rules that apply to all cookies. The first is to make sure cookies are completely cool before storing them. If you don't, the steam from the warm cookies will turn the whole batch soggy.

The second rule is to not store cookies of different types together. They'll absorb flavors from each other, and the moisture from soft cookies will soften crisp cookies.

Freezing Cookies

Theoretically, you can pop cookies into airtight containers and freeze them for six months. In real life, we find that six weeks is a better estimate. Cookies grow stale and pick up "off" flavors in the freezer. Rich butter cookies stay freshest longest, and can be frozen for two to three months if they're kept in airtight tins.

Soft, cakelike cookies, sticky bars, and many filled cookies do not freeze well. Cookies that have chocolate glazes, buttercream icings, or other potentially sticky toppings should be frozen in single layers on cookie sheets, then put into tins with waxed paper between layers.

Mailing Cookies

Some cookies are simply too fragile, too sticky, or too perishable to be shipped across the country or the world to your cousin Agatha.

To mail cookies, first wrap any softer cookies or bars (such as brownies) individually in plastic wrap. If mailing a few cookies of the same variety, put them in a small tin or box. Place a sheet of waxed paper over the cookies, then fill any spaces between and above the cookies solidly with crushed or shredded paper or plastic bubble wrap.

When we mail an assortment of various cookies, we put them in paper cupcake liners, which we arrange in flat tins. Again, pack the spaces well with shredded paper or bubble wrap.

The tin or box should then go into either a larger box or a padded mailing bag. Cushion the cookie tin or box by filling all the nooks and crannies in the mailing box or bag with shredded or crumpled paper, ungreased popped popcorn, or foam packing peanuts.

Needless to say, you should use a mailing service that will get the cookies to their destination within two or three days—fourth-class mail doesn't cut it here. If you're mailing them overseas (to, say, military personnel), choose cookies that are sturdy and high enough in fat or liquid to stay reasonably fresh for a couple of weeks. Good candidates are oatmeal cookies, hermits, molasses cookies, and sturdy slice-and-bake or rolled cookies. If you're shipping cookies a long distance or in the summer, skip any that have chocolate chips or glazes; the chocolate will melt in warm temperatures.

Using the Recipes

In our recipes, "room temperature" refers to butter that is still cool enough to hold its shape, but can easily be cut with a butter knife. *Softened* butter means butter that is soft enough to be whipped, but not yet melted.

Unless otherwise indicated, all-purpose flour refers to bleached flour, although in most cases you can substitute unbleached flour. In recipes that specifically call for unbleached flour, do not substitute bleached.

Unless otherwise specified, an *egg* refers to a large egg.

We define a *soft* dough as one that is very sticky; the typical chocolate chip cookie dough is a good example. A *stiff* dough is one that holds in a ball and cleans the sides of the mixer bowl. A *medium* dough falls somewhere between; it is not overly sticky, but is not firm enough to clean the bowl. A *crumbly* dough doesn't hold together in a ball, but is scattered in pieces.

Chopped nuts refers to nuts in fairly small pieces, say, between ⅛ and ¼ inch. *Coarsely chopped* is closer to ¼ inch. *Finely chopped* is one step above ground.

The *yield* given for each cookie is, of course, just an average. You may get a slightly larger or smaller yield, depending on how you size the cookies.

Tips alert you to anything special you need to know about this cookie, as well as ways to vary it to suit your taste.

We also suggest the best way to store each cookie. An *airtight container* refers to a tightly sealed canister, cookie tin, or similar container. A *covered container* would be a cookie jar or other container that keeps air directly off the cookies, but is not airtight. Filled or sticky cookies often call for being stored loosely wrapped on a plate. This keeps them from turning into a gooey mess.

We've also included advice on whether a cookie should be mailed or not. A *no* means the cookie is too fragile, too soft or sticky, or is likely to go stale quickly.

DROP COOKIES

It's no surprise that many of America's favorite cookies are drop cookies—oatmeal, chocolate chip, peanut butter, and the buttermilk cookies Grandma used to serve with a glass of cold milk. We're a nation that loves convenience, and drop cookies are convenient. Most require little or no chilling, shaping, or filling. You just mix up the dough, drop it from a spoon or roll it into balls, and bake.

Drop cookies also radiate a homey appeal. With their clean, smooth contours and precise sizes, supermarket and bakery cookies cannot match the rough-hewn charm of homemade drop cookies, no two of which are alike.

Although most drop cookies are a cinch to make, there are a few "rules" to keep in mind. When a recipe calls for dropping dough by the teaspoonful or tablespoonful, it refers to measuring spoons, not your silverware. Using a measuring spoon helps keep cookies more evenly sized. Use a second spoon, a butter knife, or a mini-spatula to push the dough from the spoon. You also can buy cookie scoops, which look like ice cream scoops, only smaller. They work quite well.

Some recipes call for rolling the dough into balls, so that the finished cookie is more uniformly round. Pay attention to the size we specify if you expect to get the same yield; a one-inch ball of dough may be smaller than you think it is. (See fig. 1.1.) If the dough is too soft and sticks to your hands, refrigerate it for 10 to 15 minutes before rolling it. Although rolling the dough into balls gives the cookies a more even shape, it is optional. You can always drop the dough from a spoon.

Since drop cookies spread during baking, it's important not to crowd them. Leave at least one-and-a-half inches between mounds of dough.

At altitudes of 5,000 feet and above, drop cookies that contain a lot of leavening may flatten too much, crack on top, and get tough during

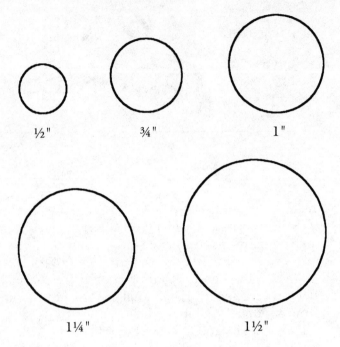

½"   ¾"   1"

1¼"   1½"

Figure 1.1

baking. If you live at high altitude, bake a test batch of four or five cookies to see if the recipe needs adjustment. If the cookies seem too chewy and heavy, increase the oven temperature by 25 degrees and bake for the same length of time. Or, decrease the amount of baking powder, baking soda, or cream of tartar by one-fourth to three-fourths teaspoon (the higher you live, the more leavening you should subtract). A third alternative is to add another one to four tablespoons of flour to the dough, plus one-half tablespoon water for each tablespoon of flour.

For a few of the cookies that are especially affected by altitude, we've provided high-altitude baking tips after the recipe.

Soft Orange Frosted Cookies

Yield
26 cookies

½ cup (1 stick) unsalted butter, at room temperature
⅓ cup confectioners' sugar
1 egg
1½ cups all-purpose flour
½ cup cornstarch
¾ teaspoon baking powder
¼ teaspoon salt
About ½ cup fresh orange juice
1 teaspoon orange extract
Orange Frosting (page 283)

Preheat oven to 350 degrees. Lightly grease or spray cookie sheets.

Cream butter and sugar on medium speed until very light, about 5 minutes. Beat in egg. Whisk together flour, cornstarch, baking powder, and salt; add to batter. Stir in enough orange juice to make a soft dough. Mix in orange extract.

Drop dough by tablespoonfuls onto cookie sheets 3 inches apart. Press cookies lightly with a fork to flatten them slightly.

Bake in the center of the oven for 10 to 12 minutes, or until the cookies are firm to the touch and golden brown on bottom. Remove to wire racks to cool.

Spread Orange Frosting on cooled cookies. Let frosting set before serving.

Tip: Cookies are soft but will firm up as they stand.

Store: In an airtight container

Freeze: Yes. Place on a cookie sheet in a single layer and freeze until frosting is hard, then place in an airtight tin and return to the freezer.

Mail: Yes

Soft Brown Sugar Cookies with Burnt Butter Icing

Yield
40 cookies

½ cup (1 stick) unsalted butter, at room temperature
1½ cups packed dark brown sugar
2 eggs
1 teaspoon vanilla extract
2½ cups all-purpose flour
½ teaspoon baking powder
1 teaspoon baking soda
¼ teaspoon salt
1 cup plain low-fat yogurt
Burnt Butter Icing (page 285)

Cream butter and sugar on medium speed until light. Blend in eggs, one at a time, mixing well after each addition. Stir in vanilla.

In a separate bowl, whisk together flour, baking powder, baking soda, and salt. Add flour mixture to batter, alternately with yogurt, to make a smooth dough. Cover lightly and refrigerate for 1 hour.

Preheat oven to 350 degrees. Lightly grease or spray cookie sheets.

Drop batter by tablespoonfuls onto cookie sheets, spacing cookies 2 inches apart. With the help of a second spoon, shape cookies into rounded forms.

Bake cookies for 15 minutes, or until firm to the touch and golden brown on the bottom. Let stand on cookie sheets for 2 minutes, then remove to wire racks to cool.

When cool, lightly frost cookies with Burnt Butter Icing. Let icing set before serving.

Store: In single layers on plates, wrapped with foil. These are best served within a day of baking.

Freeze: No

Mail: No

Grandma Chamberlin's Buttermilk Nutmeg Cookies

Yield
60 cookies
(with chopped
nuts or raisins)

Virginia's maternal grandmother frequently made these classic drop cookies for her children, and then her grandchildren. Virginia's mother continued the tradition, and now Virginia makes them for her daughter as well.

½ cup (1 stick) unsalted butter, softened
½ cup vegetable shortening
2 cups sugar
2 eggs
1 cup buttermilk or sour milk (see Tip)
4 cups flour
2 teaspoons baking powder
1 teaspoon baking soda
½ teaspoon salt
1 to 1½ teaspoons ground nutmeg, to taste
1 cup chopped pecans or raisins (optional)
Pecan halves

Preheat oven to 375 degrees. Lightly grease or spray cookie sheets.

Cream butter, shortening, and sugar on medium speed until light. Beat in eggs and buttermilk. Whisk together flour, baking power, soda, salt, and nutmeg; stir into mixture to make a very soft dough. Stir in chopped pecans or raisins if desired.

Drop by tablespoonfuls onto baking sheets. Put a pecan half in the center of each cookie before baking. Bake in the center of the oven for 10 minutes, or until lightly browned on edges.

Tip: If you do not have buttermilk, you can make sour milk by putting 1 tablespoon vinegar or lemon juice in a measuring cup; add enough skim or 1% milk to make 1 cup. Let stand 5 minutes.

High altitude: These cookies baked fine at 5,000 feet. At altitudes above that, you may have to decrease the baking powder to 1½ to 1¾ teaspoons.

Store: In a covered (not airtight) container. Cookies have the best texture when served fresh from the oven.

Freeze: Yes

Mail: Yes

New York Black and Whites

Yield
20 cookies

¾ cup vegetable shortening, at room temperature
1½ cups sugar
2 eggs
1 cup buttermilk
3 cups cake flour
1 teaspoon baking soda
1 teaspoon baking powder
¼ teaspoon salt
1 teaspoon vanilla extract

Chocolate frosting:

½ cup (1 stick) unsalted butter, at room temperature
⅓ cup buttermilk
⅓ cup unsweetened cocoa
3 cups confectioners' sugar
1 teaspoon vanilla extract
½ teaspoon chocolate extract

Vanilla frosting:

½ cup (1 stick) unsalted butter, at room temperature, cut in chunks
3 cups confectioners' sugar
1½ teaspoons vanilla extract
2 to 4 tablespoons milk or cream, as necessary to provide a smooth spreadable consistency

Preheat oven to 375 degrees. Lightly grease or spray cookie sheets.

Cream shortening and sugar on medium speed until creamy and light, about 2 minutes. Add remaining ingredients and continue blending until combined. Dough will be soft.

Using a ¼ cup measure, scoop out a scant cupful (about 3 tablespoonfuls) of batter. Using a spoon or small plastic spatula, scrape out batter and shape into a circle on cookie sheet. With back of the spoon or spatula, flatten cookie slightly. Set cookies about 2 inches apart.

Bake cookies in the center of the oven for 12 to 15 minutes or until cookies feel firm and a tester inserted into the center of a cookie comes out dry. Remove cookies to a wire rack and cool completely.

While cookies are baking, prepare the frostings. To prepare the chocolate frosting, cream butter with an electric mixer or food processor until smooth. Add remaining ingredients and beat or process only until frosting is smooth and spreadable.

To prepare vanilla frosting, use the same procedure.

Spread half of each cookie with chocolate frosting and the other half with vanilla frosting. Return cookies to the rack. Let frosting set before serving or storing.

Tip: These cookies are large, about 3 to 3½ inches in diameter. You can make smaller ones by cutting the amount of dough in half for each cookie.

Store: Individually wrapped with plastic wrap. Place on a plate and wrap with foil, or store in an airtight container.

Freeze: Yes. Freeze unfrosted and frost before serving. Or, place in a single layer on a cookie sheet and freeze until frosting is hard, then place in an airtight tin and return to the freezer.

Mail: Yes; pack individually.

Chocolate Buttermilk Cookies

Yield
44 cookies

½ cup (1 stick) unsalted butter, at room temperature
1 cup packed light brown sugar
1 egg
1 teaspoon vanilla extract
2 ounces unsweetened chocolate, melted and cooled
2 cups all-purpose flour
½ teaspoon baking soda
¼ teaspoon salt
½ teaspoon ground cinnamon
½ cup buttermilk
¾ cup chopped pecans, preferably toasted
Chocolate Buttermilk Frosting (page 284)

Preheat oven to 350 degrees. Lightly grease or spray cookie sheets.

Cream butter and sugar until light, about 2 minutes. Beat in egg, vanilla, and cooled chocolate until well blended. Whisk together flour, baking soda, salt, and cinnamon; stir into batter. Blend in buttermilk and pecans to make a stiff dough.

Drop dough by teaspoonfuls onto cookie sheets, spacing cookies about 1½ inches apart. With your fingers, pat dough to smooth out any rough spots.

Bake in the center of the oven for 12 to 14 minutes, until cookies are firm to the touch and golden brown on the bottom. Remove cookies to wire racks to cool.

While cookies are cooling, prepare the frosting. Frost the cooled cookies. Let frosting set before serving.

Tip: To make these cookies look like turtles, cut 22 extra pecan halves in half and insert at one end of each cookie before baking to make a "head." Cut 12 pecan halves in quarters and use these pieces for "tails." Use additional small pecan pieces for legs.

Store: In an airtight container

Freeze: Yes. Freeze unfrosted and frost before serving. Or, place on a cookie sheet in a single layer and freeze until frosting is hard, then place in an airtight tin and return to the freezer.

Mail: Yes

Great Pumpkin Cookies

Yield
6 jumbo (6- to
7-inch) cookies

1 cup (2 sticks) unsalted butter or margarine, at room temperature
⅓ cup granulated sugar
½ cup plus 2 tablespoons packed dark brown sugar
1 cup canned pumpkin
1 egg
1 teaspoon vanilla extract
2 cups all-purpose flour
1 teaspoon baking soda
1 teaspoon baking powder
¾ teaspoon ground cinnamon
¼ teaspoon ground allspice
⅛ teaspoon ground nutmeg
1 cup dark raisins

Preheat oven to 350 degrees. Lightly grease or spray cookie sheets.

Cream butter and both sugars on medium speed until light, about 2 to 3 minutes. Stir in pumpkin, egg, and vanilla. Whisk together flour, baking soda, baking powder, and spices. Stir into batter to make a medium dough. Stir in raisins.

Use flour or butter to "draw" 6- to 7-inch circles on cookie sheets, leaving 1½ to 2 inches between circles. Using a ½-cup measure, scoop out a heaping ½ cup of dough and set it in the center of the circle. Using the back of a tablespoon, smooth out the batter in a circular motion to about 4 to 5 inches in diameter.

Bake the cookies in the center of the oven for 15 to 18 minutes, or until firm. Remove cookies from the oven and let cool on cookie sheets for 5 minutes, then remove to wire racks to cool completely.

Tips: You can frost the cookies with Orange Frosting (page 283). You can also pipe a greeting or a jack-o'-lantern face on the plain or frosted cookies with decorator's gel or icing.

Store: Individually wrapped, in an airtight container

Freeze: Yes

Mail: No; they grow stale too quickly.

Sour Cream Tangerine Cookies

Yield
55 to 60
cookies

½ cup (1 stick) unsalted butter, at room temperature
1½ cups sugar
2 eggs
¾ teaspoon orange extract
3 tablespoons grated tangerine zest or orange zest
1 cup sour cream
2½ cups all-purpose flour
1 teaspoon baking soda
½ teaspoon salt
Sugar for sprinkling (optional)
Enough sliced almonds to put 1 on each cookie

Preheat oven to 375 degrees. Lightly grease or spray cookie sheets.

Cream butter and sugar on medium speed until light, about 2 minutes. Beat in eggs, orange extract, and tangerine zest. Mix in sour cream. Whisk together flour, baking soda, and salt. Stir into batter to make a soft dough.

Drop dough by scant tablespoonfuls onto cookie sheets, using a second spoon to help push batter onto sheets. Space cookies about 2 inches apart. If desired, sprinkle each cookie with sugar. Insert an almond slice decoratively in the center of each cookie. Bake cookies in the middle of the oven for 14 to 15 minutes, or until golden on the bottom and still soft on the top. Let cool 2 minutes on cookie sheets, then remove to wire racks to cool completely.

Store: On a plate, wrapped with foil. Use waxed paper between layers.
Freeze: Yes
Mail: Yes

Snickerdoodles

Yield
48 cookies

These crackled, cinnamon-scented sugar cookies were a favorite of late-nineteenth-century "Hoosier" poet James Whitcomb Riley, and are served to tourists every year on October 7, his birthday, at his home in Greenfield, Indiana.

½ cup (1 stick) unsalted butter, at room temperature
½ cup vegetable shortening, at room temperature
1½ cups sugar
2 eggs
2⅔ cups all-purpose flour
2 teaspoons cream of tartar
1 teaspoon baking soda
½ teaspoon salt
2 tablespoons sugar mixed with 1 tablespoon ground cinnamon

Preheat oven to 375 degrees. Spray or lightly grease baking sheets.

Cream butter and shortening with 1½ cups sugar on medium speed until light and fluffy, about 2 minutes. Beat in eggs, one at a time. Whisk together flour, cream of tartar, baking soda, and salt. On low speed, beat into egg mixture until well blended.

Pinch off pieces of dough and roll into 1-inch balls. (If dough is too soft to handle, refrigerate for 15 to 30 minutes.) Roll in cinnamon sugar. Place on prepared baking sheets, leaving at least 1½ inches between cookies.

Bake for 10 to 12 minutes, until cookies are golden, flattened, and crackled on top. Remove to wire racks to cool.

High altitude: Decrease cream of tartar to 1½ teaspoons.
Store: In an airtight container
Freeze: Yes
Mail: Yes

Spicy Molasses Crinkles

Yield
24 cookies

Most of the food served in Virginia's dorm at Indiana University all those years ago was not what you would call memorable. One exception was a delightfully spicy, chewy molasses cookie. Memories of it inspired this recipe, which has become one of Virginia's greatest baking hits.

¾ cup (1½ sticks) unsalted butter, at room temperature
⅓ cup packed dark brown sugar
½ cup granulated sugar
½ cup unsulphured dark molasses
1 egg
1 teaspoon vanilla extract
2⅓ cups all-purpose flour
½ teaspoon salt
2 teaspoons baking soda
2 teaspoons ground cinnamon
1¾ teaspoons ground ginger
½ teaspoon ground allspice
Coarse or granulated sugar (optional)

Preheat oven to 350 degrees. Lightly grease or spray cookie sheets.

Cream butter and both sugars on medium speed until fluffy and light, about 2 to 3 minutes.

Beat in molasses, egg, and vanilla. Whisk together flour, salt, baking soda, and spices. Mix into dough until well blended. Dough should be fairly soft, but not too sticky to handle. If it is too sticky, refrigerate it for 15 minutes.

Pinch off pieces of dough and roll into 1¼-inch balls. If desired, roll cookies in coarse or granulated sugar. Place on cookie sheets at least 2 inches apart.

Bake for 10 to 12 minutes. Cookies will puff up, then flatten. Cookies are done when tops look crackled and are dry around the edges; the cookies should still be soft in the center. Let cool on cookie sheets for 5 minutes, then remove to wire racks to finish cooling.

Tip: When cookies rise rapidly in the oven, then collapse, the surface gets pulled apart, resulting in crinkly tops. That's why crinkly cookies such as snickerdoodles and molasses cookies contain so much leavening.

High altitude: Increase the amount of flour to 2½ cups; reduce the amount of baking soda to 1½ teaspoons.

Store: In a covered (not airtight) container

Freeze: Yes

Mail: Yes

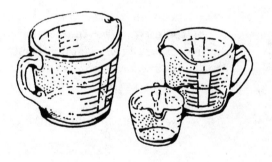

Classic Buttery Chocolate Chip Cookies

Yield
**54 cookies
(with nuts)**

1¼ cups (2½ sticks) unsalted butter, at room temperature
1 cup packed light brown sugar
½ cup granulated sugar
2 eggs
2½ teaspoons vanilla extract
2½ cups plus 1 tablespoon all-purpose flour
1 teaspoon baking soda
¾ teaspoon salt
12 ounces semisweet chocolate chips
1 cup coarsely chopped walnuts or pecans (optional)

Preheat oven to 375 degrees. Lightly grease or spray cookie sheets.

Cream butter and sugars on medium speed until well blended and smooth. Beat in eggs and vanilla.

Whisk together flour, baking soda, and salt. Add to butter-egg mixture and stir in to make a soft dough. Stir in chocolate chips and nuts.

Drop mixture by rounded tablespoonfuls onto baking sheets. Bake in the center of the oven for about 9 to 10 minutes, or until golden on the edges and bottoms. Let cool on baking sheets for a minute, then remove to racks to cool completely.

Store: In an airtight container
Freeze: Yes
Mail: Yes

Everything-but-the-Kitchen-Sink Chocolate Chip Cookies

Yield
34 to 36
large cookies

We gave these cookies their name because they seem to have a bit of everything—including plenty of flavor.

1 cup (2 sticks) unsalted butter, at room temperature
¾ cup granulated sugar
¾ cup packed light brown sugar
1 tablespoon vanilla extract
1 tablespoon coffee liqueur
1 tablespoon Frangelico (hazelnut liqueur)
2 eggs
2½ cups all-purpose flour
1 teaspoon baking soda
½ teaspoon salt
12 ounces milk chocolate chips
6 ounces (1 cup) semisweet chocolate chips
1 cup English toffee bits, butterscotch chips,
    or other chips or candy bits of your choice
1 cup chopped walnuts
½ cup chopped pecans
½ cup chopped hazelnuts

Preheat oven to 325 degrees. Lightly grease or spray cookie sheets.

Beat butter, sugars, vanilla, and liqueurs on medium speed until light and fluffy. Beat in eggs. Whisk together flour, baking soda, and salt, then stir into butter mixture to make a soft dough. Mix in all the chips and nuts.

Drop by ¼-cupfuls onto cookie sheets, spacing 2 inches apart. Bake in the center of the oven until golden, about 16 to 17 minutes. Let cool on cookie sheets briefly, then transfer to wire racks to cool.

Tip: You can omit the hazelnut liqueur and use an additional tablespoon of coffee liqueur, or vice versa. Or, leave out the liqueurs altogether, and reduce the amount of flour to 2¼ cups.

Store: In an airtight container
Freeze: Yes
Mail: Yes, except in the summer

Mocha Chocolate Chip Cookies

Yield
48 to 50
cookies
(with nuts)

1 cup unsalted butter, at room temperature
1 cup packed light brown sugar
½ cup plus 1 tablespoon granulated sugar
2 eggs
1 tablespoon coffee-flavored liqueur, or vanilla extract
2½ cups all-purpose flour
2 teaspoons unsweetened cocoa
¾ teaspoon baking soda
¾ teaspoon salt
2 tablespoons powdered (not granulated) instant coffee, preferably espresso or French roast
12 ounces semisweet chocolate chips
1 cup chopped almonds or hazelnuts (optional)

Preheat oven to 375 degrees. Lightly grease or spray cookie sheets.

In a large mixing bowl, beat butter to soften it, then add sugars and cream until light. Beat in eggs and liqueur or vanilla.

Whisk together flour, cocoa, baking soda, salt, and instant coffee powder. Add to butter-egg mixture and stir in just until blended. Stir in chocolate chips and nuts.

Drop mixture by tablespoonfuls onto baking sheets. Bake in the center of the oven for about 9 to 10 minutes, or until golden on the edges and bottoms. Let cool on cookie sheets for a minute, then remove to wire racks to cool completely.

Tip: If you don't have instant powdered coffee on hand, grind regular ground or granulated coffee crystals in a coffee grinder or blender until the coffee has the consistency of fine powder.

Store: In an airtight container

Freeze: Yes

Mail: Yes

Old-Fashioned Chunky Oatmeal Cookies

Yield
45 to 48
cookies

1 cup (2 sticks) unsalted butter, at room temperature
¼ cup packed light brown sugar
2 teaspoons vanilla extract
2 eggs
2½ cups quick-cooking (not instant) oats
2 cups all-purpose flour
1 teaspoon baking soda
½ teaspoon salt
¾ teaspoon ground cinnamon
¼ teaspoon ground nutmeg
1 cup dark raisins
½ cup chopped walnuts or pecans

Preheat oven to 325 degrees. Lightly grease or spray cookie sheets.

Cream butter and sugar on medium speed until light. Add vanilla and eggs. Stir in oats, flour, baking soda, salt, cinnamon, nutmeg, raisins, and nuts. Dough will be stiff.

Drop dough by tablespoonfuls onto cookie sheets, using a second spoon to help shape cookies.

Bake in the center of the oven for 15 minutes, or until cookies are firm on top and golden on the bottom. Let cookies stand on the cookie sheets for 1 to 2 minutes, then remove to a wire rack to cool.

Tip: Skip the raisins or nuts, or replace ½ cup of the raisins with semisweet, milk chocolate, or white chocolate chips.

Store: In a covered container
Freeze: Yes
Mail: Yes

Fudgy Rich Chocolate Delights

Yield
27 to 28
cookies

These are like rich brownies that are moist in the center. You can change around the chips and nuts to suit your taste.

5 ounces semisweet or bittersweet chocolate
¼ cup (½ stick) unsalted butter, at room temperature
1 egg
1 egg white
½ cup plus 2 tablespoons sugar
1 tablespoon instant coffee or espresso powder
1 teaspoon vanilla extract
⅓ cup all-purpose flour
¼ teaspoon baking powder
¼ teaspoon salt
¾ cup white or semisweet chocolate chips
1½ cups assorted chopped nuts, such as walnuts, pecans, hazelnuts, or almonds

Preheat oven to 325 degrees. Lightly grease or spray cookie sheets.

Melt chocolate together with butter in a microwave on 80 percent power or in the top of a double boiler over hot water, stirring occasionally. Cool.

Beat egg, egg white, and sugar on medium to high speed until thick and light, about 4 to 5 minutes. Stir in coffee and vanilla. Slowly stir in chocolate mixture until well blended. Whisk together flour, baking powder, and salt, then add to chocolate mixture. Do not overmix. Batter will be loose; it thickens as it stands. Fold in chocolate chips and nuts.

Using a tablespoon or small ice cream scoop, scoop out batter, 2 tablespoons at a time. Shape into mounds with the aid of 2 spoons. Set cookies about 2 inches apart on cookie sheets.

Bake in the center of the oven for 14 to 16 minutes, or until cookies look firm and set.

Cool cookies on cookie sheets for 2 to 3 minutes, then remove to a wire rack to cool completely.

Tip: If you don't have instant powdered coffee on hand, grind regular ground or granulated coffee crystals in a coffee grinder or blender until the coffee has the consistency of fine powder.

Store: In an airtight container

Freeze: Yes

Mail: Yes

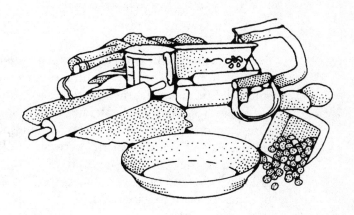

Mark Jensen's Chewy Oatmeal Cookies

Yield
48 cookies

These cookies have a lot of sugar and a high ratio of oats to flour, making them flat and chewy. Mark once ran out of ingredients for another oatmeal cookie recipe, and improvised with this one. The resulting cookies were so popular, he's been making them ever since.

1 cup (2 sticks) margarine, at room temperature
2 cups sugar
1½ tablespoons dark molasses
1 teaspoon vanilla extract
2 eggs
1½ cups all-purpose flour
½ to 1 teaspoon salt, to taste
1 teaspoon baking soda
3 cups quick-cooking (not instant) oats
¾ to 1 cup raisins, to taste

Preheat oven to 350 degrees. Lightly grease or spray cookie sheets.

Cream margarine, sugar, and molasses on medium speed until smooth. Stir in vanilla, then eggs.

Whisk together flour, salt, and baking soda. Add to creamed mixture. Stir in oats and raisins. Drop by tablespoonfuls onto cookie sheets, leaving at least 2 inches between cookies.

Bake in the center of the oven for 10 to 15 minutes, or until golden. Let stand on cookie sheets for 1 to 2 minutes, until firmed up, then remove to wire racks.

Tip: Although it may be tempting to replace the margarine with butter, don't. Mark says butter makes the cookies *too* flat.

Store: In a closed (not airtight) container
Freeze: Yes
Mail: Yes

Lacy Oatmeal Cookies with Dried Cranberries

Yield
48 cookies

½ cup (1 stick) unsalted butter, at room temperature
½ cup packed light brown sugar
½ cup granulated sugar
1 egg
1 cup all-purpose flour
1 cup old-fashioned oats
1½ teaspoons baking powder
1½ teaspoons baking soda
¼ teaspoon salt
1 tablespoon milk
1 cup dried cranberries

Preheat oven to 350 degrees. Lightly grease or spray cookie sheets.

Cream butter on medium speed until light. Add sugars and cream until smooth and light, about 2 minutes. Add egg and combine. Mix in flour, oats, baking powder, baking soda, salt, and enough milk to make a lumpy batter. Fold in dried cranberries.

Drop cookies by teaspoonfuls onto cookie sheets, 2 inches apart. Bake in the center of the oven for 5 to 8 minutes. Cookies will be golden brown on the bottom and firm on the top. Remove to a wire rack to cool.

Tip: Cranberries add color and a wonderful tart accent, but if they are not available, substitute raisins or currants.

High altitude: To adjust for high altitude (5,000 feet), reduce the amount of baking powder to 1 teaspoon.

Store: In an airtight container
Freeze: Yes
Mail: Yes

Double Butterscotch Cookies with Toasted Pecans

Yield
54 cookies

We once had a conversation with a baker who insisted with some agitation that the "butterscotch" cookie recipe in the newspaper was missing the butterscotch. It dawned on us that she defined "butterscotch" as orange-yellow candies and artificially flavored baking morsels. We suspect she is not alone. Please note that in olden days, "butterscotch" meant simply a mixture of butter and brown sugar—hence the "double butterscotch" of the recipe title.

1 cup (2 sticks) unsalted butter, at room temperature
1 cup packed light brown sugar
2 eggs
1 tablespoon vanilla extract
2½ cups all-purpose flour
1 teaspoon baking soda
½ teaspoon salt
12 ounces butterscotch morsels
1 cup toasted, chopped pecans

Preheat oven to 350 degrees. Lightly grease or spray cookie sheets.

Cream butter and sugar on medium speed until light, about 2 minutes. Beat in eggs and vanilla. In a separate bowl, whisk together flour, baking soda, and salt. Beat dry ingredients into butter-sugar mixture to make a soft dough. Stir in butterscotch morsels and pecans.

Drop dough by tablespoonfuls onto cookie sheets. Bake for 9 to 10 minutes, or until light golden. Let cookies stand on baking sheets for a minute, then remove to wire racks to cool.

Tips: See page 303 for instructions on toasting nuts. These are also good with toasted almonds.

These cookies can be baked as bars. Spread the dough into a lightly greased 10 × 15-inch jelly roll pan. Bake for 20 to 25 minutes, until golden.

Store: In an airtight container
Freeze: Yes
Mail: Yes

Maple Pecan Cookies

Yield
30 cookies

½ cup (1 stick) unsalted butter, at room temperature
¼ cup ricotta cheese, at room temperature
1 teaspoon maple extract or flavoring
1 cup sugar
1 egg
2 cups all-purpose flour
½ teaspoon baking soda
¼ teaspoon salt
½ cup chopped pecans

Preheat oven to 350 degrees. Lightly grease or spray cookie sheets.

Soften butter for 1 to 2 minutes at medium speed. Add ricotta and beat at high speed until creamy. Stir in maple extract and sugar. Beat in egg. Blend in flour, baking soda, and salt at high speed to make a medium dough. Stop mixing and scrape down sides of bowl as necessary. Stir in nuts.

Using two spoons as guides, drop dough by teaspoonfuls onto prepared cookie sheets, spacing cookies about 1½ inches apart. Bake in the center of the oven for 10 minutes, or until cookies are firm to the touch and a light golden brown on the bottom. Remove from the oven and let stand on cookie sheets for 5 minutes, then remove to a wire rack to cool completely.

Tips: You can sprinkle a small amount of chopped nuts on the cookies before baking. Another alternative is to frost the cookies with a maple frosting when they are cool. To make a maple frosting, cream ¼ cup (½ stick) unsalted butter at room temperature. Beat in 1 cup confectioners' sugar, 1 teaspoon maple extract, and 2 to 4 tablespoons milk to make a creamy frosting.

Store: In an airtight container
Freeze: Yes
Mail: Yes

Caramel-Dipped Cookies

Yield
75 cookies

1 cup (2 sticks) unsalted butter, at room temperature
⅓ cup confectioners' sugar
2 cups sifted all-purpose flour
1½ teaspoons vanilla extract
1 cup chopped pecans

Coating:

⅔ pound square candy caramels (36 to 37 caramels), unwrapped
¼ cup water
1¼ cups chopped pecans

Preheat oven to 350 degrees.

Cream butter and sugar on medium speed until light, about 2 minutes. Add flour and vanilla; mix well to make a stiff dough. Stir in nuts.

Pinch teaspoonfuls of batter and shape into mounds on ungreased cookie sheets. Leave at least 1½ inches between cookies.

Bake in the center of the oven for 10 to 12 minutes, until cookies are firm to the touch and golden color on the bottom. Let cookies stand for 1 minute on cookie sheets, then remove them to a wire rack to cool.

In a small, heavy saucepan, melt caramels and water over medium-low heat until smooth, stirring often. Cool slightly. Have cookies and 1¼ cups chopped nuts handy. Dip bottom of one cookie in caramel sauce and then in nuts. Continue until all of the cookies have been dipped. Let caramel set before serving cookies.

Tip: You can substitute walnuts for the pecans.

Store: In an airtight container

Freeze: Yes, before they're dipped

Mail: No, too sticky

Malted Milk Chocolate Cookies

Yield
42 to 45
cookies

1 cup (2 sticks) unsalted butter, at room temperature
½ cup sugar
1 egg yolk
1 teaspoon vanilla extract
⅔ cup plain malted milk powder
½ teaspoon salt
1¾ cups all-purpose flour
6 ounces milk chocolate, coarsely chopped

Preheat oven to 350 degrees.

Cream butter and sugar until light and fluffy. Beat in egg yolk and vanilla, then beat in malted milk powder and salt.

Stir flour into butter mixture to make a stiff dough.

Pinch off pieces of dough and roll into 1-inch balls. Place on ungreased cookie sheets. Bake in the center of the oven for 12 to 15 minutes, until cookies are set and golden on the bottom. Remove to wire racks to cool.

When cookies are cool, place chopped chocolate in a microwave-proof bowl or in the top of a double boiler. Melt in the microwave on 80 percent power, stirring until melted and smooth.

Dip the top of each cookie in the melted chocolate, swirling to completely coat top of cookie. Or, spread the melted chocolate over the top of each cookie with the back of a teaspoon. Place on wire racks until chocolate has set. If kitchen is warm, refrigerate cookies for about 10 minutes to set chocolate.

Store: In single layers on plates, wrapped with foil. Keep cookies cool.
Freeze: Yes, before dipping
Mail: Yes, for plain cookies; no for the dipped ones

Banana Chip Cookies

Yield
40 cookies

½ cup (1 stick) unsalted butter, at room temperature
1 cup sugar
1 egg
2 ripe bananas, peeled and mashed (about ⅔ cup)
1½ cups all-purpose flour
1¾ cup quick-cooking (not instant) rolled oats
½ teaspoon baking soda
¼ teaspoon salt
½ teaspoon ground cinnamon
1 cup dried banana chips

Preheat oven to 400 degrees. Lightly grease or spray cookie sheets.

Cream butter and sugar on medium speed until light, about 2 minutes.

Mix in egg; beat well. Add mashed bananas and continue beating until batter is smooth. Mix together flour, oats, baking soda, salt, and cinnamon. Stir into batter to make a medium dough. Divide banana chips in half. Mix half of the chips into the dough. Crush remaining half of chips and save them to put on top of the cookies.

Drop dough by heaping teaspoonfuls onto cookie sheets, spacing cookies about 2 inches apart. Top with crushed banana chips, pressing lightly into dough. Bake cookies in the center of the oven for 12 to 15 minutes, until just firm to the touch and a light golden color. Let stand on cookie sheets for a minute, then remove to wire racks to finish cooling.

Tip: If you want more banana chips in the cookies, it is fine to add another ¼ to ½ cup of chips. If you prefer, you can use all of the banana chips in the dough instead of putting some on top.

Store: In an airtight container

Freeze: Yes

Mail: Yes

*P*ineapple Cookies

Yield
22 to 24
cookies

½ cup (1 stick) unsalted butter, at room temperature
¾ cup confectioners' sugar
1 tablespoon pineapple juice
1 tablespoon minced dried pineapple
1½ cups all-purpose flour
¼ cup plain low-fat yogurt
⅓ cup diced dried pineapple

Cream butter and sugar on medium speed until light, about 2 minutes. Stir in pineapple juice and minced dried pineapple. Blend in flour and yogurt to make a soft but workable dough.

Gather dough into a ball. Knead on a lightly floured board for 1 to 2 minutes. Wrap in plastic wrap and refrigerate for 30 minutes to 1 hour.

Preheat oven to 350 degrees. Lightly grease or spray cookie sheets.

Drop dough by heaping teaspoonfuls onto cookie sheets. Set 2 or 3 pieces of diced dried pineapple on the top of each cookie. Press them slightly into the dough so that they will not fall off after baking. Bake cookies in the center of the oven for 12 to 14 minutes, until golden on the bottom, but still pale on top. Cool on cookie sheets for 2 to 3 minutes, then gently transfer to wire racks to finish cooling.

Tips: You can substitute orange juice and bits of candied orange peel for the pineapple. This recipe can easily be doubled. For more evenly shaped cookies, press dough through a pastry bag fitted with a ½-inch round tip.

Store: In an airtight container
Freeze: Yes
Mail: Yes

Mrs. Gutmann's Candied Ginger Cookies

Yield
20 to 24
cookies

Ginger is Joanna Gutmann's favorite spice, and she loves to experiment with it. These cookies, which are loaded with sweet-hot candied ginger, are her husband David's favorites.

½ cup (1 stick) unsalted butter, at room temperature
⅓ cup granulated sugar
⅓ cup light brown sugar
1 egg
½ teaspoon vanilla extract
1½ cups all-purpose flour
½ teaspoon cream of tartar
¼ teaspoon baking soda
¼ teaspoon salt
½ teaspoon ground ginger
¼ teaspoon ground cinnamon
½ cup candied ginger, minced

Cream butter and both sugars on medium speed until light, about 2 to 3 minutes. Blend in egg and vanilla. Whisk together flour, cream of tartar, baking soda, salt, and spices. Stir into batter to make a soft dough. Mix in candied ginger.

Gather dough in a ball. Cover with plastic wrap or aluminum foil and refrigerate for 45 minutes to 1 hour, until firm.

Preheat oven to 350 degrees. Lightly grease or spray cookie sheets.

Break off small pieces of dough and shape into ¾-inch balls. If dough is too sticky, sprinkle with a small amount of flour and knead until flour is incorporated.

Set cookie balls about 2½ inches apart on cookie sheet. Flatten them slightly with the bottom of a glass or a fork.

Bake cookies for 8 to 10 minutes, until they look set and are golden on the bottom. Let stand on cookie sheets for 1 to 3 minutes, then remove to wire racks to cool.

Tip: You can buy the candied ginger, or make your own (page 291) for even better-tasting cookies.

Store: In an airtight container

Freeze: Yes

Mail: Yes

Two-Cereal and Sunflower Seed Cookies

Yield
65 cookies

1 cup vegetable shortening
1 cup packed light brown sugar
1 cup granulated sugar
2 eggs
1 teaspoon vanilla extract
2 cups all-purpose flour
1 teaspoon baking powder
1 teaspoon baking soda
¼ teaspoon salt
1 cup granola
1 cup cornflakes
1 cup sunflower seed kernels

Preheat oven to 350 degrees. Lightly spray or grease cookie sheets.

Cream shortening with sugars on medium speed until light and fluffy, about 2 minutes. Mix in eggs, one at a time, beating well after each addition. Mix in vanilla.

In a separate bowl whisk together the flour, baking powder, baking soda, and salt. Stir dry ingredients into creamed mixture until combined. Stir in granola, cornflakes, and sunflower seeds to make a stiff dough.

Pinch off enough dough to make a 1-inch ball. Set cookie balls about 2 inches apart on cookie sheet. Set in the center of the oven and bake for 12 to 15 minutes, or until golden on top and firm. Let cookies stand for 2 to 3 minutes before removing them to a wire rack to cool.

Tips: Be sure to let cookies stand a few minutes on cookie sheets to firm up before you remove them to a rack to cool. You can use any kind of granola you like; for fun, vary it from batch to batch.

Store: In an airtight container

Freeze: Yes

Mail: Yes

Hermit Drops

Yield
30 cookies

¼ cup (½ stick) unsalted butter or margarine, at room temperature
¼ cup vegetable shortening
1 cup packed dark brown sugar
¼ cup orange juice
1 egg
¾ teaspoon ground cinnamon
¼ teaspoon ground nutmeg
⅛ teaspoon ground cloves
1¾ cups all-purpose flour
¼ teaspoon salt
¾ cup golden raisins
¾ cup chopped pecans or walnuts
½ cup chopped candied orange peel

Preheat oven to 375 degrees. Lightly grease or spray cookie sheets.

Cream butter or margarine and shortening with sugar on medium speed until light, about 2 minutes. Mix in orange juice, egg, cinnamon, nutmeg, and cloves. Stir in flour, salt, raisins, nuts, and candied orange peel. Batter will be somewhat stiff.

Drop batter by rounded teaspoonfuls onto cookie sheets, spacing cookies about 1½ inches apart. Press cookies slightly with the bottom of a glass dipped in sugar.

Bake cookies in the center of the oven for 12 to 14 minutes, or until golden on the bottom. Cool on cookie sheets for 1 to 2 minutes, then remove to a wire rack to cool completely.

Store: In an airtight container
Freeze: Yes
Mail: Yes

Date and Pecan Drops

Yield
36 cookies

6 tablespoons (¾ stick) unsalted butter or
    margarine, at room temperature
½ cup sugar
1 egg yolk
¼ cup fresh orange juice
1½ cups all-purpose flour
1½ teaspoons baking powder
¼ teaspoon salt
2 tablespoons grated orange zest
¾ cup pitted, chopped dates
½ cup walnuts or pecans, chopped
¾ cup walnut or pecan halves for decoration

Cream butter on medium speed. Add sugar and continue beating
until light, about 2 minutes. Stir in egg yolk and juice. Whisk together
flour, baking powder, and salt, then stir into batter. Stir in orange zest,
chopped dates, and chopped nuts. Dough should be stiff but workable.

Gather dough in a ball and wrap in plastic wrap or aluminum foil.
Refrigerate for 30 minutes.

Preheat oven to 350 degrees. Lightly grease or spray cookie sheets.

Break off enough dough to make a ¾-inch ball. Roll it between
your hands to shape. Set cookie balls 2 inches apart on cookie sheet.
Press a walnut or pecan half firmly into top of each cookie.

Bake in the center of the oven for 15 to 20 minutes or until edges
begin to brown. Let cookies stand on cookie sheets for 2 minutes, then
remove to a wire rack to cool.

Store: In an airtight container
Freeze: Yes
Mail: Yes

Chunky Peanut Cookies

Yield
58 to 60
cookies

1 cup vegetable shortening
1 cup packed dark brown sugar
½ cup granulated sugar
2 eggs
1½ teaspoons vanilla extract
2 cups all-purpose flour
½ teaspoon baking soda
¼ teaspoon salt
1½ cups candied peanuts (such as Beer Nuts), or roasted,
    salted peanuts

Preheat oven to 375 degrees. Lightly grease or spray cookie sheets.

Cream shortening and sugars on medium speed until light. Mix in eggs and vanilla. Whisk together flour, baking soda, and salt. Stir into shortening mixture. Dough will be soft. Stir in nuts.

Drop about 2 teaspoons of batter from a teaspoon, using a second spoon as an aid. Bake in the center of the oven for 12 minutes, or until cookies have firmed up and are golden brown on the bottom. Cool cookies 2 minutes on cookie sheets, then remove to a wire rack to finish cooling.

Store: In an airtight container
Freeze: Yes
Mail: Yes

Fruit Florentines

Yield
28 cookies

These luscious fruity, chocolate-coated cookies, which border on confections, are time-consuming to prepare, but worth the effort.

⅓ cup unsalted butter (5 tablespoons plus 1 teaspoon), cut into chunks
⅓ cup packed dark brown sugar
¼ cup light corn syrup
2 tablespoons milk or cream
¾ cup ground almonds
½ cup all-purpose flour, sifted
¼ cup chopped candied orange peel
¼ cup chopped candied cherries
12 ounces bittersweet or semisweet chocolate, coarsely chopped or
    broken into small pieces

Preheat oven to 350 degrees. Line 2 or 3 cookie sheets with aluminum foil, and lightly grease or spray the foil.

Combine butter, sugar, corn syrup, and milk in a small, heavy saucepan. Cook ingredients over medium heat until butter is melted, stirring often with a wooden spoon.

Remove pan from heat and stir in ground almonds, flour, and candied orange peel and cherries. Batter should be smooth and soft but not runny; add more flour or milk if necessary.

Drop batter by teaspoonfuls onto foil-lined cookie sheets, allowing at least 2½ to 3 inches between cookies, as batter spreads.

Bake for about 10 minutes, or until cookies have spread and become lacy. Remove from oven. Cookies are completely pliable while still hot. Try to push cookies with a spatula or knife into a circle shape if they become distorted during baking. Let cool on cookie sheets for 3 to 5 minutes, then carefully peel them off the foil. Set on a sheet of lightly greased or sprayed aluminum foil.

When cookies have cooled completely, set on a wire rack. Melt chocolate in a microwave on 80 percent power or in the top of a double boiler over hot water until melted, stirring occasionally. Using a pastry brush, coat the bottom of each cookie with chocolate. Return to wire rack, chocolate side up, and set in a cool place until chocolate sets completely. (If your kitchen is warm, you may need to refrigerate cookies for about 5 minutes to set the chocolate.)

Store: In single layers on plates, wrapped with foil. Keep cool.

Freeze: No

Mail: No

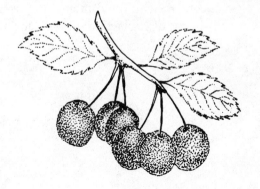

Potato Chip and Chocolate Chip Cookies

Yield
50 to 52
cookies

1 cup unsalted butter, at room temperature
¾ cup sugar
1 teaspoon vanilla extract
2 cups all-purpose flour
1 cup finely crushed potato chips, plus an
   optional ¾ to 1 cup crushed chips for rolling
1 cup mini chocolate chips or chopped nuts

Preheat oven to 350 degrees.

Cream butter and sugar on medium speed until well blended, about 1 minute. Beat in vanilla. Stir in flour to make a stiff dough. Work in 1 cup crushed potato chips and the chocolate chips; it's easiest to do this with your hands.

Pinch off pieces of dough and roll into 1-inch balls. If desired, roll cookies in additional crushed potato chips. Place on ungreased cookie sheets. Bake in the center of the oven for 10 to 12 minutes, or until bottoms of cookies are golden and tops are just beginning to turn a little golden.

Let cool on cookie sheets for 1 minute, then remove to wire racks.

Tips: You can omit the chocolate chips or chopped nuts.

Store: In an airtight container

Freeze: Yes

Mail: Yes

Lemony Pine Nut Cookies

Yield
45 to 48
cookies

1½ cups sugar
3 eggs, beaten
2½ cups all-purpose flour
2 tablespoons grated lemon zest
6 tablespoons confectioners' sugar, sifted
½ cup pine nuts

Preheat oven to 325 degrees. Lightly spray or grease cookie sheets.

In the top of a double boiler over hot, not boiling water, combine sugar and eggs. Stir over medium heat until mixture is warm. Remove pan from heat. Whisk mixture until foamy; cool.

Gradually add flour and lemon zest; blend well.

Drop batter by teaspoonfuls, about 1 inch apart on cookie sheets. Let cookies stand 10 minutes. Sprinkle with confectioners' sugar and pine nuts. Press pine nuts into the dough so that they will not fall off after baking.

Bake cookies in the center of the oven for 15 minutes, or until firm to the touch but not brown. Remove from cookie sheets and cool on a wire rack.

Tips: These cookies harden quickly, so enjoy them soon after baking. Instead of sprinkling cookies with sugar, you can brush them with a lightly beaten egg white and sprinkle pine nuts on top, pressing them into the cookies slightly so that they will not fall off after baking.

Store: In an airtight container

Freeze: Yes

Mail: No

Toasted Pine Nut Cookies

Yield
40 cookies

1 cup (2 sticks) unsalted butter, at room temperature
1 cup granulated sugar
⅓ cup packed light brown sugar
2 eggs
1¼ teaspoons vanilla extract
2 cups all-purpose flour
¼ teaspoon baking soda
¼ teaspoon salt
½ cup butterscotch morsels, or white or chocolate chips
2 cups toasted pine nuts

Preheat oven to 350 degrees. Lightly grease or spray cookie sheets.

Cream butter and sugars on medium speed until light, about 2 minutes. Add eggs, one at a time, beating well after each addition. Stir in vanilla. Whisk together flour, baking soda, and salt, then stir into batter to make a soft dough. Stir in chips and toasted pine nuts.

Drop cookies by tablespoonfuls onto cookie sheets. Leave 2 to 3 inches between cookies, as they spread. Bake in the center of the oven for 12 to 15 minutes. Cookies will be golden on the bottom and around the edges.

Cool on cookie sheets for 2 to 3 minutes, then remove to wire racks to cool completely.

Store: In an airtight container
Freeze: Yes
Tip: See page 303 for directions on toasting nuts.
Mail: Yes

Cornmeal Cookies with Roasted Pumpkin Kernels

Yield
30 cookies

½ cup plus 2 tablespoons (1¼ sticks)
   unsalted butter, at room temperature
½ cup sugar
1 egg
¾ teaspoon vanilla extract or coconut flavoring
1¼ cups all-purpose flour
½ cup white or yellow cornmeal
½ teaspoon ground cinnamon
1 cup roasted pumpkin seed kernels, divided

Preheat oven to 350 degrees. Lightly grease or spray cookie sheets.

Cream butter and sugar on medium speed until light, about 2 minutes. Mix in egg and vanilla. Stir in flour, cornmeal, and cinnamon to make a soft to medium dough. Stir in ¾ cup of the roasted pumpkin kernels by hand.

Using 2 spoons, drop heaping teaspoonfuls of batter onto cookie sheet. Round batter with the back of the spoon. Stick 2 or 3 of the reserved pumpkin kernels into the top of each cookie.

Bake in the center of the oven for 15 to 20 minutes, or until cookies are golden colored and set on top.

Let cookies cool about 3 minutes on the cookie sheets, then remove to wire racks to cool completely.

Tip: Crunchy, green roasted pumpkin seed kernels are available in the nut sections of most large supermarkets and health food stores. Sometimes they are called Chinese pumpkin seeds, or are labeled by their Spanish name, *pepitas.*

Store: In an airtight container
Freeze: Yes
Mail: Yes

Almond Wafers

Yield
25 cookies

½ cup (1 stick) unsalted butter, at room temperature
½ cup sugar
½ teaspoon almond extract
½ cup sifted all-purpose flour
½ cup ground almonds

Preheat oven to 375 degrees. Lightly grease or spray cookie sheets.

Cream butter and sugar on medium speed until light, about 2 minutes. Blend in almond extract. Stir in flour and mix well to make a thick batter. Stir in almonds.

Drop batter by teaspoonfuls, 2 inches apart, on cookie sheets. If the batter is too thick, add water by the tablespoonful until the batter is loose enough to drop from a spoon onto the pan.

Bake for 6 to 7 minutes, or until cookies are golden around the edges.

Cool cookies for 5 minutes on cookie sheets, then remove to wire racks to cool completely.

Store: In an airtight container
Freeze: Yes
Mail: Yes

*O*vernight Mint Chocolate Chip Meringues

Yield
22 cookies

2 egg whites, at room temperature
½ cup sugar
⅛ teaspoon salt
1 teaspoon peppermint extract
½ teaspoon cream of tartar
6 ounces semisweet chocolate chips

Preheat oven to 350 degrees. Lightly grease or spray cookie sheets, then dust lightly with flour. Or, line pans with foil.

With an electric mixer on high speed, beat the egg whites until they form soft peaks. Sprinkle half of the sugar over egg whites and incorporate. Continue until all of the sugar has been added and meringue stands in stiff, glossy peaks. Sprinkle with salt, peppermint extract, and cream of tartar. Mix ingredients together. Fold chocolate chips into batter.

Using 2 spoons as guides, drop batter by heaping teaspoonfuls onto prepared cookie sheets, leaving about 1½ inches between cookies.

Set cookies in the center of the oven. Turn off the oven. Do not open the oven door. Leave cookies in the oven overnight. Cookies should be white and firm. Remove cookies from cookie sheets.

Tip: Always mix and bake meringues on a clear, dry day for best results. On a humid day, they will absorb moisture and get too sticky.

Store: In an airtight container

Freeze: Yes

Mail: No

Chocolate Nut Meringues

Yield
at least
42 cookies

4 egg whites
1 cup confectioners' sugar
2½ cups finely ground almonds or walnuts
1½ cups (about 9 ounces) semisweet chocolate chips
¼ cup all-purpose flour

On high speed, beat egg whites until soft peaks form. Sprinkle half of the confectioners' sugar over egg whites. Continue beating until stiff, glossy peaks form. With a spatula, gently fold in remaining ½ cup of sugar, ground nuts, and chocolate chips. Fold in flour. Cover bowl and refrigerate for 1 hour.

Preheat oven to 350 degrees. Lightly grease or spray cookie sheets, then dust lightly with flour. Or, line pans with foil.

With the aid of 2 spoons, shape tablespoonfuls of dough into mounds spaced about 1½ inches apart on the cookie sheets.

Set cookies in the center of the oven. Immediately turn heat down to 275 degrees. Bake cookies 1 hour, then turn off oven. Do not open the oven door. Let cookies cool completely in the oven with the door closed.

Carefully lift cookies from cookie sheets with a spatula.

Tip: The number of cookies that the recipe makes depends on the size of the cookie. We like them on the small side, about ¾ inch across. In that case you would get about 75 cookies.

Store: In an airtight container

Freeze: Yes

Mail: No

Hazelnut Nuggets

Yield
42 cookies

3 egg whites, at room temperature
Pinch of cream of tartar
1 cup confectioners' sugar
2 tablespoons Frangelico (hazelnut liqueur)
1½ cups finely ground hazelnuts

Preheat oven to 300 degrees. Lightly grease or spray cookie sheets, then dust lightly with flour. Or, line pans with foil.

In a very clean mixing bowl, beat egg whites and cream of tartar until foamy. Gradually beat in sugar. Continue beating on high speed until egg whites hold in stiff peaks, but are still glossy. Beat in Frangelico. Fold in hazelnuts.

Drop meringue by rounded teaspoonfuls onto cookie sheets. Bake in the center of the oven for about 20 to 25 minutes, or until cookies are crisp and light tan. This will make cookies that are crunchy on the outside and still slightly chewy in the center; if you like them dry and crunchy throughout, bake 30 minutes.

Remove from baking sheets to wire racks until completely cool.

Tip: For fancier cookies, use a pastry bag and a ½-inch star tip; pipe the meringue onto the baking sheets. Although roasting and skinning the hazelnuts makes for a better-textured cookie, it's not essential.

Store: In an airtight container

Freeze: Yes

Mail: Yes

Coconut Macaroons

Yield
20 to 22
cookies

3 cups grated or shredded sweetened coconut
2 tablespoons all-purpose flour
1 cup sugar
1 tablespoon corn syrup
2 tablespoons butter
1 egg, lightly beaten

Preheat oven to 350 degrees. Lightly grease cookie sheets.

In a mixing bowl toss the coconut with flour; set aside.

Mix together the sugar, corn syrup, butter, and egg in the top of a double boiler. Set over simmering water and cook over medium heat for 10 to 12 minutes, stirring occasionally. Syrup will thicken slightly.

Stir only enough of the syrup into the coconut to moisten. Using 2 spoons, drop and shape into rounds on prepared cookie sheets, using about 2 teaspoons of coconut mixture per cookie. Space cookies about 2 inches apart.

Bake in the center of the oven for 20 to 25 minutes. Cookies will turn a light golden brown on top and be golden brown on the bottom. Remove cookies from oven and let cool on cookie sheets for 3 to 5 minutes, then remove to a wire rack.

Tips: Set half of a candied cherry or a piece of candied pineapple on the top of each cookie before it is baked.

For more evenly shaped cookies, press the dough through a pastry bag fitted with a ½-inch round tip.

Store: In an airtight container
Freeze: Yes
Mail: Yes

Almond Paste Macaroons

Yield
38 to 40
cookies

1 can (8 ounces) almond paste
1 cup sugar
3 egg whites
¾ teaspoon vanilla extract
½ teaspoon almond extract
3 tablespoons all-purpose flour
⅓ cup confectioners' sugar
¼ teaspoon salt

Break up almond paste into small pieces and place in a mixing bowl. Beat in sugar and egg whites until mixture is blended and soft. Stir in remaining ingredients.

Line 2 large baking sheets with parchment. Drop batter by teaspoonfuls onto cookie sheets, leaving 1½ inches between cookies. Let cookies stand at room temperature for 1½ hours to dry out. Do not let them stand longer than that.

Preheat oven to 300 degrees. Bake cookies in the center of the oven for 30 minutes, or until they color slightly and are firm to the touch. Take 2 clean kitchen towels, soak them in water and squeeze dry. Spread each towel out on a counter. Carefully lift the cookies, still on the baking parchment, onto the towels. (This will create steam to release the cookies.) Let stand for about 5 to 10 minutes, or until you can easily remove cookies from parchment. Completely cool cookies on a rack.

Store: In an airtight container
Freeze: Yes
Mail: Yes

BARS AND PAN COOKIES

The cookies in this chapter fall into three categories: those that most closely resemble cakes, those that take after pies, and those that are simply rectangular cookies.

The good old all-American brownie best represents the cake-style bar. The only difference between brownies and some fudgy cakes we have tasted is that the brownies were square and the cakes were cut into wedges. To make cake-style bars, you whip up a batter, spread it in a cake or jelly roll pan, and bake it.

Those gooey lemon bars and nut meringue bars rank among the most beloved of the pie-style cookie bars, which have a butter cookie crust that is baked, topped with a filling, then returned to the oven to set the topping. A variation on the theme consists of bottom and top crusts with a filling between.

Pan cookies consist of a standard cookie dough that is spread into a larger pan so that it bakes as one sheet, rather than individual cookies. Two longtime favorites, shortbread and toffee bars, always get patted into pans, but many other doughs, such as chocolate chip and oatmeal, can be baked as pan cookies too.

Convenience is the chief virtue of pan cookies. When your daughter tells you that, by the way, she "volunteered" you to bake treats for to-morrow's school party, it takes less time and effort to bake a panful of chocolate chip dough and cut it into squares than it does to drop dough onto cookie sheets.

Baking bar cookies requires few tricks. You should use the size of pan specified, of course. If it's a two-step bar cookie, with a shortbread crust, be sure to bake the crust thoroughly before adding the topping. When in doubt, we find that it's better to slightly overbake it. Other-wise, it will absorb too much moisture from the filling and turn pasty.

To distribute a liquid filling evenly over the crust, rock the pan gently back and forth. (Don't forget that it's hot!)

For the sake of convenience, our recipes call for simply patting the dough for bottom crusts into the pan. If you prefer a neater look, you can chill the dough until firm, roll it out to a rectangle about ¼ inch thick, trim to fit, then ease it into the pan.

Treat bars with custard fillings as you would custard pies. Let them cool, then keep them in the refrigerator and eat them within a day or two.

Do not underbake cake-style bars, or they'll be gummy. Brownies are an exception; if you like them extra fudgy, underbake them slightly. (On the other hand, remember that they *are* brownies, not fudge. To our displeasure, we have tasted "brownies" so raw the sugar in the dough was still gritty.)

If you want to try turning a favorite drop cookie recipe into a pan cookie, mix up the dough as usual, spread it into a 9 × 13-inch cake pan or a 10 × 15-inch jelly roll pan, depending on how much dough there is (it should be about ½ inch deep in the pan), and bake about 10 minutes longer than you normally would.

Removing baked bar cookies of any kind from the pan is easier if you use a thin, flexible spatula, such as an icing knife. If you prefer, you can line the pan with two thicknesses of foil. Use the foil to lift the cooled cookies from the pan, then cut them into bars. This saves wear and tear on your pans.

Classic Chocolate Lover's Brownies

Yield
16 brownies

1 cup (2 sticks) unsalted butter, cut into bits
5 ounces unsweetened chocolate, coarsely chopped
1¾ cups sugar
3 eggs
1 tablespoon vanilla extract
¼ teaspoon salt
1¼ cups all-purpose flour

Preheat oven to 350 degrees. Spray a 9-inch square baking pan lightly with nonstick cooking spray, or use a nonstick pan.

Place butter and chocolate in a microwave-proof bowl or in the top of a double boiler. Microwave on medium-high (80 percent) or heat over hot water, stirring occasionally, until melted and smooth.

With a wooden spoon, vigorously stir in sugar until well blended. Beat in eggs, one at a time, then vanilla and salt. Stir in flour just until completely incorporated. Batter will be thick. Spread in prepared pan.

Bake in the center of the oven for about 35 to 40 minutes, until brownies are firm and a tester inserted near the center comes out mostly clean. Let cool completely, then cut into bars.

Tip: These are about 1½ inches tall. If you prefer a thinner brownie, bake them in a 9 × 13-inch pan.

Store: On a plate, wrapped with foil. Use waxed paper between layers.

Freeze: Yes

Mail: Yes; wrap individually.

Marbeled Chocolate–Peanut Butter Brownies

Yield
42 brownies

Chocolate batter:

¾ cup (1½ sticks) unsalted butter, cut into bits
3 ounces unsweetened chocolate, coarsely chopped
1¼ cups sugar
2 eggs, at room temperature
1½ teaspoons vanilla extract
¼ teaspoon salt
1 cup all-purpose flour

Peanut butter batter:

¾ cup creamy peanut butter
½ cup sugar
1 egg
¾ teaspoon vanilla extract
¼ cup milk
2 tablespoons all-purpose flour

Preheat oven to 350 degrees. Spray a 9 × 13-inch baking pan lightly with nonstick cooking spray, or use a nonstick pan.

To make chocolate batter: Place butter and chocolate in a microwave-proof mixing bowl or in the top of a double boiler. Microwave on medium-high (80 percent) or heat over hot water, stirring occasionally, until melted and smooth.

Beat in sugar on medium speed until well blended. Beat in eggs, one at a time, then vanilla and salt. Stir in flour. Pour batter into prepared pan.

To make the peanut butter batter: In another bowl, beat peanut butter with sugar, egg, vanilla, milk, and flour until smooth. Drop peanut butter batter by large spoonfuls over chocolate batter. With a butter knife, "cut" the peanut butter batter into the chocolate batter, lifting the chocolate batter and swirling to make a marbled pattern.

Bake in the center of the oven for 25 to 35 minutes, or until a tester inserted near the center comes out clean. Let cool in the pan, then cut into bars.

Tip: Cut these carefully. The peanut butter layer forms a slightly sugary crust on top that can separate if the bars aren't handled gently.

Store: On a plate, wrapped with foil. Use waxed paper between layers.

Freeze: Yes

Mail: No

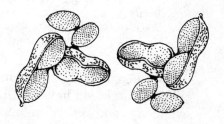

Toffee Brownies

Yield
16 brownies

½ cup (1 stick) unsalted butter, cut into bits

2 ounces unsweetened chocolate

2 eggs

1 cup sugar

1 teaspoon vanilla extract

½ cup plus 2 tablespoons all-purpose flour

½ teaspoon ground cinnamon

¼ teaspoon salt

½ cup chopped pecans or hazelnuts

1 package (2.52 ounces) Toblerone candy or other chewy toffee candy of your choice, chopped

Preheat oven to 350 degrees. Butter and flour an 8-inch square baking pan.

Place butter and chocolate in a microwave-proof mixing bowl or in the top of a double boiler. Microwave on medium-high (80 percent) or heat over hot water, stirring occasionally, until melted and smooth.

Beat eggs on high speed until light, about 2 minutes. Beat in sugar. With a spatula, stir in butter and chocolate. Stir in vanilla. Stir in flour, cinnamon, and salt. Stir in nuts and chopped candy. Spoon the thin batter into prepared baking pan and smooth the top.

Bake brownies in the center of the oven for about 40 minutes or until a toothpick inserted in the center of the brownies comes out with moist crumbs. Set pan on a wire rack to cool.

With the aid of a sharp knife, cut cooled brownies into 16 squares and remove with a pastry knife or spatula to a serving dish.

Tip: You can sprinkle the brownies with sifted confectioners' sugar just before serving.

Store: On a plate, wrapped with foil. Use waxed paper between layers.

Freeze: Yes

Mail: Yes; wrap individually.

Chocolate Cherry Bars with Amaretto Cream Cheese

Yield
48 brownies

Chocolate-cherry layer:

1 cup (2 sticks) unsalted butter, cut into bits
6 ounces best-quality bittersweet chocolate
1 cup sugar
2 tablespoons unsweetened cocoa
3 eggs, lightly beaten
1 teaspoon vanilla extract
¼ teaspoon salt
1 cup all-purpose flour
3 ounces (about ½ cup) dried tart cherries

Cream cheese layer:

8 ounces cream cheese
½ cup sugar
1 egg
2 tablespoons amaretto (see Tips)
¼ cup flour

Preheat oven to 350 degrees. Lightly butter a 9 × 13-inch pan.

To make chocolate layer: Place butter and chocolate in a microwave-proof mixing bowl or in the top of a double boiler. Microwave on medium-high (80 percent) or heat over hot water, stirring occasionally, until melted and smooth. Stir in unsweetened cocoa and sugar. Let cool slightly, then beat in eggs, vanilla, and salt. Stir in flour, then cherries. Spread evenly over bottom of pan.

To make cream cheese layer: Beat together cream cheese, sugar, egg, amaretto, and flour until smooth. Spread evenly over chocolate layer.

Bake in the center of the oven for 35 to 40 minutes, or until a tester inserted in the center comes out with just a few crumbs clinging to it. Let cool in the pan, then cut into small bars.

Tip: If you prefer not to use amaretto, substitute 1 teaspoon almond extract and cut the amount of flour in the topping to 1 tablespoon.

Store: In single layers on plates, wrapped with foil.

Freeze: No

Mail: No

Blond Brownies

Yield
16 brownies

¼ cup (½ stick) unsalted butter, melted
1 cup packed light brown sugar
2 eggs
¾ teaspoon vanilla extract
1 cup all-purpose flour
1 teaspoon baking powder
¼ teaspoon salt
½ cup white chocolate chips
½ cup golden raisins

Preheat oven to 350 degrees. Grease and flour an 8-inch square baking pan.

Pour melted butter in a mixing bowl. Stir in sugar, eggs, and vanilla. Whisk together flour, baking powder, and salt. Stir into butter-sugar mixture. Stir in white chocolate chips and golden raisins. Batter will be thick.

Spoon it into prepared pan and smooth top of batter with back of spoon. Bake in the center of the oven for 35 minutes or until a tester inserted in the center of the brownies comes out dry.

Cool brownies in the pan. Cut and remove while still slightly warm, then remove to a wire rack to finish cooling.

Tips: You can change the types of chips and nuts to suit your taste. You can also sprinkle the brownies with sifted confectioners' sugar before serving.

Store: On a plate, wrapped with foil. Use waxed paper between layers.

Freeze: Yes

Mail: No

Marty Pille's Date Nut Bars

Yield
24 bars

Her mother died when she was a child, and Marty found this recipe among her things. She made date nut bars for her father for years, and they have become a favorite of her husband, Bob. There's just enough batter in these rich bars to hold the dates and nuts together.

2 eggs
½ cup sugar
½ teaspoon vanilla extract
½ cup flour
½ teaspoon baking powder
½ teaspoon salt
1 cup walnuts, chopped medium
2 cups dates, diced medium
Confectioners' sugar

Preheat oven to 325 degrees. Lightly grease or spray an 8-inch square cake pan.

Beat eggs until foamy; beat in sugar and vanilla. Sift together flour, baking powder, and salt; stir into egg mixture. Mix in walnuts and dates. Spread in pan. Bake in the center of the oven for 25 to 30 minutes, until top has a dull crust. Do not overbake. Cool in the pan, then cut into small bars and dust with confectioners' sugar.

Store: In a covered (not airtight) container
Freeze: No
Mail: Yes; wrap individually.

Black Walnut Apple Bars

Yield
42 bars

1½ cups all-purpose flour
1¼ cups packed light brown sugar
½ cup (1 stick) unsalted butter, softened
¾ cup finely chopped black walnuts (or regular walnuts)
1 teaspoon ground cinnamon
¾ teaspoon baking soda
½ teaspoon salt
½ cup unsweetened applesauce
1 teaspoon vanilla extract
1 egg
1½ cups peeled, finely chopped tart apples
  (such as Granny Smith or Jonathan)

Preheat oven to 350 degrees. Lightly grease or spray a 9 × 13-inch baking pan.

Combine flour, brown sugar, butter, black walnuts, and cinnamon until crumbly. Pat 2½ cups of mixture firmly over bottom of pan; set aside.

To remaining flour-sugar mixture, add baking soda, salt, applesauce, vanilla, and egg. Beat until smooth. Stir in apples.

Spread evenly over bottom crust; top layer will be thin. Bake in the center of the oven for 20 to 25 minutes, until golden and firm. Let cool in pan, then cut into bars.

Store: On a plate, loosely wrapped with foil. Use waxed paper between layers.

Freeze: No

Mail: No

Applesauce Bars

Yield
24 bars

1¼ cups sifted all-purpose flour
¾ teaspoon baking soda
1 teaspoon ground cinnamon
¼ teaspoon ground allspice
¼ teaspoon salt
¼ cup (½ stick) unsalted butter, at room temperature
¾ cup sugar
1 egg
½ cup applesauce (homemade or store-bought)
½ cup golden raisins

Preheat oven to 375 degrees. Lightly grease or spray a 7 × 11-inch baking pan.

Sift together flour, baking soda, cinnamon, allspice, and salt. Set aside.

Cream butter and sugar on medium speed. Add egg and continue beating until light. Stir in flour mixture and applesauce until combined. Stir in raisins.

Spoon batter into prepared pan. Bake in the center of the oven 25 to 30 minutes, until cookies are golden and a cake tester inserted in the center comes out clean.

Cool in pan, then cut into bars.

Store: On a plate, wrapped with foil. Use waxed paper between layers.

Freeze: No

Mail: No

Lemon-Lime Squares with a Twist

Yield
16 squares

The "twist" in these tart-sweet bars is the lime zest in the crust.

Crust:

1 cup all-purpose flour
6 tablespoons (¾ stick) unsalted butter
   or margarine, at room temperature
¼ cup confectioners' sugar
1 tablespoon very finely grated lime zest

Topping:

4 eggs
1 cup granulated sugar
¼ cup freshly squeezed lemon juice
¼ cup freshly squeezed lime juice
3 tablespoons all-purpose flour
½ teaspoon baking powder
Sifted confectioners' sugar

Preheat to 350 degrees.

Mix the flour, butter, confectioners' sugar, and lime zest on low speed (or with a wooden spoon), just until mixed. Pat dough evenly into an ungreased 8-inch square cake pan.

Bake for 15 minutes, until shortbread is firm to the touch but not browned. Remove from the oven.

While the crust bakes, prepare the topping. Beat eggs, granulated sugar, and lemon and lime juices on medium speed for about 8 minutes, until mixture is a pale lemon color. Mix in flour and baking powder, and blend just until combined.

Pour topping over hot crust. Return to the oven and bake an additional 20 to 25 minutes, until filling is firm to the touch and does not wiggle.

Let cool completely in the pan, then refrigerate for 15 minutes. With a small, sharp knife, cut evenly into squares. If filling starts to stick to knife, wipe knife blade off frequently with a wet paper towel. Remove cookies from pan with a small spatula.

Sprinkle with confectioners' sugar just before serving.

Tips: Because lime zest (the green part of the peel) can be somewhat bitter, it should be grated as finely as possible. For best results, use a vegetable peeler to remove the zest from 1½ medium limes or 2 small ones. Chop the zest, then put it in a food processor or mini-chopper with the confectioners' sugar called for in the crust. Process until the green flecks are almost as fine as sand. Add to the remaining dry ingredients in the crust.

Store: In single layers on plates, in the refrigerator. Wrap loosely with foil.

Freeze: No

Mail: No

*K*ey Lime Bars

Yield
42 bars

Crust:

1½ cups all-purpose flour
2 tablespoons confectioners' sugar
½ teaspoon salt
6 tablespoons (¾ stick) cold unsalted butter, cut into small bits
3 tablespoons cold vegetable shortening, cut into small bits
4 to 5 tablespoons ice water

Filling:

½ cup Key lime juice (preferably fresh)
3 egg yolks
1 (14-ounce) can sweetened condensed milk

Meringue:

3 egg whites
1 teaspoon Key lime juice
¾ cup confectioners' sugar

Preheat oven to 400 degrees.

To make the crust: Whisk together flour, sugar, and salt. (Or, mix in a food processor.) Add butter and vegetable shortening and cut into dry ingredients to make a uniformly crumbly mixture. Add enough ice water to make a dough that clings together (or forms a ball around the blade, if you're using a food processor).

Lightly pat dough evenly into an ungreased 9 × 13-inch baking pan. Prick dough all over with a fork. Bake in the center of the oven for 10 to 12 minutes, until a light golden color.

While crust bakes, make filling: Whisk together lime juice, egg yolks, and condensed milk until smooth.

Remove crust from oven. Turn oven temperature down to 350 degrees.

Pour filling evenly over hot crust. Return to oven for another 7 to 8 minutes, just until filling is set.

Meanwhile, make meringue: Beat egg whites with lime juice until foamy, then gradually beat in sugar. Continue beating on high speed until meringue forms stiff, glossy peaks.

Remove lime bars from oven and spread meringue evenly over the top. Return to oven for 8 to 10 minutes, until meringue is a light golden color.

Let cool in pan, then cut into bars.

Store: In single layers on plates, in the refrigerator. Wrap loosely with foil.

Freeze: No

Mail: No

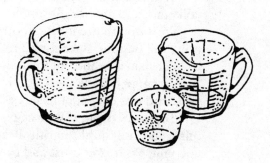

Banana-Coconut Bars

Yield
48 bars

Crust:

½ cup (1 stick) unsalted butter, at room temperature
¼ cup confectioners' sugar
1 egg yolk
⅛ teaspoon salt
⅛ teaspoon ground allspice or nutmeg
1 cup all-purpose flour

Topping:

2 large or 3 medium bananas
Freshly squeezed lime juice
3 eggs
1 egg white
1 cup sugar
2 tablespoons dark rum, or 1 teaspoon rum extract
2 tablespoons flour
¼ teaspoon baking powder
1 cup shredded sweetened coconut, preferably toasted (page 299)

Preheat oven to 350 degrees.

To make crust: Cream butter and sugar until light. Beat in egg yolk, salt, and allspice. Stir in flour to make a fairly stiff dough.

Press dough evenly over bottom of an ungreased 9 × 13-inch pan; crust will be thin. Bake for 12 to 14 minutes, until golden.

Peel bananas and cut into very thin slices. Dip in fresh lime juice, then arrange banana slices evenly over hot crust, covering the entire crust and not overlapping slices.

To make topping: Beat eggs, egg white, sugar, 2 tablespoons lime juice, and rum until smooth. Beat in flour and baking powder, then coconut. Pour over crust and bananas.

Return to oven for 20 to 25 minutes, until topping is completely set. Let cool completely, then cut into bars.

Tip: It helps to dip the knife in hot water when slicing these.

Store: In single layers on plates, in the refrigerator. Wrap loosely with foil and eat within 24 hours.

Freeze: No

Mail: No

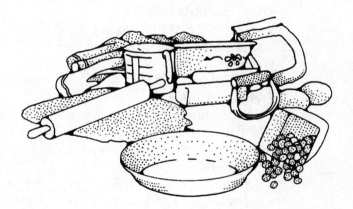

Pumpkin Currant Bars

Yield
30 bars

Crust:

¾ cup (1½ sticks) unsalted butter, at room temperature
½ cup confectioners' sugar
2 cups all-purpose flour

Topping:

½ cup currants or dark raisins
3 tablespoons dark rum, or hot water
1 can (16 ounces) solid pack pumpkin
3 eggs
½ teaspoon ground cinnamon
⅛ teaspoon ground nutmeg
⅛ teaspoon ground allspice
½ cup ricotta cheese
½ cup granulated sugar
⅓ cup firmly packed dark brown sugar
2 tablespoons all-purpose flour
½ teaspoon baking powder

Preheat oven to 350 degrees.

Soften butter on medium speed. Add sugar and beat until smooth. Add flour and beat until ingredients are mixed. Press dough evenly over bottom of 9 × 13-inch pan. Bake crust for 20 to 25 minutes, until it begins to brown.

While crust bakes, make topping: Put currants or raisins in a small bowl. Stir in rum. Set aside.

Spoon pumpkin into a mixing bowl. Blend in remaining ingredients, including drained currants, until smooth.

Remove baked crust from oven. Spoon topping evenly over hot crust. Return pan to the oven. Continue baking for 25 minutes, or until a knife inserted in center of bars comes out clean. Cool. Cut into bars.

Store: In single layers on plates, in the refrigerator. Wrap loosely with foil.

Freeze: Yes

Mail: No

Blueberry Cheesecake Squares

Yield
16 squares

Crust:

1½ cups graham cracker crumbs
2 tablespoons sugar
½ teaspoon cinnamon
3 tablespoons butter, melted and cooled
1 egg white, lightly beaten

Topping:

8 ounces cream cheese, at room temperature
½ cup sugar
1 tablespoon flour
1 egg yolk, lightly beaten
2 tablespoons lemon juice
¾ teaspoon vanilla extract
¼ teaspoon almond extract
2 cups blueberries, fresh or frozen

Preheat oven to 325 degrees.

To make crust, mix graham cracker crumbs with sugar and cinnamon. Beat butter with egg white and add to crumb mixture; work in thoroughly with a fork. Pat mixture evenly over bottom of an 8-inch square nonstick cake pan (or use a regular pan, and lightly butter or spray it). Bake for 5 minutes. Remove from oven and set aside to cool.

To make topping: Beat all ingredients except blueberries together until smooth. Fold in blueberries.

Spread topping gently over crust. Bake in the center of the oven for about 30 minutes. Topping should be puffy and no longer look wet. Let cool in pan, then cut into squares.

Store: In single layers on plates, in the refrigerator. Wrap loosely with foil.

Freeze: No

Mail: No

Almond Squares

Yield
48 bars

Crust:

½ cup (1 stick) cold unsalted butter, cut into chunks
7 to 8 ounces almond paste
3 tablespoons confectioners' sugar
¼ teaspoon salt
1 to 1¼ cups all-purpose flour

Topping:

2 eggs
1 egg white
¾ cup sugar
1 tablespoon finely grated lemon zest
½ teaspoon almond extract
2 cups sliced and/or slivered almonds, preferably toasted

Preheat oven to 350 degrees.

To make the crust, put butter, almond paste, confectioners' sugar, and salt in a food processor bowl. Process on high speed until smooth. Add enough flour, pulsing several times, to make a moist, crumbly dough.

Press dough evenly over bottom of an ungreased 9 × 13-inch pan. Bake in the center of the oven for 12 to 15 minutes, or until pale golden.

Make the topping: Beat eggs, egg white, and sugar on high speed until mixture falls off the beater in ribbons when the beater is lifted. Stir in lemon zest, almond extract, and almonds. Pour over hot crust, spreading evenly over crust. Return to oven for about 20 minutes, or until topping is golden. Let cool, then cut into rectangles.

Tips: The topping on these tends to shatter when you cut into them, which is part of their charm. The amount of almond paste will vary according to whether you buy it in the tube (7 ounces) or can (8 ounces).

Store: In an airtight container

Freeze: Yes

Mail: No

Maple Walnut Sticks

Yield
40 bars

Crust:

¾ cup (1½ sticks) unsalted butter, at room temperature
½ cup confectioners' sugar
2 egg yolks
¼ teaspoon salt
1⅔ cups all-purpose flour

Topping:

1 egg
2 egg whites
¾ cup dark maple syrup
1 teaspoon maple extract, or vanilla extract
¼ teaspoon salt
2 tablespoons flour
2 cups coarsely chopped, toasted walnuts

Preheat oven to 350 degrees.

To make the crust: On medium speed, cream butter with sugar until fluffy. Beat in egg yolks and salt. Stir in flour to make a stiff dough. Pat dough evenly over bottom of an ungreased 9 × 13-inch pan.

Bake crust in the center of the oven for 15 minutes, until set and beginning to turn golden.

To make the topping: Beat egg, egg whites, maple syrup, extract, and salt until smooth. Sprinkle flour over mixture and beat until dissolved. Stir in walnuts.

Pour the walnut mixture over the hot crust. Using pot holders, pick up pan and carefully rock back and forth to distribute walnut topping evenly over crust.

Return to oven and bake another 20 to 25 minutes, or until topping is firm, golden, and slightly puffed. Let cool in pan, then cut lengthwise 4 times and across 10 times to make 40 skinny bars.

Tip: Use a dark maple syrup in these cookies. The maple extract helps accentuate the maple flavor.

Store: In an airtight container

Freeze: Yes

Mail: Yes

Hazelnut Lovers' Bars

Yield
48 bars

Crust:

¾ cup (1½ sticks) unsalted butter, at room temperature
½ cup packed light brown sugar
1 egg yolk
½ teaspoon vanilla extract
1½ cups all-purpose flour
½ teaspoon salt

Topping:

3 egg whites
Pinch of salt
½ cup sugar
1 teaspoon vanilla extract
1¼ cups chopped, skinned, roasted hazelnuts
½ cup Nutella (see Tip)

Preheat oven to 350 degrees. Spray a 9 × 13-inch baking pan with non-stick cooking spray.

To make the crust: Cream butter and sugar until light. Beat in egg yolk and vanilla. Mix flour with salt, then stir into butter mixture to make a moist, crumbly dough.

Press dough evenly over bottom of prepared pan. Bake in the center of the oven for 15 minutes, or until light golden.

While crust bakes, make topping: Beat egg whites and salt until foamy. Gradually beat in sugar. Continue beating on high speed until meringue is glossy and stands in stiff peaks. Fold in vanilla and hazelnuts.

Remove baked crust from oven and drop dollops of Nutella on top. Return to oven for 30 seconds to a minute, until Nutella softens enough to be easily spreadable. Spread evenly over crust, then spread meringue-nut mixture evenly over top. Return to the oven for another 20 minutes, or until golden. Let cool, then cut into rectangles.

Tips: Nutella, a spread made of milk chocolate, oil, milk, and hazelnuts, is available in some large supermarkets, in European delis and groceries, and in specialty shops. In the supermarket, you'll most likely find it by the peanut butter or by the ice cream toppings.

Store: In an airtight container

Freeze: Yes

Mail: Yes

Peanut-Chocolate Bars

Yield
42 to 48 bars

Crust:

¾ cup (1½ cups) unsalted butter, at room temperature
½ cup packed light brown sugar
1 egg yolk
½ teaspoon vanilla extract
1½ cups all-purpose flour
½ teaspoon salt

Topping:

1¼ cups unsalted, chopped peanuts
¾ cup almond paste
¼ cup sugar
3 tablespoons unsalted butter or margarine
  at room temperature, cut in chunks
1 egg white
3 tablespoons Drambuie, or dark rum
9 ounces (about 1½ cups) semisweet chocolate chips

Preheat oven to 350 degrees. Spray a 9 × 13-inch baking pan with non-stick cooking spray.

To make the crust: Cream butter and sugar until light. Beat in egg yolk and vanilla. Mix flour with salt, then stir into butter mixture to make a moist, crumbly dough.

Press dough evenly over bottom of prepared pan. Bake in the center of the oven for 10 minutes, or until firm.

While crust bakes, make topping: In a large bowl combine peanuts, almond paste, sugar, butter, egg white, and Drambuie.

Remove baked crust from oven and scatter chocolate chips evenly over hot crust. Spread peanut filling evenly over crust. Return to oven for about 20 minutes, or until topping is golden and firm.

Let cool in pan, then cut into rectangles or diamonds.

Tip: Any sort of nut, coarsely chopped, could substitute for the peanuts. If you like these even sweeter, use milk chocolate chips.

Store: In an airtight container
Freeze: Yes
Mail: Yes

Linzer Bars

Yield
36 small
squares

¾ cup (1½ sticks) unsalted butter, at room temperature
1¾ cups all-purpose flour
2 tablespoons unsweetened cocoa
1 cup ground almonds
½ cup sugar
1 teaspoon ground cinnamon
¼ teaspoon ground cloves
¼ teaspoon salt
Grated zest of 1 lemon
3 egg yolks
1 teaspoon vanilla extract
1 jar (12 ounces) raspberry jam

Preheat oven to 350 degrees. Use a nonstick 9-inch square baking pan, or use a regular pan and lightly grease or spray it.

Mix butter and flour on medium speed until well blended. Mix in cocoa, almonds, sugar, cinnamon, cloves, salt, lemon zest, egg yolks, and vanilla to make a soft dough. Gather dough into a ball. Divide it in half.

Gently pat half of the dough into the baking pan, building up a ½-inch ridge around edges. Using the back of a spoon, spread jam evenly over crust. Set aside.

Roll remaining dough between 2 sheets of waxed paper to ¼-inch thickness. (If dough is too soft and sticky to roll, wrap in plastic wrap or foil and refrigerate for 30 minutes.) Remove top sheet of waxed paper and cut dough into ¼-inch-wide strips. Place dough strips over jam-filled crust in a lattice design. It will be necessary to piece together some of the strips to make them fit.

Bake in the center of the oven for 40 minutes, or until lattice crust is firm. Remove from the oven and let cool in the pan. Cut into rectangles or squares, and remove from pan carefully with a wide knife.

Store: On a plate, wrapped with foil. They'll keep at room temperature for several hours, or can be refrigerated for up to two days.

Freeze: Yes

Mail: No

Chocolate Mint Squares

Yield
48 bars

Crust:

1 (9-ounce) package dark chocolate wafer cookies,
  finely crushed (about 2⅓ cups crumbs)
½ cup melted unsalted butter
1 egg yolk

Filling:

2½ cups confectioners' sugar
1½ teaspoons peppermint extract
1¼ teaspoons vanilla extract
1 to 2 tablespoons milk, as needed
2 or 3 drops of green food coloring (optional)

Topping:

9 ounces bittersweet chocolate, broken into
  bits, or 1½ cups semisweet chocolate chips
¼ cup unsalted butter, cut into bits
Milk as needed

Make the crust: Preheat oven to 350 degrees. In a medium bowl, combine crumbs with butter and egg yolk, stirring and tossing with a fork until ingredients are thoroughly mixed. Pat evenly over the bottom of an ungreased 9 × 13-inch baking pan. Bake for 8 minutes, or until crumb mixture is firm. Let cool completely.

Make the filling: Beat all ingredients together to make a smooth, easily spreadable buttercream. Spread evenly over cooled crust. Refrigerate for 20 to 30 minutes until buttercream is firm.

Make the topping: Place chocolate and butter in a microwave-proof bowl or in the top of a double boiler. Microwave on medium-high (80 percent) or heat over hot water, stirring occasionally, until melted and smooth. Chocolate should pour easily from a spoon; if necessary, thin with additional butter or a tablespoon or so of milk. Spread chocolate evenly over chilled buttercream.

Return cookies to refrigerator for at least 2 hours, until firm. Cut into bars; cutting is easier if you clean off the knife between cuts.

Store: In single layers on plates, in the refrigerator. Wrap loosely with foil.

Freeze: Yes

Mail: No

Apricot Bars

Yield
18 bars

Crust:

¾ cup (1½ sticks) unsalted butter, at room temperature
1¾ cups all-purpose flour
¾ cup sugar

Topping:

1½ cups dried apricots
¾ cup water
1 cup apricot preserves
¼ cup packed dark brown sugar
4 eggs, well beaten
¼ teaspoon salt
1 teaspoon vanilla extract
⅓ cup sliced almonds for garnish (optional)

Preheat oven to 350 degrees. Lightly grease or spray a 9-inch square baking pan.

Place butter, flour, and sugar in a food processor; pulse until combined into a crumbly dough. Spread half of the mixture on the bottom of the baking pan, reserving remainder for the top of cookies. Bake in the center of the oven for 20 minutes.

While crust is baking, prepare topping. Put chopped dried apricots in a pan with water and cook over medium heat for 8 minutes or until all of the water is absorbed. Cool for 5 minutes. Purée apricots in a food processor or grinder; put in a bowl. Mix in apricot preserves, sugar, eggs, salt, and vanilla.

Remove pan from oven and spread topping over crust. Sprinkle remaining flour and butter mixture over top of apricots.

Bake in the center of the oven for 35 to 45 minutes. Top will have cracks in the crust. Remove pan from oven and sprinkle with almonds. Cool completely, then cut into bars.

Tip: This is a very rich cookie; cut in small pieces.

Store: In single layers on plates, in the refrigerator. Wrap loosely with foil.

Freeze: Yes

Mail: No

Goat Cheese Diamonds

Yield
48 cookies

Crust:

¾ cup (1½ sticks) unsalted butter, at room temperature
¾ cup packed light brown sugar
1¾ cups all-purpose flour
1 cup very finely chopped toasted hazelnuts, walnuts, or a combination
   of the two

Topping:

12 ounces cream cheese, at room temperature
4 ounces fresh goat cheese, at room temperature
1 cup sugar
1 egg, lightly beaten
3 tablespoons lemon juice
1 teaspoon vanilla extract

Preheat oven to 350 degrees. Butter a 9 × 13-inch cake pan.

To make crust: Cream butter and brown sugar. Stir in flour and nuts to make a moist, crumbly dough. Measure out a scant 2 cups of the mixture for topping. Press the remaining mixture evenly over the bottom of the pan.

Bake in the center of the oven for 20 minutes, or until golden.

To make the topping, beat the cream cheese, goat cheese, and sugar until smooth. Beat in egg, lemon juice, and vanilla. Pour this mixture over the hot crust. Sprinkle evenly with reserved flour-nut mixture and pat topping gently into place. Return the cookies to the oven for another 25 to 30 minutes, or until the topping is golden. Let cool, then refrigerate at least 4 hours.

Cut into small diamonds or rectangles, cleaning the knife off between cuts.

Store: In single layers on plates, in the refrigerator. Wrap loosely with foil.

Freeze: Yes

Mail: No

Pistachio Orange Bars

Yield
16 squares

Crust:

½ cup (1 stick) unsalted butter, at room temperature
6 tablespoons sugar
1 cup all-purpose flour
⅔ cup very finely chopped shelled pistachios (salted are okay)

Topping:

¾ cup fresh orange juice
1 tablespoon grated orange zest
½ cup sugar
3 eggs, lightly beaten
2 tablespoons all-purpose flour
½ teaspoon orange flower water (see Tip), or orange extract
About 2 tablespoons finely chopped pistachios

Preheat oven to 350 degrees. Lightly grease or spray an 8-inch square cake pan.

To make crust: Cream butter and sugar until smooth. Stir in flour and nuts to make a crumbly dough. Measure out 1 cup of the mixture for topping and set aside. Press the remaining mixture evenly over the bottom of the pan.

Bake in the center of the oven for 15 minutes, or until set and beginning to turn golden around the edges.

While crust bakes, make the topping: Whisk together orange juice, orange zest, sugar, eggs, flour, and orange flower water or extract. Slowly pour this mixture over hot baked crust, being sure not to disturb crust. Return to oven and bake another 20 to 25 minutes, or until filling is no longer liquid. Sprinkle remaining crumb mixture evenly over top, and press gently. Sprinkle with chopped pistachios. Return to oven for another 8 to 10 minutes, or until crumb topping has firmed up.

Let cool, then refrigerate at least 2 hours. Cut into squares, cleaning knife off between cuts.

Tip: Orange flower water gives the topping an intense, almost perfumed flavor. It is available in some specialty shops. Orange extract is not as exotic, but makes a perfectly good substitute.

Store: In single layers on plates, in the refrigerator. Wrap loosely with foil.

Freeze: No

Mail: No

Raspberry Oatmeal Bars

Yield
32 bars

¾ cup (1½ sticks) unsalted butter, at room temperature
1 cup packed light brown sugar
1¾ cups all-purpose flour
½ teaspoon baking soda
½ teaspoon ground cinnamon
¼ teaspoon salt
1½ cups old-fashioned oats
1 large jar (18 ounces) raspberry jam or orange marmalade

Preheat oven to 400 degrees. Lightly grease or spray a 9 × 13-inch baking pan.

Cream butter and sugar on medium speed until light, about 2 minutes. Whisk together flour, baking soda, cinnamon, and salt, then stir into butter mixture. Dough will be crumbly and dry. Blend in oats.

Press half of the mixture into the bottom of the pan. Gently spread the jam over the crust. Sprinkle remaining crumb mixture over the top of the jam. Gently press the crumbs to the jam.

Bake in the center of the oven for 20 minutes, until the top begins to turn golden. Remove bars from the oven and cool for 15 minutes. Cut into bars.

Store: On a plate, wrapped with foil. Use waxed paper between layers. After 1 day at room temperature, refrigerate. Bring to room temperature before serving.

Freeze: Yes

Mail: No

Date-Filled Bars

Yield
40 bars

Filling:

1 package (8 ounces) pitted dates, chopped
1 cup firmly packed light brown sugar
1 cup water
1 cup chopped pecans

Crust:

2½ cups old-fashioned oats
1¾ cups all-purpose flour
1½ teaspoons baking soda, dissolved in 1 tablespoon hot water
1 cup firmly packed light brown sugar
¼ teaspoon salt
1 cup (2 sticks) unsalted butter, softened

Preheat oven to 350 degrees. Grease a 9 × 13-inch baking pan.

To make filling: In a small or medium saucepan, mix together chopped dates, brown sugar, and water. Cook over medium heat, stirring often, until filling thickens, about 10 minutes. Stir in nuts. Cool.

While filling cools, prepare crust. Put oats, flour, baking soda, sugar, and salt in the bowl of an electric mixer. Stir ingredients together. Cut in butter. Press half of the crust mixture over bottom of prepared pan. Spread cooled filling over the crust. Sprinkle remaining crumbs over top of the date filling. Press gently with the tips of your fingers so that the crumbs adhere slightly to the filling.

Bake in the center of the oven for 35 minutes. Cool bars in the pan for 10 minutes, then score into bars with a sharp knife. Continue cooling in pan.

Store: On a plate, wrapped with foil. Use waxed paper between layers.
Freeze: Yes
Mail: No

Apple-Filled Oatmeal Cinnamon Bars

Yield
42 bars

Filling:

1½ pounds tart apples, peeled, cored, and coarsely chopped
2 tablespoons lemon juice
⅔ cup granulated sugar
2 tablespoons cornstarch
⅛ teaspoon ground nutmeg

Crust:

½ cup (1 stick) unsalted butter, softened
3 tablespoons canola or other vegetable oil
¾ cup packed light brown sugar
1¼ cups whole wheat flour
2 teaspoons ground cinnamon
½ teaspoon baking powder
½ teaspoon salt
1½ cups quick-cooking (not instant) oats

To make filling: Combine apples and lemon juice in a large, non-aluminum saucepan. Mix sugar with cornstarch and nutmeg; stir into apples. Cook over medium heat, stirring frequently, for about 10 minutes, or until filling is thick. Let cool completely.

Preheat oven to 375 degrees.

To make crust: Cream butter, oil, and brown sugar until smooth. Whisk together flour, cinnamon, baking powder, and salt. Beat into butter-sugar mixture just until blended. Stir in oats to make a crumbly dough.

Reserve 1⅓ cups oat mixture for topping. Pat remaining oat mixture evenly over bottom of ungreased 9 × 13-inch pan. Spread cooled apple filling over crust. Sprinkle reserved oat mixture evenly over apple filling, and press gently with fingers.

Bake for 25 to 30 minutes, until golden. Let cool completely, then cut into bars.

Tip: You can make the filling well in advance; just cover and refrigerate. Let it come to room temperature before spreading it on the crust.

Store: On a plate, wrapped with foil. Use waxed paper between layers.

Freeze: No

Mail: No

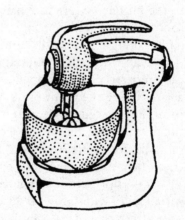

Five-Spice Shortbread

Yield
16 pieces

This very untraditional shortbread would be delicious after a Chinese dinner.

1 cup (2 sticks) unsalted butter, softened, cut into bits
⅓ cup packed light brown sugar
1 teaspoon vanilla extract
2 cups all-purpose flour
¼ cup cornstarch
⅛ teaspoon salt
¾ teaspoon Chinese five-spice powder

Preheat oven to 350 degrees. Line two 8-inch round cake pans with aluminum foil, pressing foil evenly into pan to fit well. Grease foil.

In a large bowl, beat butter, sugar, and vanilla until fluffy, about 2 to 3 minutes.

Whisk together flour, cornstarch, salt, and five-spice powder. Add to the butter mixture in 2 batches, beating lightly with a wooden spoon. Dough will be rough, but pliable. With lightly floured hands, gather dough into a ball. Cut it into 2 equal pieces with a knife.

Again with lightly floured hands, press each half of the dough into the prepared pans. Crimp edges or press down gently with the tines of a fork. Using the point of a small, sharp knife, score each pan of shortbread into 8 wedges (be careful not to cut more than halfway through the dough), much as if you were marking a pie to be cut later.

Bake for 18 to 20 minutes, or until shortbread is a uniform honey color, firm to the touch but not brown around the edges.

Cool shortbread completely in the pan. Score the shortbread again with a knife. Grasp foil on 2 sides and lift carefully to remove shortbread from pan. Break gently into wedges.

Tips: Traditional Chinese five-spice powder is a blend of star anise, fennel, cloves, cinnamon, and Szechuan peppercorns. (Some commercial blends vary from that formula.) It gives this shortbread an intriguing, aniselike flavor. Five-spice is available in many supermarkets and wherever Chinese foodstuffs are sold.

If you like your shortbread a little crunchier, bake for an additional 5 minutes.

For chocolate-chip shortbread, omit the five-spice powder and stir ½ cup mini-chocolate chips into the finished dough with a wooden spoon.

Store: In an airtight tin

Freeze: Yes

Mail: Yes; wrap separately

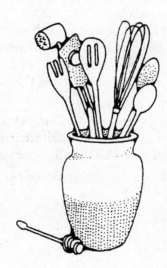

Toffee Bars

Yield
48 bars

Crust:

1 cup (2 sticks) unsalted butter, at room temperature
1 cup packed light brown sugar
1 egg yolk
1 teaspoon vanilla extract
¼ teaspoon salt
2 cups all-purpose flour

Topping:

7 to 8 ounces milk chocolate, broken into pieces
1 cup chopped roasted almonds

Preheat oven to 350 degrees.

Cream butter and sugar until smooth. Stir in egg yolk, vanilla, salt, and flour to make a stiff dough. Pat dough evenly over bottom of 9 × 13-inch pan. Bake in the center of the oven for 20 minutes, or until golden.

Remove from oven and scatter milk chocolate pieces over crust.

Return to oven for 1 minute. Remove again and spread chocolate evenly over crust. Sprinkle with almonds. Let sit at cool room temperature until completely cool, then cut into squares.

Tip: You can use commercially roasted almonds, or roast your own (see page 303). Although we have seen this recipe made with semisweet chocolate, milk chocolate gives it a true toffee flavor.

Store: In airtight containers, with waxed paper between layers.

Freeze: Yes

Mail: Yes

Buttered Candy Fingers

Yield
50 fingers

Virginia created these bars for her husband, a longtime fan of Butterfinger candy bars. Similar candy bars could be used. They're a great cookie for potlucks—easy to make and popular with both kids and adults.

¾ cup (1½ sticks) unsalted butter, at room temperature
¾ cup packed light brown sugar
¼ teaspoon salt
1¾ cups all-purpose flour
4 regular (2.1-ounce) or 2 king-size (3.7-ounce) Butterfinger bars, finely crushed

Preheat oven to 350 degrees. Lightly grease or spray a 9 × 13-inch cake pan.

Cream butter and sugar until well blended. Beat in salt, then stir in flour to make a stiff dough. Pat mixture evenly over bottom of pan.

Bake in the center of the oven for 10 minutes. Remove from oven, and sprinkle crushed candy bars evenly over top. Return to oven for another 10 minutes, or until edges of crust that show are golden and crushed candy has fused into a topping.

Let cool in pan, then cut lengthwise 5 times and across 10 times to make 50 skinny bars.

Tips: It's easiest to crush the candy bars if you first freeze them for about 15 minutes. Break them into pieces, then crush them in a food processor. Or, break into pieces and put between two sheets of waxed paper, then pound evenly with a rolling pin until finely crushed.

You can use a different kind of candy bar in this recipe. It should have a high percentage of sugar and a crispy-crunchy, rather than soft, center.

Store: In an airtight container
Freeze: Yes
Mail: Yes

Pecan Praline Grahams

Yield
35 cookies

35 graham cracker strips (strip = half of a square cracker)
1 cup (2 sticks) unsalted butter or a combination
    of butter and margarine, cut into chunks
1 cup firmly packed light brown sugar
1¼ cups chopped pecans

Preheat oven to 350 degrees. Lightly grease or spray a 9 × 13-inch cookie sheet with raised sides.

Arrange the graham cracker halves close together in rows on the cookie sheet. Set aside.

Put the butter and sugar in a small saucepan. Bring mixture to a boil over medium heat, stirring occasionally. Remove pan from heat and stir in the pecans.

Pour hot praline mixture evenly over the crackers. With the back of a spoon spread the pecans evenly over the crackers.

Bake crackers for 8 to 10 minutes. Check cookies after 5 minutes. Do not let the crackers brown.

Remove from oven. Let cookies stand for 10 to 15 minutes. Using a spatula or frosting knife, remove cookies to a wire rack to cool.

Store: In single layers on plates, wrapped with foil.
Freeze: No
Mail: No

Cashew Bars with Candied Papaya

Yield
48 bars

½ cup unsalted butter, softened
½ cup cashew butter (see Tips)
½ cup packed light brown sugar
⅓ cup granulated sugar
1 egg
1 teaspoon vanilla extract
1¾ cups all-purpose flour
¼ to ½ teaspoon salt (see Tips)
½ teaspoon baking soda
½ teaspoon ground cinnamon
½ cup chopped roasted cashews
½ cup finely diced candied or dried papaya

Preheat oven to 350 degrees. Lightly butter or spray a 10 × 15-inch pan.

Cream butter and cashew butter with sugars until light. Beat in egg and vanilla.

Whisk together flour, salt, baking soda, and cinnamon. Stir into butter mixture until well incorporated. Stir in cashews and papaya.

Spread dough evenly in prepared pan. Bake for 20 to 25 minutes, or until golden. Cut into rectangles when cool.

Tips: You can buy cashew butter in health food stores and some supermarkets. You also can grind your own from shelled, roasted cashews. Place cashews in a food processor or blender, along with a small amount of oil or water, and grind to a paste. Use the lesser amount of salt if you use salted cashew butter or grind your own butter from salted cashews.

Store: In an airtight container
Freeze: Yes
Mail: Yes

Backpacker's Bars

Yield
42 bars

Rich in carbohydrates and low in fat, these bars are meant for an energy boost when you're on the trail, on your bike, or even in your garden. They freeze well and cost less than commercial energy bars.

¾ cup peanut butter or other nut butter (such as almond or cashew)
¾ cup honey
½ cup nonfat dry milk
⅓ cup skim milk or water
1 teaspoon baking soda
¼ teaspoon salt
1 teaspoon ground cinnamon
½ cup wheat germ
2 cups rolled oats
½ cup whole wheat flour
¾ cup currants or raisins
2 tablespoons sesame seeds

Preheat oven to 350 degrees. Lightly grease or spray a 10 × 15-inch baking sheet with sides.

Cream peanut butter and honey with dry milk and skim milk until smooth. Stir in baking soda and salt, then remaining ingredients to make a stiff dough; it may be easiest to knead in ingredients with your hands.

With oiled hands, spread mixture evenly in baking sheet. Bake in the center of the oven for 10 to 12 minutes, until golden. Let cool, then cut into rectangles.

Store: In covered (not airtight) container
Freeze: Yes
Mail: Yes; wrap individually.

ROLLED AND REFRIGERATOR COOKIES

Rolled cookies and refrigerator cookies are essentially the same. Nearly any dough that you can roll into a log and slice, you can also roll out thinly and cut with cookie cutters. The refrigerator cookie is the more convenient of the two varieties; the rolled cookie is the more elegant. The only real difference between the two is that you can put slightly chunkier ingredients, such as dried raisins or chopped nuts, into refrigerator cookies. You cannot roll out a dough with chunky ingredients; it will tear.

Rolled cookies are more forgiving than pie crusts, but they're similar to crust and tart doughs in that they will suffer from overworking or the wrong temperature. A properly prepared dough rolls out seamlessly, then bakes into either a short, melt-in-the-mouth cookie or a crispy one, depending on the proportion of fat to flour and sugar.

Nearly all rolled cookies require that the dough be chilled. Chilling accomplishes two things: It makes the fat in the dough (usually butter) more solid so it won't stick all over the table and the rolling pin, and it allows the proteins (gluten) in the flour to "rest" so the dough is firm rather than elastic.

If the chilled dough is too hard to roll, on the other hand, it will crack. Dough that is hard should sit at room temperature for 10 to 15 minutes to soften slightly. Before rolling, pat it firmly all over with the rolling pin to help make it more pliable.

If dough starts to soften up and stick as you're rolling out batches of cookies—as it probably will if your kitchen is warm—put it in the freezer for 5 to 10 minutes.

One mistake many home bakers make when rolling out cookies is to use too much flour on the work surface and the dough. An overabundance of flour will damage the delicate balance of fat, flour, and liquid, resulting in a tough, pasty-tasting cookie.

Lightly flour the rolling pin and the board and sprinkle both with only as much additional flour as is needed to keep the dough from sticking. Placing a pastry cloth on the board and a cloth sleeve on the rolling pin can help because the fabric retains flour better than a smooth surface.

If you roll out many cookies and pie crusts, consider investing in a marble pastry slab and a marble rolling pin. Marble stays cool in even the warmest kitchen, and helps keep the dough from heating up and getting sticky.

If the dough sticks all over the lightly floured board, chill the dough a little longer. If that still doesn't get rid of the stickiness, work in just a smidgen more flour.

Roll the cookies with quick, even strokes from the center. Push and coax the dough; don't smash it.

Making rolled cookies interesting is no problem. Cookie cutters come in an amazing array of shapes these days, from dinosaurs to skyscrapers. We recommend tin cutters over plastic ones because they produce more sharply defined edges. To make even more interesting cookies, you can buy a set of mini-cookie cutters, which range in size from about ½ inch to ¾ inch across, and cut out shapes within the cookie. If you can't find your biscuit cutters, you can cut out cookies with a drinking glass that has a fairly sharp rim.

Cut straight up and down with the cutters in a single, quick motion. If you twist the cutter, you'll blur the outlines of the cookie or, in the case of a leavened cookie, pinch the edges so it might not rise as much as it should. Cut the cookies as close together as possible. The fewer scraps, the better. Bake cookies of a similar size in the same batch. Brush any flour off the cookies with a pastry brush before baking them. The scraps can be rerolled and cut again, but these cookies will not be as tender as the "first cut."

Refrigerator or icebox cookies (to use Grandma's term) are always chilled. If they weren't, they would not only have an inappropriate name, but also you would not be able to slice them into neat rounds. The method for making refrigerator cookies is to roll the dough into a log, then chill it until firm. To bake, simply cut off slices of the thickness you want, plop onto baking sheets, and bake. You can even wrap it well and freeze it for up to one month. Let it thaw for a couple of hours in the refrigerator, or until it can easily be sliced.

Use a thin, flexible spatula (a pancake turner) to transfer rolled or refrigerator cookies to cookie sheets. Softer doughs may stretch a little; ease them back into shape gently with your fingers.

Use caution in substituting fats. Butter is the best fat for rolled cookies. Because it is highly saturated, it becomes hard when chilled and makes rolling out the dough easier. It results in a tender cookie. Shortening has similar properties, but lacks flavor; it makes a flaky cookie, similar to pie crust. Margarine rarely makes a good substitute for butter in rolled cookies that are high in fat; it is not as hard as butter.

Double Chocolate Sugar Cookies

Yield
**42 large
cookies**

2½ cups all-purpose flour
2 tablespoons plus 1 teaspoon Dutch-process cocoa
2 teaspoons baking powder
¼ teaspoon baking soda
¼ teaspoon salt
½ cup (1 stick) unsalted butter, at room temperature
1 cup sugar
2 eggs
1 teaspoon vanilla extract
Additional sugar for rolling and topping

Topping:

¾ cup ground pistachios, or other nuts of your choice
4 ounces semisweet chocolate
1 teaspoon vegetable oil

Preheat oven to 375 degrees. Lightly grease or spray cookie sheets.

Sift together flour, cocoa, baking powder, baking soda, and salt. Set aside.

Cream butter with sugar on medium speed until light, about 2 minutes. Add the eggs and vanilla, beating well. Gradually add the flour mixture. Blend well.

Gather dough into a ball and cover with aluminum foil. Refrigerate for 1 to 2 hours, until firm.

Divide dough in half. Use a pastry cloth and rolling pin sleeve.

Sprinkle the pastry cloth lightly and evenly with sugar. Roll out one half of the dough to ¼-inch thickness. Using a 2½- to 3-inch cutter, cut out cookies, then lift with a spatula onto cookie sheets, leaving about 1½ inches between cookies. Sprinkle with sugar and pistachios. Gently press nuts into cookies.

Bake 8 to 9 minutes, or until cookies are firm and edges are just beginning to brown. Remove to a wire rack to cool.

Place chocolate in a microwave-proof bowl or in the top of a double boiler. Microwave on medium-high (80 percent) or heat over hot water, stirring occasionally, until melted and smooth. Mix in oil and stir until chocolate is smooth. Spoon chocolate into a small, heavy-duty plastic storage bag or a pointed paper cup. Force chocolate into one side of the bag, near a corner (or the bottom of the cup). Cut a tiny snip off the corner of the bag or the pointed end of the cup. Squeeze chocolate from bag or cup onto cookies, drizzling it in a free-form design. Let set.

Store: In an airtight container
Freeze: Yes
Mail: Yes

Cappuccino Cookies with Chocolate Drizzle

Yield
46 to 48
cookies

4 ounces semisweet chocolate
1 cup (2 sticks) unsalted butter, at room temperature
½ cup granulated sugar
½ cup firmly packed dark brown sugar
1 egg
1 tablespoon instant coffee dissolved in 1 tablespoon hot water
2 cups all-purpose flour
1 teaspoon ground cinnamon
⅛ teaspoon ground nutmeg
¼ teaspoon salt

Place 2 ounces of the chocolate in a microwave-proof bowl or in the top of a double boiler. Microwave on medium-high (80 percent) or heat over hot water, stirring occasionally, until melted and smooth. Set aside.

Cream the butter on medium speed until light, about 2 minutes. Increase speed to high and add the sugars and egg. Continue beating until mixture is smooth. Stir in coffee and melted chocolate; mix well.

Blend in flour, cinnamon, nutmeg, and salt. Shape dough into 2 logs, each about 2 inches in diameter. Cover with plastic wrap or aluminum foil. Refrigerate for 45 minutes.

Preheat oven to 350 degrees. Lightly grease or spray cookie sheets. Cut ¼-inch-thick slices from logs of dough. Transfer cookies to cookie sheets. Bake in the center of the oven for 8 to 10 minutes or until cookies are firm to the touch and a light golden brown on the bottom. Remove cookies to wire racks to cool.

Melt remaining chocolate. Using a spoon, drizzle chocolate decoratively over cookies. Let chocolate harden before serving cookies.

Tip: You can drizzle the cookies with white chocolate instead of dark chocolate.

Store: In an airtight container

Freeze: Yes

Mail: Yes

Streusel-Topped Cookies

Yield
46 cookies

¾ cup (1½ sticks) unsalted butter, at room temperature
½ cup sugar
1 teaspoon vanilla extract
2 cups all-purpose flour, sifted
1 teaspoon baking powder
¼ teaspoon salt
¾ cup blanched, ground almonds

Streusel:

⅓ cup (5½ tablespoons) butter or margarine, at room temperature,
   cut into chunks
1 scant cup all-purpose flour, sifted
⅓ cup sugar
½ teaspoon ground cinnamon
⅛ teaspoon ground nutmeg
Candied pineapple pieces or candied cherries cut in half

Cream butter on medium speed until light, about 2 minutes. Add sugar and vanilla, and beat until combined. Stir in sifted flour, baking powder, and salt. Completely mix ingredients together. Blend in almonds. Dough will be crumbly.

Gather dough into a ball and cover with plastic wrap or aluminum foil. Refrigerate for 45 minutes.

Preheat oven to 375 degrees. Lightly grease or spray cookie sheets.

Roll out dough on a lightly floured board or pastry cloth to ¼-inch thickness. Use a 2-inch cookie cutter to cut dough into circles. Set the circles on the cookie sheets.

To prepare streusel: Cream butter on medium speed for about 2 minutes. Add remaining ingredients except fruit. The mixture will be crumbly. Spread streusel evenly over the cookies. Set a piece of pineapple or a cherry half in the center of each cookie.

Bake in the center of the oven for 12 minutes, or until the cookies are a light golden color. The cookies brown quickly, so watch carefully. Let cookies sit on cookie sheets for 2 minutes, then remove to wire racks.

Store: In an airtight container
Freeze: Yes
Mail: Yes

Double Vanilla Sugar Wafers

Yield
36 to 40
cookies

1¼ cups all-purpose flour
¾ cup vanilla sugar (page 294; see Tip)
½ teaspoon baking powder
¼ teaspoon salt
½ cup cold unsalted butter, cut into pieces
1 egg yolk
1 teaspoon vanilla extract
1 to 2 tablespoons cold milk
Additional vanilla sugar for sprinkling

Mix flour, sugar, baking powder, and salt in a mixing bowl or a food processor. Cut in butter until mixture resembles coarse crumbs. In a small bowl, beat egg yolk, vanilla extract, and 1 tablespoon milk. Add to flour-butter mixture and stir or process, adding more milk if necessary, to make a dough that holds together. Wrap dough in plastic wrap or foil and chill for at least 1 to 2 hours, until firm.

Preheat oven to 350 degrees.

Roll dough on a lightly floured board or pastry cloth to ⅛ inch thick. Cut with a biscuit cutter into 2-inch rounds, rerolling scraps.

Transfer to cookie sheets. Sprinkle lightly with additional vanilla sugar. Bake in the center of the oven for 10 to 12 minutes, or until cookies are just a pale golden color, but not brown. Transfer to wire racks to cool.

Tip: If you do not have vanilla sugar on hand (and we recommend always having it on hand—it's wonderful stuff), place ¾ cup plain sugar in a food processor or blender. Add the seeds scraped from ½ vanilla bean and process to distribute the vanilla throughout. Then use in the recipe.

These cookies may be slightly chewy when they're warm; as they stand, they get crunchier.

Store: In an airtight container

Freeze: Yes

Mail: Yes

Buttered Lime Thins

Yield
55 to 60 cookies

1 cup (2 sticks) unsalted butter, at room temperature
1 cup sugar
1 tablespoon finely grated lime zest
1 tablespoon fresh lime juice
1 egg yolk
¼ teaspoon salt
1½ cups all-purpose flour

Cream butter and sugar until fluffy. Beat in lime zest, juice, egg yolk, and salt. Stir in flour to make a medium dough. Wrap dough tightly in plastic wrap and chill for at least 1 hour, or until firm.

Preheat oven to 350 degrees.

Roll dough out on a lightly floured pastry board or cloth to ⅛ inch thick. Cut into 2-inch rounds with a biscuit or cookie cutter. Transfer to ungreased cookie sheets. Bake in the center of the oven for 9 to 11 minutes, just until edges turn golden. Let cool on baking sheets for 1 minute, then remove to wire racks.

Store: In an airtight container
Freeze: Yes
Mail: Yes

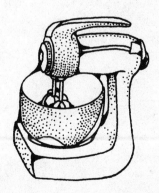

Lemon Anise Thins

Yield
48 cookies

½ cup (1 stick) unsalted butter, at room temperature
¾ cup sugar
1 tablespoon finely grated lemon zest
¼ teaspoon salt
1 cup all-purpose flour
2 teaspoons anise seed
Additional sugar for sprinkling

Cream butter and sugar on medium speed until light. Beat in lemon zest and salt. Stir in flour to make a stiff dough. Stir in anise seed. Wrap tightly in plastic wrap and chill for at least 1 hour.

Preheat oven to 350 degrees. Lightly grease or spray baking sheets.

On a lightly floured board or pastry cloth, roll out dough to slightly less than ⅛-inch thickness. Use a biscuit cutter to cut into 2-inch rounds. Sprinkle lightly with sugar.

Bake in the center of the oven for about 10 minutes, or until pale golden. Remove immediately to wire racks.

Tip: Fennel can be substituted for anise; crush or finely chop the seeds before adding.

Store: In an airtight container
Freeze: Yes
Mail: Yes

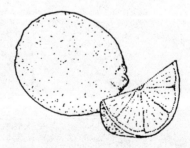

Mrs. Redfield's Stars

Yield
30 cookies

Mrs. Redfield's daughter, Joanna Gutmann, whose Candied Ginger Cookies are on page 38, says many of her childhood memories came wrapped around cookies. These stars seemed especially magical.

4 egg whites, room temperature
¼ teaspoon salt
3 cups confectioners' sugar
2 cups blanched almonds, grated
2 tablespoons freshly squeezed lemon juice
2 tablespoons grated lemon zest
1 tablespoon ground cinnamon
2 cups confectioners' sugar for rolling out cookies

Beat egg whites with salt on high speed until soft peaks form. Gradually add the 3 cups of sugar, and continue beating until stiff, glossy peaks form. Remove ¼ cup of this meringue and set aside in the refrigerator. Into remainder of meringue, fold grated almonds, lemon juice, zest, and cinnamon.

Cover mixture in the bowl and refrigerate for 1 hour.

Preheat oven to 275 degrees. Lightly grease and flour 2 cookie sheets.

Sprinkle a pastry cloth or a large sheet of waxed paper with the 2 cups of sugar. Cover rolling pin with a pastry sleeve. Divide dough into four parts, and gently roll out 1 part at a time on the sugared cloth or paper. Cut out cookies with a sugared star-shaped cutter. Set stars on cookie sheets about 2 inches apart. Brush them with reserved meringue.

Bake in the center of the oven for 30 minutes, or until stars are firm to the touch but not browned. Cool cookies on cookie sheets 1 to 2 minutes, then remove to wire racks.

Tips: You can garnish cookies with colored sugar if desired. This is a fragile batter, but the cookies are well worth the effort. When beating egg whites, always have them at room temperature for greater volume.

Store: In an airtight container
Freeze: Yes
Mail: No

Autumn Leaves

Yield
45 cookies

Painting these cookies with the colored glaze is optional, of course, but makes them pretty, fun, and seasonal. This is a good project to do with children.

1 cup (2 sticks) unsalted butter or margarine,
    or a combination of the two
¾ cup sugar
½ cup pure maple syrup, preferably dark amber
⅓ cup milk
3½ cups all-purpose flour
½ teaspoon baking soda
¼ teaspoon salt
Paint Glaze (page 289), tinted with red, yellow,
    and/or orange food coloring

Cream butter and/or margarine on medium speed until light, about 2 minutes. Add sugar and continue beating until smooth and combined. Blend in maple syrup, then milk. Whisk together flour, baking soda, and salt, then stir into batter to make a soft, pliable dough.

Gather dough in a ball and cover with plastic wrap or foil. Refrigerate for 1 hour, until firm.

Preheat oven to 375 degrees. Lightly grease or spray cookie sheets.

Divide dough in quarters. Roll out dough, one quarter at a time, on a lightly floured board or pastry cloth to between ⅛ and ¼ inch thick. Cut out cookies with a maple or oak leaf cutter (or use a tree-shaped cutter).

Set cookies on cookie sheets. Bake in the center of the oven for 8 to 10 minutes, until cookies are golden on the bottom and still pale on top. Transfer to wire racks to cool.

Using a pastry brush or a clean, wide artist's brush, brush the cooled cookies with glaze, using one or two colors per cookie. Leave some small areas unpainted to create the effect of shading. Allow frosting to set before serving.

Store: In an airtight container
Freeze: Yes
Mail: Yes

Spiral Cookies

Yield
40 cookies

If you can't make up your mind between a vanilla and a chocolate cookie, these attractive spirals offer a tasty compromise.

¾ cup (1½ sticks) unsalted butter or margarine
   or a combination, at room temperature
½ cup sugar
2 egg yolks
2 cups all-purpose flour
3 tablespoons water
2 tablespoons unsweetened cocoa
1 teaspoon vanilla extract
1 egg white, lightly beaten

Cream butter and sugar on medium speed until light, about 2 minutes. Beat in egg yolks, flour, and 2 tablespoons of water to make a stiff, maybe crumbly dough that holds together when you knead it lightly.

Divide dough in half. Blend cocoa and 1 tablespoon of water into one half of the dough. Blend vanilla into the remaining half.

On a lightly floured pastry cloth, roll out each dough half to a rectangle about 12 inches long and ¼ inch thick.

Brush the vanilla dough with the beaten egg white. Set the chocolate dough on top. Roll up the double layer of dough, jelly roll–style. Cover with plastic wrap and refrigerate for 45 minutes.

Preheat oven to 375 degrees. Lightly butter cookie sheets.

Unwrap cookie roll and cut into ¼-inch-thick slices. Place cookies on prepared cookie sheets. Bake for 10 to 12 minutes, until cookies are firm and lightly golden on the bottom. Cool on cookie sheets for 2 to 3 minutes. Slide a pastry knife under cookies to loosen them, then remove to wire racks to finish cooling.

Store: In an airtight container
Freeze: Yes
Mail: No

Fern Taylor's Ribbon Cookies

Yield
65 cookies

Every year Mrs. Taylor makes dozens and dozens of Christmas cookies in assorted fancy shapes, and every year her daughter's friends eat way too many of them. We especially like these pretty pastel ribbons, which are good all year long. Note that the dough has to chill for a long time, until it is very firm.

1 cup (2 sticks) unsalted butter, at room temperature
1¼ cups sugar
1 egg
1 teaspoon vanilla extract
2¼ cups all-purpose flour
¼ teaspoon salt
1¼ teaspoons baking powder
1 square unsweetened chocolate, melted and cooled, or 3 tablespoons
     unsweetened cocoa mixed with 1 tablespoon melted shortening
¼ cup very finely chopped pecans or walnuts
Red food coloring

Cream butter on medium speed until light and fluffy. Gradually add sugar, beating well. Add egg and vanilla and beat well. Whisk together flour, salt, and baking powder; then add to batter and mix well to make a fairly stiff dough.

Divide dough into 3 equal parts. Stir melted chocolate and nuts into one part. Knead a few drops of red food coloring into a second part. Leave the third part plain.

Line a 9 × 5 × 3-inch loaf pan with waxed paper. Press the plain part of the dough evenly over bottom of pan, packing dough in firmly. Spread the chocolate layer evenly over that. Top with the pink layer and spread until smooth.

Fold waxed paper over the top of the dough and press gently with fingers to smooth out top and press layers together.

Refrigerate for 12 to 24 hours, until very firm.

Preheat oven to 350 degrees. Turn dough out onto a clean cutting board and peel off the waxed paper. Cut the loaf in half lengthwise, then cut each portion of dough into ⅛-inch slices. Place about 1 inch apart on ungreased cookie sheets. Bake for about 10 minutes, until set. Cookies should not brown. Let stand on cookie sheets for a few seconds, then remove to wire racks to cool.

Store: In an airtight container

Freeze: Yes

Mail: Yes

Checkerboard Cookies

Yield
35 to 40
cookies

Make vanilla and chocolate doughs as directed in recipe for Spiral Cookies (page 111).

Roll each portion of dough between ¼ and ½ inch thick. Cut six ½-inch-wide strips from the vanilla dough and six ½-inch-wide strips from the chocolate dough. Gather up the remaining dough and knead lightly to make a marbled chocolate-vanilla dough. Roll it out thinly to use as a covering. Brush with egg white. Set 4 of the dough strips on the covering dough, alternating the flavors. Then set another 4 strips on top of that, reversing the colors so you have a chocolate strip sitting atop vanilla, and so on. Repeat for remaining layer. Tightly wrap the covering dough around the strips, making a round or square log. Cover with plastic wrap and refrigerate for at least 45 minutes.

Preheat oven to 375 degrees. Lightly butter 2 cookie sheets. Cut the roll in ¼-inch slices. Set on cookie sheets. Bake cookies for 10 to 12 minutes or until they are just firm and lightly golden on the bottom. Cool on cookie sheets for 2 to 3 minutes. Slide a pastry knife under cookies to loosen them, then remove to wire racks to finish cooling.

Storage: Store, covered with foil or plastic wrap or in airtight tins, at room temperature for up to 3 days.

Store: In an airtight container

Freeze: Yes

Mail: No

Cream Cheese and Cherry-Berry Triangles

Yield
64 cookies
(when cookies
are cut in half)

1 cup (2 sticks) unsalted butter, at room temperature
3 ounces cream cheese, at room temperature, cut in chunks
½ cup sugar
2 cups all-purpose flour
½ cup dried cherries, chopped
½ cup dried blueberries
1 teaspoon almond extract

Cream butter and cream cheese until blended, about 2 to 3 minutes. Blend in sugar. Add flour and mix well. Stir in cherries, blueberries, and almond extract to make a medium dough.

Gather dough into one piece. Using a spatula or a dough scraper, pat dough into a triangle-shaped roll. Cover with plastic wrap or aluminum foil. Refrigerate for at least 1 hour.

Preheat oven to 350 degrees. Lightly grease or spray cookie sheets.

Cut ¼-inch slices from the dough roll. If cookies are large, cut in half to make skinny triangles. Transfer to cookie sheets.

Bake in the center of the oven for 8 to 10 minutes, or until cookies are firm and golden on the bottom. Let cool on cookie sheets for 2 to 3 minutes, then remove to wire racks to cool completely.

Tip: You can substitute dried, chopped cranberries for the cherries.
Store: In an airtight container
Freeze: Yes
Mail: Yes

Pie Crust Cookies with Cinnamon Sugar

Yield
30 to 40
cookies,
depending on
size and shape

For centuries, children have loved snacking on the "cookies" baked from leftover scraps of pie pastry. This is a more formal version of those tantalizing scraps. It's easier, too—you don't have to make a pie.

2 cups all-purpose flour
3 tablespoons sugar
½ teaspoon salt
½ cup cold vegetable shortening
¼ cup (½ stick) cold unsalted butter, cut into bits
1 teaspoon lemon juice or cider vinegar
5 to 6 tablespoons ice water
3 tablespoons sugar mixed with 2 teaspoons cinnamon

Place flour, sugar, and salt in a mixing bowl or a food processor bowl. Mix thoroughly. Cut in shortening and butter until mixture resembles coarse crumbs. Add lemon juice or vinegar and enough ice water to make a dough that just clings together. Cover dough with plastic wrap or foil and refrigerate for 30 minutes.

Preheat oven to 400 degrees.

Roll dough out on a lightly floured board or pastry cloth to ⅛ inch thick. Cut into desired shapes. Transfer to ungreased cookie sheets. Sprinkle with cinnamon sugar.

Bake in the center of the oven for 10 to 12 minutes, until golden. Remove to wire racks to cool.

Store: In an airtight container
Freeze: Yes
Mail: Yes

After-Dinner Mints

Yield
54 to 55
cookies

These intensely minty treats are a cross between a cookie and a candy.

⅔ cup Burnt Butter (page 292), at room temperature
1 cup confectioners' sugar
1½ teaspoons mint extract
½ teaspoon vanilla extract
Drop or two of green food coloring (optional)
Pinch of salt
1 cup all-purpose flour
Confectioners' sugar for rolling
Green decorating sugar (optional)

The butter should be opaque but not hard; if it has been refrigerated, let it stand at room temperature until it softens.

Beat butter with sugar until creamy. Beat in extracts and food coloring (if using), then salt. Stir in flour to make a very soft dough.

Scrape dough onto a sheet of plastic wrap, cover tightly, and refrigerate at least 2 to 3 hours, or until firm.

Preheat oven to 300 degrees. Sprinkle confectioners' sugar over a clean board or pastry cloth. Place dough on surface, and sprinkle with more confectioners' sugar. Roll out dough to ⅛ inch thick. Using small cutters (about 1½ inches long), cut cookies into desired shapes—leaves are nice. Use a small, flexible spatula to transfer to ungreased baking sheets. If desired, sprinkle very lightly with green decorating sugar. Cookies should be firm and cool when they go into the oven; if dough has softened, refrigerate cookies for 5 to 10 minutes before baking.

Bake in the center of the oven for 5 to 7 minutes, or just until dry and set; cookies should not brown. Remove immediately to wire racks to cool.

Tips: Either peppermint extract or spearmint extract is good in these cookies. Or, use the extract labeled "mint," which often is a combination of the two. Although browned butter makes these cookies wonderful, it's not essential. You can substitute ½ cup (1 stick) regular butter, softened, plus 2 tablespoons vegetable oil.

Store: In an airtight container
Freeze: Yes
Mail: No

Ginger Thins

Yield
45 to 55
cookies,
depending on
size of cutters

7 tablespoons unsalted butter or margarine, at room temperature
¾ cup sugar
1 egg, beaten
1½ teaspoons dark corn syrup
2 cups all-purpose flour
1 teaspoon baking soda
1½ teaspoons ground ginger
¼ teaspoon ground nutmeg
¼ teaspoon ground cloves

Cream butter and sugar until smooth. Add egg and corn syrup.

Whisk together flour, baking soda, and spices, then stir into batter to make a somewhat stiff but workable dough. Gather dough into a ball. Cover with plastic wrap and refrigerate for at least 1 hour.

Preheat oven to 375 degrees. Lightly grease or spray cookie sheets.

Divide dough into thirds for easy handling. Roll each piece of dough on lightly floured board or pastry cloth as thinly as possible. Cut cookies with your favorite cookie cutter. Transfer to cookie sheets.

Bake 6 to 8 minutes, until cookies are firm and beginning to brown on the bottom. Transfer to wire racks to cool.

Tips: For a more intense flavor, you can use finely grated fresh ginger instead of ground ginger.

These also make good drop cookies. Break off small pieces of the chilled dough and roll into ¾-inch balls. Set on cookie sheets and flatten lightly with a fork or the bottom of a glass. Bake for about 12 minutes. The recipe will make 36 drop cookies.

Store: In an airtight container

Freeze: Yes

Mail: Yes

*B*uttered Honey Thins

Yield
50 to 54
cookies

½ cup unsalted butter, at room temperature
6 tablespoons honey
1 tablespoon finely grated orange zest
1 teaspoon finely grated lemon zest
⅛ teaspoon salt
1¾ cups all-purpose flour

Cream butter and honey on medium speed until blended. Beat in orange zest, and lemon zest, and salt. Stir in flour to make a medium dough. Wrap dough in plastic wrap or foil and refrigerate at least 1 hour, or until firm enough to roll.

Preheat oven to 350 degrees. Lightly grease or spray cookie sheets.

Roll out dough on a lightly floured board or cloth as thinly as possible—¹⁄₁₆ inch is ideal. Cut into 2-inch rounds with a biscuit or cookie cutter. Carefully transfer to cookie sheets. Bake in the center of the oven for about 10 minutes, or until golden on top. Let stand on cookie sheets for 1 minute, then remove to wire racks.

Store: In an airtight container
Freeze: Yes
Mail: Yes

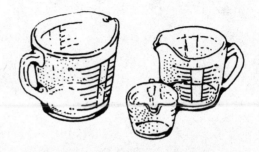

Whole Wheat Hazelnut Slices

Yield
30 cookies

¾ cup (1½ sticks) unsalted butter, at room temperature
¾ cup packed light brown sugar
1 teaspoon vanilla extract
¼ teaspoon salt
1¼ cups whole wheat flour
1 cup finely ground roasted, skinned hazelnuts

Cream butter and brown sugar on medium speed until light and fluffy. Beat in vanilla and salt. Stir in flour, then hazelnuts to make a crumbly dough.

Knead dough briefly, then place on waxed paper and roll into a log about 2 inches in diameter. Refrigerate at least 1 to 2 hours, until firm.

Preheat oven to 350 degrees.

With a sharp (not serrated) knife, cut off slices of dough ¼ inch thick. Dough will be a bit crumbly; use firm strokes to cut the cookies. Transfer to ungreased baking sheets; reshape cookies with your fingers if necessary.

Bake in the center of the oven for 8 to 10 minutes, until edges of cookies are tinged with brown. Let cool on baking sheets for 1 to 2 minutes, then remove to wire racks.

Store: In an airtight container
Freeze: Yes
Mail: Yes

Lavender Orange Crisps

Yield
55 to 60
crisps

½ cup sugar
1 to 1½ teaspoons dried lavender leaves or flowers, to taste
2 teaspoons minced or grated orange zest
½ cup (1 stick) unsalted butter, at room temperature
1 tablespoon orange liqueur, or 1½ teaspoons
    orange extract and 1½ teaspoons water
⅛ teaspoon salt
1 cup all-purpose flour

Place sugar, lavender, and orange zest in a food processor or mini-chopper. Process on high until lavender and orange zest are very finely minced and distributed throughout the sugar.

In a large mixing bowl, cream butter. Add lavender sugar and cream on medium speed until light and fluffy. Beat in orange liqueur or extract and salt. Stir in flour to make a medium dough.

Wrap dough in plastic wrap and refrigerate for at least 1 to 2 hours, until firm.

Preheat oven to 375 degrees.

Roll out on a lightly floured board or pastry cloth very thinly, between 1/16 and ⅛ inch thick. Cut into small cookies, using 1½-inch cutters (fluted ones are nice).

Place on ungreased baking sheets and bake in the center of the oven for 7 to 9 minutes, until golden but not brown. Keep an eye on cookies; they burn easily.

Let cool on pans for about 30 seconds, then remove to racks to finish cooling.

Tips: Try to roll these as uniformly as possible. If they're different thicknesses, some of the cookies may burn before others are done.

These cookies have a crunchy, crackerlike consistency.

If you do not grow your own lavender, you can find dried lavender in some health food stores with the dried herbs. Do not buy the kind intended for potpourri, which may not be suitable for food. These cookies are also good with dried rosemary; crush the seeds or finely chop them before adding to the dough.

Store: In an airtight container

Freeze: Yes

Mail: Yes

Rosemary Currant Cookies

Yield
60 cookies

1 cup (2 sticks) unsalted butter, at room temperature
1 cup sugar
2 eggs
1 teaspoon baking soda
½ teaspoon cream of tartar
¼ teaspoon salt
2½ cups all-purpose flour
½ teaspoon vanilla extract
2 tablespoons crushed dried rosemary, or to taste
1 cup dried currants

Cream butter and sugar on medium speed until light, about 2 minutes. Add eggs, one at a time, beating well after each addition. Add baking soda, cream of tartar, and salt. Stir in flour, one cup at a time, until mixed well. Add vanilla, crushed rosemary, and currants to make a medium dough. On a floured surface or a sheet of waxed paper, shape dough into a log. Wrap in plastic wrap or waxed paper and refrigerate for 2 hours or longer, until firm.

Preheat oven to 350 degrees. Lightly grease or spray cookie sheets.

With a very sharp (or serrated) knife, cut dough into ⅛-inch slices. Transfer cookies to cookie sheets. If necessary, press edges lightly with fingers to make them rounder. Bake in the center of the oven for about 10 minutes, or until firm, golden on the bottom and still pale on top.

Let cookies stand for 2 to 3 minutes on cookie sheets, then remove to wire racks to cool.

Tip: If you really like rosemary, just add more by ½-teaspoon increments. If you want less herb taste, reduce the amount. This is an ideal cookie to serve with port or sherry.

Store: In an airtight container

Freeze: Yes

Mail: Yes

Lemon Basil Refrigerator Cookies

Yield
36 cookies

1 cup unsalted butter, at room temperature
1 cup confectioners' sugar
1 tablespoon grated lemon zest
1 teaspoon vanilla extract
2 teaspoons freshly squeezed lemon juice
2 tablespoons minced fresh basil
¼ teaspoon salt
2½ cups all-purpose flour
1 egg white, lightly beaten with 1 teaspoon water
Sugar for sprinkling

Cream butter and sugar until light and fluffy. Beat in lemon zest, vanilla, lemon juice, basil, and salt. Stir in flour just until incorporated.

Divide dough in half. Place each half of dough on a sheet of waxed paper. With your hands and the waxed paper, roll dough into a log about 2 inches in diameter. If dough is too sticky to handle, refrigerate for 15 to 30 minutes. Roll log up in waxed paper, tucking in ends.

Repeat with remaining half of dough. Refrigerate dough for at least 4 to 6 hours, or until very firm.

Preheat oven to 350 degrees. Lightly grease or spray cookie sheets.

Cut ⅛-inch slices from logs of dough. Transfer to cookie sheets. Dab or brush each cookie very lightly with beaten egg white, then sprinkle lightly with sugar. Bake in the center of the oven for 8 to 9 minutes, until set and just beginning to turn golden on the edges. Remove cookies to wire racks to cool.

Tip: If you grow lemon balm, you can substitute it for the basil. The resulting cookie will have an intensely lemony flavor.

Store: In an airtight container
Freeze: Yes
Mail: Yes

Bev Bennett's Parmesan Sticks

Yield
32 crackers

Whenever Bev brings these to a party, they disappear in a wink. We like them with 1½ teaspoons hot sauce as a party appetizer. With only ½ teaspoon hot sauce, they make a good accompaniment to tart fresh fruits such as apples and grapes.

¼ cup (½ stick) unsalted butter, at room temperature
4 ounces Parmesan cheese, freshly grated
½ to 1½ teaspoons hot red pepper sauce, to taste
¾ cup all-purpose flour
Cold water if needed

Cream butter on medium speed until fluffy. Gradually add cheese. Add hot pepper sauce. Then gradually add flour. If necessary, add cold water by the teaspoonful to form a dough that will hold together.

Divide dough in half. Wrap in plastic wrap or foil and refrigerate for 15 minutes.

Preheat oven to 375 degrees.

Roll out each half of dough on a lightly floured board or pastry cloth to a rectangle about 8 × 5 inches. Trim the edges. Cut each rectangle in half widthwise to make two 8 × 2½-inch strips. Cut strips into 1-inch sticks along the length (to yield 8 sticks per strip).

Place on ungreased cookie sheets. Bake for 15 minutes, or until the crackers are faintly brown.

Tips: Be sure to use fresh Parmesan cheese and to grate it finely. For best results, use a liquid, uniform hot sauce such as Tabasco. Those that contain chunks of hot peppers will not distribute as evenly through the dough.

To make rounds instead of sticks, roll dough into a log about 1 inch in diameter, making it as smooth and round as possible. Chill for at least 1 to 2 hours, until very firm. Using a very sharp knife (a serrated knife works well), cut off slices about ⅛ inch thick. Bake as directed.

Store: In an airtight container
Freeze: Yes
Mail: Yes

Goat Cheese Pepper Puffs

Yield
48 crackers

Serve these with goat cheese (of course), plain, or with fruit. They go well with dried fruits, such as apricots.

3½ to 4 ounces mild goat cheese, at room temperature
4 tablespoons softened unsalted butter
¾ teaspoon salt
½ teaspoon freshly ground black pepper (a coarse grind is best)
1 cup all-purpose flour
1 to 3 tablespoons milk or cream, as needed

Cream goat cheese until fluffy. Beat in 2 tablespoons of the softened butter, salt, and pepper. Stir in flour, then enough milk to make a soft dough that holds together. Refrigerate for 30 minutes, or until dough firms up.

Preheat oven to 400 degrees. Lightly grease or spray cookie sheets.

Roll dough on a lightly floured board or pastry cloth to a rectangle about 10 × 14 inches. It should be about ⅛ inch thick. Brush evenly with remaining 2 tablespoons softened butter. Starting with the short end of the dough, fold the left third of the dough over the center, then fold the right third over that, to make 3 layers. Roll out again to ⅛ inch thick.

Cut out dough with a plain or scalloped 1½-inch round cookie cutter. Transfer to cookie sheets. Bake in the center of the oven for 10 to 12 minutes, or until golden and puffy. Remove to wire racks to cool.

Tip: These should be a nice golden color. If they are still fairly pale, they will not be as crisp. When in doubt, overbake slightly rather than underbake.

Store: In an airtight container
Freeze: Yes
Mail: No

Whole Wheat Chedder Rounds

Yield
28 to 30
crackers

This is a good cracker to have on a party buffet. Or, serve it with an after-meal assortment of fresh fruits.

¼ pound grated extra-sharp or spicy Cheddar cheese
¼ cup (½ stick) unsalted butter, at room temperature
¾ cup whole wheat flour
¼ cup all-purpose flour
½ teaspoon baking powder

Cream cheese and butter until smooth and fluffy, about 2 to 3 minutes. Stir in whole wheat flour, all-purpose flour, and baking powder to make a medium dough.

Roll dough into a log about 1¼ inches in diameter. Cover with plastic wrap or foil and refrigerate for at least 1 hour, until firm.

Preheat oven to 350 degrees. Lightly grease or spray cookie sheets.

Cut off slices of dough between ⅛ and ¼ inch thick. Transfer to cookie sheets. Bake in the center of the oven for 12 to 14 minutes, until crackers are a light golden color. Let stand on cookie sheets for 1 to 2 minutes, then remove to wire racks to cool.

Tips: You can sprinkle extra cheese on top of the crackers during the last 5 minutes of baking.

You also can bake these as drop cookies. You do not need to chill the dough. Break off small pieces of dough and shape into ¾-inch balls. Set on cookie sheets and flatten with a fork.

Store: In an airtight container
Freeze: Yes
Mail: Yes

Blue Cheese Walnut Crackers

Yield
24 to 28
crackers

These taste especially nice with pears and a good port or Cognac.

¼ cup (½ stick) unsalted butter or margarine, at room temperature
⅓ cup finely crumbled blue cheese, at room temperature
1 egg
2 teaspoons freshly squeezed lime juice
1¼ cups all-purpose flour
½ teaspoon baking powder
¼ teaspoon salt
½ cup finely chopped walnuts

Cream butter and blue cheese for 2 minutes, or until smooth. Mix in egg and lime juice. Whisk together flour, baking powder, and salt; add to batter and mix well to make a medium, slightly sticky dough. Stir in walnuts.

Gather dough into a ball, then roll into a log shape, using a floured pastry cloth to roll dough if it is sticky. Cover with plastic wrap or foil. Refrigerate for 45 minutes or until firm.

Preheat oven to 350 degrees. Lightly grease or spray cookie sheets.

With a sharp knife cut ¼-inch slices from dough. Set crackers on cookie sheets.

Bake in the center of the oven for 17 to 20 minutes or until crackers are beginning to turn golden on the top. Let stand on cookie sheets for 1 to 2 minutes, then remove to wire racks to cool.

Tip: For a garnish you can brush uncooked wafers with slightly beaten egg white and sprinkle with extra ground or chopped walnuts.

Store: In an airtight container
Freeze: Yes
Mail: Yes

Curried Almond Cookies

Yield
30 crackers

We like these crackers, with just a hint of spice, with a mild cheese such as Brie or Montrachet. They pair well with tropical fruits such as mangos or papayas, as well as with grapes and apples.

1 tablespoon vegetable oil
¾ teaspoon curry powder
¼ teaspoon ground ginger
¼ teaspoon ground coriander
1 tablespoon finely minced onion
1 cup all-purpose flour
½ teaspoon salt
1 teaspoon sugar
¼ cup (½ stick) unsalted butter, softened
2 to 3 tablespoons yogurt or buttermilk
¼ cup finely chopped almonds

Heat the oil over medium heat in a small frying pan. Add the curry powder, ginger, coriander, and onion. Sauté for 30 seconds to 1 minute, until fragrant.

In a large bowl, stir together the flour, salt, and sugar. Beat in the spice mixture, butter, and yogurt to make a medium-stiff dough.

Sprinkle the almonds over a sheet of waxed paper. Place the dough in the center of the waxed paper and pat into a log about 1 inch in diameter and 10 inches long. Roll dough log all the way around to coat with almonds. Wrap in the waxed paper and chill for at least 2 to 4 hours, until very firm.

Preheat oven to 375 degrees. With a very sharp knife, cut dough into slices slightly thicker than ⅛ inch.

Bake for 10 to 12 minutes, until golden on edges and bottom. Remove to wire racks to cool.

Store: In an airtight container
Freeze: Yes
Mail: No

SHAPED AND FILLED COOKIES

Sometimes you want a cookie with just a bit more elegance or piz-zazz, a cookie that holds its shape and adds architectural interest to a plate of treats. Or maybe you treasure the textural contrast of a creamy filling in a crisp cookie.

In this chapter, you'll find cookies that sport distinctive shapes: spheres, crescents, ovals, perfect circles. You'll also find sandwich cook-ies, cookies that hide a surprise—whether it's a candied cherry or a bit of candied pineapple—and more elaborate cookies that are filled and rolled into rich crescents or layered into little pastries.

Such cookies often take more time and effort than just dropping dough from a spoon, but they'll reward you with their spectrum of flavors and shapes.

The basic rules we've set forth in other chapters—such as chilling rolled dough—apply here, too, of course. An additional rule of thumb is that moist fillings should not be put into crisp cookies until shortly be-fore serving. Also, cookies with moist fillings should not be stored in airtight containers, for such storage will soften them.

White Chocolate Rounds

Yield
30 to 32
cookies

½ cup (1 stick) unsalted butter, at room temperature
6 tablespoons confectioners' sugar
3 ounces white chocolate, melted and cooled
1 egg white
½ teaspoon vanilla extract
⅛ teaspoon orange or lemon extract
Pinch of salt
¾ cup plus 2 tablespoons all-purpose flour

Preheat oven to 350 degrees.

Cream butter and sugar until light. Beat in white chocolate, egg white, extracts, and salt. Stir in flour to make a very soft dough.

Place dough in a pastry bag fitted with a ½-inch round or star tip. Pipe dough onto ungreased baking sheets in ¾-inch mounds, leaving at least 1½ inches between cookies. Dough mounds will look like peaks; cookies will flatten out in the oven.

Dough should be soft but not runny. If necessary, refrigerate it for 5 to 10 minutes before piping it.

Bake in the center of the oven for 8 to 9 minutes, or until cookies are just rimmed with light gold. Let cool on the cookie sheets for 1 minute, then remove to wire racks to cool completely.

Tips: If you prefer, you can drop the dough by teaspoonfuls onto baking sheets, and smooth out the dough mounds with the back of a spoon. The cookies will not be as evenly rounded, however.

These cookies are the basis of White on White Chocolate Sandwiches (page 268).

Store: In an airtight container; cookies are fragile, so stack carefully.

Freeze: Yes

Mail: No

Busia Kwiecien's Coffee Nuggets

Yield
36 small
cookies

Our friend Alan Magiera fondly remembers enjoying these dainty cookies as a child. They were one of his maternal grandmother's specialties (*Busia* is Polish for grandma). Not too sweet, they're also very popular with adults.

½ cup (1 stick) unsalted butter or margarine, at room temperature
3 tablespoons confectioners' sugar
1½ teaspoons powdered instant coffee
½ teaspoon vanilla extract
1 cup all-purpose flour
½ cup finely chopped nuts
Confectioners' sugar for rolling

Cream butter, sugar, coffee, and vanilla until light and fluffy. Add flour and nuts and mix thoroughly to make a stiff dough. Chill dough for 1 hour.

Preheat oven to 350 degrees. Using 1 teaspoon of dough per cookie, form into small balls. Bake on ungreased cookie sheets for 15 minutes, or until firm and golden on the bottom. While still warm, roll in confectioners' sugar.

Store: In an airtight container
Freeze: Yes
Mail: Yes

Chocolate Tipped Almond Crescents

Yield
48 cookies

1 cup minus 2 tablespoons unsalted butter (2 sticks
  minus 2 tablespoons), at room temperature
½ cup sugar
2½ cups all-purpose flour
½ cup ground almonds
2 egg yolks
¾ teaspoon almond extract
2 ounces white chocolate or white coating
2 ounces semisweet or milk chocolate

Cream butter and sugar on medium speed until light. Add flour, almonds, egg yolks, and almond extract. Mix well to make a soft dough. Gather dough into a ball, cover with aluminum foil or plastic wrap, and refrigerate for 30 to 45 minutes, until firm but pliable.

Preheat oven to 325 degrees. Lightly grease or spray cookie sheets.

Break off about 2 teaspoons of dough and roll into a pencil shape about 2½ inches long. Form into a crescent (half moon) shape by turning ends up, and set on cookie sheet. Repeat with remaining dough. If dough softens too much, refrigerate briefly.

Bake in the center of the oven for 30 minutes, until cookies are firm but still pale. Transfer to a wire rack to cool.

When cookies have cooled, place white and semisweet chocolates in separate microwave-proof bowls. One at a time, microwave on medium-high (80 percent), stirring occasionally, until melted and smooth. Or, melt white chocolate in the top of a double boiler over hot water; then melt semisweet chocolate the same way.

Set chocolate near the cookies for easy handling. Dip one tip of each crescent first in the white chocolate, then the other tip in the semisweet chocolate. Remove to wire racks and keep in a cool place to set chocolate.

Tips: The cookies are good without the chocolate, or sprinkled with chocolate shots while the chocolate is still wet.

White chocolate tastes better, but can be a bit tricky to work with. If you are experienced in using chocolate for dipping, use white chocolate. If not, use white coating, which is easier to handle.

Store: In an airtight container

Freeze: Yes

Mail: No

Crispy Pecan Slices

Yield
75 to 80
cookies

½ cup (1 stick) unsalted butter or margarine, softened
4 eggs
1 cup sugar
2 cups all-purpose flour
¼ teaspoon salt
¼ teaspoon baking powder
2 teaspoons vanilla extract
3 cups pecan halves, preferably toasted

Center a rack in the oven and preheat to 350 degrees.

Line 3 loaf pans, each 8 × 3¾ × 2½ inches, with aluminum foil, allowing foil to hang 1 inch over each long side of each pan. Lightly grease the foil.

Beat butter, eggs, and sugar on medium speed until mixture is fluffy and a pale lemon color. On low speed, mix in flour, salt, baking powder, and vanilla until blended. Stir in pecan halves by hand.

Spread batter evenly among the 3 pans. Bake the dough for 30 minutes. Remove from the oven. Using a pot holder, gently lift foil to remove cookies from pans. Cool, then wrap partially baked dough in foil, keeping shape intact. Freeze for at least 4 hours.

When ready to bake the pecan crisps, preheat oven to 350 degrees.

Remove dough from freezer. Use a long, sharp knife to cut cookies into ⅛-inch-thick slices. Arrange slices on an ungreased cookie sheet.

Bake for 10 to 15 minutes, until cookies are firm to the touch but not browned. Watch carefully so that they do not overbake. Let cool on cookie sheets for 3 minutes, then remove to a rack to cool completely.

Tip: Slicing cookie dough that contains nuts can be tricky; the nuts are firmer than the dough, and the dough often has a tendency to crumble. Freezing the partially baked dough makes it possible to cut a pecan-studded dough into clean slices.

Store: In an airtight container
Freeze: Yes
Mail: Yes

*S*hirley Sussman's Cranberry Slices

Yield
55 slices

Mandelbrot, Shirley's inspiration for these cookies, is made with almonds (*mandel* is the German and Yiddish word for almond). But she decided to use the same technique and branch into other flavor combinations.

3 eggs
1½ cups sugar
1 tablespoon vanilla extract
⅔ cup peanut oil
4 cups all-purpose flour
¼ teaspoon salt
4 teaspoons baking powder
½ teaspoon ground cinnamon
1 cup dried cranberries

Preheat oven to 350 degrees. Lightly grease or spray 2 cookie sheets.

Beat the eggs, sugar, and vanilla in a large bowl on high speed until light, about 2 to 3 minutes. Stir in oil and mix well. Whisk together flour, salt, baking powder, and cinnamon. Stir into batter. Mix in cranberries.

Divide dough into 4 equal pieces. Roll each piece into a 1½-inch log. Set 2 logs on each cookie sheet. Bake in the center of the oven for 15 to 18 minutes. Cookies are done when just firm to the touch, golden on the bottom, and still pale on top. Cool logs slightly. Using a sharp knife, cut the logs on the diagonal into ½-inch pieces. Cool completely.

Tips: If you like a sweeter cookie, you can mix ½ cup sugar with 2 teaspoons ground cinnamon and sprinkle this mixture over the sliced but still warm cookies. You can also add another cup of dried cranberries to the recipe, or substitute chopped walnuts or raisins for the cranberries.

Store: In an airtight container
Freeze: Yes
Mail: Yes

Little-Bit-Lighter Peanut Butter Cookie

Yield
**40 to 42
cookies**

Peanut butter cookies are notoriously high in fat. This one has a bit less fat and saturated fat, but still tastes great. For a traditional soft peanut butter cookie dough, see page 237.

¼ cup (½ stick) margarine, at room temperature
½ cup sugar
½ cup light peanut butter
¼ cup egg substitute, or 1 egg
⅓ cup freshly squeezed orange juice
1½ cups all-purpose flour
3 tablespoons unsweetened cocoa
1½ teaspoons baking powder
¼ teaspoon salt
½ cup golden raisins, or to taste (optional)

Preheat oven to 400 degrees. Lightly grease or spray cookie sheets.

Cream margarine, sugar, and peanut butter until light and smooth. Blend in egg substitute or egg, and orange juice.

Whisk together flour, cocoa, baking powder, and salt. Stir into batter to make a slightly sticky dough. Stir in raisins.

Roll 1 tablespoon of the dough into a 1-inch ball. (If dough sticks to your hands, either flour your hands or refrigerate the dough for about 15 minutes.) Place on a cookie sheet and flatten lightly with a fork, making a crosshatch design. Repeat with remaining dough, setting cookies 2 inches apart on cookie sheets.

Bake cookies 12 to 14 minutes in the center of the oven, or until light golden on top and golden brown on the bottom. Remove to wire racks to cool.

Tip: You can add ½ cup chopped peanuts or walnuts to the batter.
Store: In an airtight container
Freeze: Yes
Mail: Yes

Elephant Ears

Yield
30 to 32
cookies

½ cup sugar, or to taste
2 teaspoons ground cinnamon
2 tablespoons butter or margarine, melted and cooled
1 package (17¼ ounces, or 2 sheets) frozen puff pastry,
    thawed to room temperature in the package

In a small bowl, mix sugar and cinnamon together. Sprinkle a pastry cloth or a board with cinnamon sugar. Put each sheet of defrosted puff pastry on the sugar-sprinkled cloth and roll to a 10 × 10-inch rectangle. Brush pastry with melted butter or margarine. Sprinkle some of the sugar mixture, to taste, over each sheet of pastry.

Brush edges of each sheet of pastry with water. Roll each short end toward the center, jelly roll–fashion, making 3 turns on each side, until both rolls touch in the middle. Gently press rolls together. Chill for 45 minutes or until firm.

Preheat oven to 400 degrees. Lightly grease or spray cookie sheets.

Cut chilled rolls into ½-inch slices. Turn them on their sides. Sprinkle cookie sheet with some of the cinnamon sugar. Set on cookie sheet, about 2 inches apart, and sprinkle with more sugar.

Bake in the center of the oven for 15 minutes, or until puffy and golden brown. Watch the cookies so that they do not overcook. Remove to wire racks to cool.

Store: In an airtight container
Freeze: Yes
Mail: Yes

Sugar Pretzels

Yield
32 cookies

½ cup unsalted butter, at room temperature
¼ cup sugar
1 teaspoon vanilla extract
1 egg, lightly beaten
1½ cups sifted all-purpose flour
1 egg white, lightly beaten
Coarse sugar or ground almonds

Cream butter and sugar on medium speed until light, about 2 minutes. Mix in vanilla and egg. Blend in flour to make a soft dough. Gather it into a ball, flatten slightly, cover with plastic wrap or aluminum foil, and refrigerate for 1 hour.

Lightly grease or spray cookie sheets.

Break off a tablespoonful of dough and roll out on the counter, using your hands, to a 9- to 10-inch pencil-size rope. Twist the ends of the rope around each other, then bring the ends down to form a pretzel shape. Set on cookie sheet. Repeat with remaining dough. Refrigerate shaped cookies for 30 minutes.

Preheat oven to 375 degrees.

Brush cookies with beaten egg white and sprinkle with sugar or almonds.

Bake in the center of the oven for 10 to 12 minutes. They will be firm to the touch and just beginning to color. Let cookies stand for 2 minutes on cookie sheets, then remove to wire racks to cool.

Tip: For the holidays, you can decorate these pretzels with colored sugar.

Store: In an airtight container

Freeze: Yes

Mail: Yes

Flutes Dipped in Chocolate

Yield
30 cookies

½ cup (1 stick) unsalted butter, at room temperature
½ cup sugar
1 teaspoon coconut flavoring or extract
2 egg whites
⅔ cup all-purpose flour
2 to 3 tablespoons water as needed
2 ounces semisweet chocolate, melted
1 teaspoon butter

Preheat oven to 375 degrees. Lightly grease or spray cookie sheets.

Cream butter, sugar, and coconut flavoring on medium speed until light, about 2 minutes. Add egg whites and mix well. Gradually add flour; mix well.

Drop batter by teaspoonfuls, 3 inches apart, on cookie sheets. Work with 4 cookies at a time until you are used to this particular procedure. Spread the batter with the back of a spoon into 3-inch rounds. Batter should be thin. If batter is too thick, add water by the tablespoonful until batter is loose. Bake cookies for 5 to 6 minutes or until edges are light brown.

Working quickly, loosen a hot cookie from the pan with a spatula and quickly roll it tightly around a pencil. Transfer cookie to a wire rack to cool, seam side down. Continue with remaining cookies. If they begin to harden too much, return to the oven for 30 seconds.

When cookies are cool, place chocolate and butter in a microwave-proof bowl or in the top of a double boiler. Microwave on medium-high (80 percent) or heat over hot water, stirring occasionally, until melted and smooth.

Dip both ends of each cookie in the chocolate. Return cookies to wire racks and keep in a cool place to set chocolate.

Store: In single layers on plates, loosely wrapped with foil.
Freeze: Yes
Mail: No

Pecan Tiles

Yield
35 to 36
cookies

¼ cup unsalted butter, at room temperature
½ cup sugar
2 egg whites
¼ cup cake flour
¼ teaspoon orange or lemon extract
⅓ cup finely ground pecans

Preheat oven to 425 degrees. Lightly grease or spray sturdy cookie sheets.

Cream butter and sugar until light, about 2 to 3 minutes. Stir in egg whites and continue beating until batter is smooth. Mix in flour, extract, and pecans.

Set cookie sheet in the oven for a few minutes so that the pan will be warm. Drop batter onto pan, ¾ teaspoonful at a time. Make only 4 or 5 cookies at a time until you get used to the method of shaping the cookies. With the back of a spoon, smooth the cookie dough into a circle about 2½ inches in diameter.

Bake in the center of the oven for 5 to 6 minutes, or until cookies are golden around the edges. Remove pan from oven and allow cookies to cool about 3 to 4 minutes, until they have firmed up but are still pliable. Have a wooden spoon handy. With a spatula, remove a cookie and form it around the spoon to make a curved tile shape. The cookies will shape quickly. Remove them to a wire rack to cool completely. Continue until all of the cookies have been made.

Tips: It is important that the pan is warm so that you can spread the cookie into a round shape. It is equally important to let the cookies cool so that they can be removed from the pan when firm but pliable.

Be sure to use a heavy-duty cookie sheet. A flimsy pan may cause the cookies to crack or stick.

Store: In an airtight container; keep in a single layer.

Freeze: No

Mail: No

Chocolate Spritz Ribbons

Yield
60 cookies

2 ounces semisweet chocolate, chopped
1 cup (2 sticks) unsalted butter, at room temperature
¾ cup sugar
2 egg yolks
1 teaspoon vanilla extract
¼ teaspoon salt
2½ cups all-purpose flour
1 to 3 tablespoons milk, if needed
1 cup chocolate sprinkles, or to taste

Preheat oven to 350 degrees. Place ungreased nonstick cookie sheets in the refrigerator for at least 10 minutes.

Place chocolate in a microwave-proof bowl or in the top of a double boiler. Microwave on medium-high (80 percent) or heat over hot water, stirring occasionally, until melted and smooth. Cool.

Cream butter and sugar on medium speed until light, about 2 minutes. Add egg yolks, vanilla, and salt. Stir in chocolate and flour and mix well. Dough should be stiff, but easy to put through the cookie press. If it is too firm, add milk, a tablespoon at a time.

Fit a cookie press with the slotted form (for making ribbons) and, holding the press at a 45-degree angle, press out dough onto cookie sheet in one long strip. With a sharp knife, cut dough into 2 ½- to 3-inch cookies. Space about 1 inch apart. Top with chocolate sprinkles

Bake in the center of the oven for 5 to 8 minutes, or until cookies are just firm and golden on the bottom. Let stand on cookie sheets for 1 minute, then remove to wire racks to cool.

Store: In an airtight container
Freeze: Yes
Mail: Yes

Nutmeg Spritz Cookies

Yield
60 cookies

1 cup (2 sticks) unsalted butter, at room temperature
⅔ cup sugar
3 egg yolks
1 teaspoon vanilla extract
¼ teaspoon salt
½ cup ground almonds
2¼ cups all-purpose flour
1 to 3 tablespoons milk, if needed

Preheat oven to 350 degrees. Place ungreased nonstick cookie sheets in the refrigerator for at least 10 minutes.

Cream butter and sugar on medium speed until light. Add egg yolks, vanilla, and salt. Stir in ground nuts and flour. Dough should be stiff; if it is too firm to easily pipe through the cookie press, add milk by the tablespoon.

Fit a cookie press with the form of your choice. Spoon dough into the press.

Press out cookies, about 1 inch apart, onto chilled cookie sheets.

Bake in the center of the oven for 7 to 10 minutes, or until cookies are firm and beginning to color on the bottom. Let stand on cookie sheets for a minute, then remove to wire racks to cool.

Store: In an airtight container
Freeze: Yes
Mail: Yes

Ladyfingers

Yield
18 cookies

3 eggs, separated
½ cup sugar
½ teaspoon vanilla extract
1 teaspoon grated lime or lemon zest (optional)
⅔ cup sifted cake flour
Sifted confectioners' sugar to decorate cookies

Preheat oven to 350 degrees. Butter and flour a ladyfinger cake pan or use a nonstick cookie sheet.

Beat egg whites on high speed until soft peaks form. Slowly sprinkle 2 tablespoons of the sugar over the whites and continue beating until they form stiff peaks but are still glossy. Set aside.

In a separate bowl, beat egg yolks and remaining sugar until thick and light, about 5 minutes. Blend in vanilla and zest. Gently fold in flour, then the beaten egg whites.

Fill a pastry bag fitted with a ½-inch round opening tip with the batter. Pipe batter into prepared mold depressions or in 4-inch lengths on cookie sheet. Sprinkle cookies generously with sifted confectioners' sugar.

Bake cookies in the center of the oven for 10 minutes, or until cookies are lightly golden. Cool cookies in pan for 10 minutes before removing them with a spatula to a wire rack to finish cooling.

Tip: Ladyfingers are used in a number of dessert recipes, such as tiramisu, the Italian layered pudding. It is always good to have them on hand in the freezer.

Store: In an airtight container
Freeze: Yes
Mail: No

Sesame Thumbprints

Yield
36 cookies

These got their name from the bakers' custom of making the hollows in the cookies with their thumb. Since the cookies are hot, it's better to use a wooden spoon or dowel.

½ cup (1 stick) unsalted butter, at room temperature
½ cup sugar
1 egg yolk
1 teaspoon vanilla extract
1½ cups all-purpose flour
½ teaspoon salt
1 cup quick-cooking (not instant) oats
2 to 3 tablespoons sesame seeds
3 to 4 tablespoons apricot, strawberry, or raspberry jam

Preheat oven to 350 degrees.

Cream butter and sugar on medium speed until light. Beat in egg yolk and vanilla. Whisk flour with salt, then stir into butter-sugar mixture until incorporated. Stir in oats.

Pinch off pieces of dough and roll into balls about 1¼ inches in diameter. Roll half of each ball in sesame seeds. Place on ungreased cookie sheets, sesame side up, about 1½ inches apart. Bake in the center of the oven for 5 minutes, or until mostly set. With the handle of a wooden spoon or a dowel, press an indentation in the center of each cookie. Return to the oven for another 7 to 8 minutes, until cookies have firmed up and are golden on the bottom.

Let cool for a minute on cookie sheets, then remove to wire racks to finish cooling. Not too long before serving, fill the hollow in each cookie with a dab of jam.

Tips: If you prefer, you can fill the cookies with melted, cooled bittersweet chocolate. You can also roll them in finely chopped nuts of your choice, rather than sesame seeds.

Store: Unfilled cookies, in an airtight container. Filled cookies, on a plate wrapped with foil.

Freeze: Unfilled cookies only

Mail: No

Chocolate Cookies with a Cherry Inside

Yield
44 cookies

1¼ cups (2½ sticks) butter, at room temperature, cut in chunks
¾ cup sugar
¾ teaspoon vanilla extract
½ teaspoon chocolate extract
2 cups all-purpose flour
¼ teaspoon salt
½ cup Dutch-process cocoa
2 cups slivered almonds or walnuts
½ cup candied or drained maraschino cherries
1½ cups confectioners' sugar, for rolling cookies

Preheat oven to 350 degrees. Lightly grease or spray cookie sheets.

In a large bowl, cream butter and sugar until light, about 2 minutes. Add vanilla and chocolate extracts, flour, salt, cocoa, and almonds. Dough will be stiff.

To shape cookies, take a walnut-sized piece of dough and push a cherry into the center. Shape cookie so that the cherry is covered by dough and the cookie is rounded. Set cookies on cookie sheets, about 1½ inches apart.

Bake in the center of the oven for 12 to 15 minutes or until cookies are firm to the touch. While they are still hot, roll cookies in confectioners' sugar. Remove to wire racks to cool.

Store: In an airtight container
Freeze: Yes
Mail: Yes

Pineapple Cookie Puffs

Yield
20 cookies

½ cup (1 stick) unsalted butter or margarine,
    at room temperature, cut in chunks
6 tablespoons sugar
1¾ cups all-purpose flour
⅓ cup ground walnuts
2 to 4 tablespoons warm water
⅓ cup diced candied pineapple
Sifted confectioners' sugar to dust cookies

To prepare cookies, beat butter and sugar until light, about 2 minutes. Stir in flour and walnuts, blend together. Add only enough water to make a soft dough. Gather dough into a ball, turn out onto a lightly floured board, and knead about 1 to 2 minutes, until smooth. Cover dough with plastic wrap and refrigerate for 30 minutes.

Preheat oven to 350 degrees. Lightly grease or spray cookie sheets.

Divide dough in half and roll it out on a lightly floured pastry cloth to between ⅛ and ¼ inch thick. Cut into 1½-inch rounds with a cookie cutter.

Set 3 pieces of the pineapple in the center of one cookie. Brush the edges of another cookie with water. Set the top cookie over the bottom cookie. Press the edges together, stretching the top cookie to fit over the bottom one.

Set cookies 1½ inches apart on cookie sheets. Bake in the center of the oven for 15 to 17 minutes. Cookies will be golden on the bottom and firm to the touch. The color will remain natural. Remove cookies from oven and sprinkle with sifted confectioners' sugar. Let cookies stay on tray for 2 to 3 minutes. Using a spatula, remove them to a wire rack to cool.

When cookies are cool, sprinkle again with sifted confectioners' sugar. Remove to a dessert tray and serve.

Tip: To sprinkle confectioners' sugar, put a small amount in a tea strainer, hold it over cookies, and tap the strainer to sift the sugar.

Store: In an airtight container

Freeze: Yes

Mail: Yes

Cats' Tongues Filled with Espresso Chocolate

Yield
32 cookies

These cookies get their name from their long, narrow shape. They also taste good plain, without the chocolate filling.

1 cup (2 sticks) unsalted butter, at room temperature
1½ cups confectioners' sugar
2 tablespoons grated lime or lemon zest
1 egg
1 egg yolk
2 cups all-purpose flour, sifted
4 ounces semisweet chocolate
¼ cup heavy cream
2 teaspoons brewed espresso or other strong coffee

Preheat oven to 400 degrees. Line cookie sheets with baking parchment.

Cream butter on medium speed until light, about 2 minutes. Add sugar and blend together. Add zest, then egg and egg yolk; mix well. Sift flour over batter and incorporate. Batter will be thick.

Spoon batter into a pastry bag fitted with a ½-inch round tip. Pipe 3-inch lengths of dough, about 2 inches apart, onto cookie sheets.

Bake cookies in the center of the oven for 8 to 9 minutes, until golden brown around the edges. Let stand on cookie sheets 2 to 3 minutes, then remove to wire racks to cool completely.

While cookies are cooling, prepare filling. Place chocolate in a microwave-proof bowl or in the top of a double boiler. Microwave on medium-high (80 percent) or heat over hot water, stirring occasionally, until melted and smooth. Stir in cream and espresso. Let chocolate cool slightly, then stir. Using a pastry brush, brush the flat side of half of the cookies with chocolate. Top with the remaining cookies, flat side touching the chocolate. Let cookies remain on racks in a cool place until chocolate has set.

Tip: You can also make the cookies by spreading the dough into 3-inch pencil shapes with a teaspoon.

Store: Wrapped in aluminum foil, in an airtight container
Freeze: Yes
Mail: No

Black Walnut Sandwich Cookies

Yield
24 (2-inch)
sandwich
cookies

¾ cup (1½ sticks) unsalted butter, at room
  temperature, cut into chunks
¼ cup sugar
1 egg
⅓ cup ground black or regular walnuts
2 cups all-purpose flour
¼ teaspoon salt

Filling:

¼ cup (½ stick) butter
1 cup strawberry jam
⅓ cup ground black (or regular) walnuts
Sifted confectioners' sugar for garnish

Beat the butter, sugar, egg, and ground black walnuts on medium speed until light, about 2 to 3 minutes. Mix in flour and salt. Dough will be stiff. Gather dough into a ball, cover with aluminum wrap or plastic wrap, and refrigerate for 30 minutes.

Preheat oven to 350 degrees. Lightly grease or spray cookie sheets.

Divide dough in half. Roll out one half at a time to ⅛-inch thickness. For best results, use a lightly floured pastry cloth and a floured sleeve for the rolling pin. Cut cookies into 1½- or 2-inch rounds. Bake in the center of the oven for about 12 minutes, or until cookies just begin to turn color.

While cookies are baking, prepare the filling: Melt butter in a small saucepan. Mix in remaining ingredients and cook, stirring continuously for 1 to 2 minutes, only until jam melts and butter is absorbed. Remove from heat and let cool.

Spread filling on flat side of half the warm cookies. Cover with another cookie, flat side down, press gently together, and let cookies sit until filling sets. Sprinkle cookies with sifted confectioners' sugar.

Tip: You can substitute regular walnuts if you prefer, or use raspberry jam instead of strawberry.

Store: In an airtight container

Freeze: Yes

Mail: No

New England Whoopee Pies

Yield
18 cookies

⅓ cup vegetable shortening
1 cup sugar
1 egg
1½ teaspoons baking soda
⅓ cup unsweetend cocoa
½ teaspoon chocolate extract
2 cups all-purpose flour
1 cup milk
1 cup marshmallow fluff

Preheat oven to 425 degrees. Lightly grease or spray cookie sheets.

Cream shortening and sugar on medium speed until light, about 2 minutes. Beat in egg, baking soda, cocoa, and chocolate extract. Mix in flour alternately with milk to make a medium dough.

Drop dough by heaping tablespoonfuls onto cookie sheets, spacing cookies about 2 inches apart. Bake in the center of the oven for 6 to 7 minutes, until cookies are rounded and just firm to the touch.

Cool cookies 2 minutes in the pan. Using a spatula, remove cookies to a wire rack to cool. When the cookies have cooled completely, spread flat side with marshmallow fluff and secure another cookie on top. Cover cookies individually with plastic wrap.

Tips: You can fill the pies with jam of your choice if desired, instead of the marshmallow fluff. The pies are large, but you can bake them half the size if you prefer.

Store: On a plate, wrapped with foil, for up to a day. For longer storage, wrap each cookie in plastic wrap.

Mail: No

Date and Nut Sandwich Cookies

Yield
36 cookies

½ cup (1 stick) unsalted butter, at room temperature, cut into chunks
½ cup vegetable shortening
2 cups packed light brown sugar
2 eggs
½ cup buttermilk
3½ cups all-purpose flour
¼ teaspoon salt
1 teaspoon baking soda
¼ teaspoon ground cinnamon
¼ teaspoon ground allspice

Filling:

2 cups pitted, chopped dates
¾ cup granulated sugar
¾ cup water
½ cup chopped walnuts, or other nuts of your choice

Cream butter and shortening on medium speed until light, about 2 minutes. Mix in sugar and beat until well blended. Add eggs, one at a time, beating well after each addition. Mix in buttermilk. Stir in flour, salt, baking soda, and spices. Dough will be soft. If dough is too sticky, knead in an additional 2 to 4 tablespoons flour.

Gather dough into a ball, cover with plastic wrap or aluminum foil, and refrigerate for 1 hour.

While dough is chilling, prepare filling. Place all of the filling ingredients except nuts in a small or medium-sized, heavy saucepan. Bring mixture to a boil over medium heat. Reduce heat to a simmer and continue cooking for 10 minutes or until filling thickens. Stir often. Mix in nuts.

Preheat oven to 350 degrees. Lightly grease or spray cookie sheets.

Divide dough in half. Roll out one half of dough at a time on a lightly floured pastry cloth to between ⅛ and ¼ inch thick. Cut out cookies with a 1½-inch cookie cutter. Spoon ½ teaspoon of filling in center of a dough cutout. Dip your finger in water and run it around the edges. Place another dough cutout on top and seal edges by pressing with your fingers or the tines of a fork. Continue until all of the cookies have been prepared. Set cookies 3 inches apart on cookie sheets, as they spread during baking.

Bake cookies in the center of the oven for 11 to 14 minutes, until cookies are golden on the bottom and slightly browned on top. Let cookies cool 2 minutes on the cookie sheet, then remove to wire racks.

Tips: Lightly flour the bottom of the cookie cutter if it sticks to the dough. Cookies spread, so be sure to leave ample space between them.

Store: In an airtight container

Freeze: Yes

Mail: No

Whole Wheat Fig Apple Bars

Yield
32 to 36 bars

Crust:

1¼ cups whole wheat flour
1 cup unbleached all-purpose flour
¼ teaspoon salt
¾ teaspoon baking soda
½ teaspoon ground cinnamon
½ cup (1 stick) unsalted butter or margarine cut into bits
1 cup unsweetened applesauce

Filling:

10 ounces (2 heaping cupfuls) dried figs,
   stemmed and coarsely chopped
6 ounces dried apples
2 tablespoons honey
1 cup apple, raspberry, or grape juice
1½ teaspoons vanilla extract

To make crust: Place flours, salt, baking soda, and cinnamon in a large bowl. Beat in butter until crumbly. Stir in applesauce to make a somewhat stiff but sticky dough. Refrigerate for 1 hour, or until dough has firmed up a bit and is not as sticky.

Meanwhile, make filling: Place all ingredients in a non-aluminum saucepan. Cook over medium heat, stirring frequently, until fruit is very soft. Let cool slightly, then purée in a food processor to make a thick paste. Or, put through a food mill or food grinder. (Mixture is very thick for a blender; if you must use a blender, purée it in 2 or 3 batches and thin slightly with a little extra fruit juice.)

Preheat oven to 375 degrees. Lightly grease or spray a large cookie sheet.

Divide dough into three parts. On a floured board or pastry cloth, roll out each part to a rectangle slightly larger than 6 × 13 inches. Trim ragged edges. Spread cooled fig filling lengthwise down one half of dough. Filling should be thick. Fold remaining half of dough over filling and pinch edges to seal. Pat cookie rolls along sides and on top to distribute filling and make rolls as evenly shaped as possible. Place on cookie sheet. Repeat with remaining dough and filling.

Bake fig rolls in the center of the oven for 25 to 30 minutes, until outsides are crisp and bottoms are golden. Let cool on pans for a minute, then carefully transfer to wire racks. When completely cool, use a sharp knife to slice off 1-inch-wide pieces.

Store: On a plate, wrapped with foil

Freeze: Yes

Mail: No

Poppy Seed and Raisin Crescents

Yield
48 cookies

½ cup (1 stick) unsalted butter, at room temperature
½ cup (1 stick) unsalted margarine, at room temperature
2½ cups all-purpose flour
1 cup sour cream
1 can (12½ ounces) poppy seed filling
1½ cups golden raisins or currants
2 egg whites, slightly beaten
Sugar to sprinkle on top of the cookies

Cream butter and margarine on medium speed until light. Add flour and sour cream. Blend ingredients together and increase speed to high. Continue mixing to form a sticky dough. Remove dough, then shape into a ball. Roll dough lightly in flour and wrap in plastic wrap. Refrigerate for at least 1 hour.

When ready to prepare cookies, cut dough into 4 equal parts. Knead each half briefly until pliable. If dough is too sticky, sprinkle with a small amount of flour and incorporate until dough is soft and pliable, but not sticky.

Preheat oven to 350 degrees. Lightly grease or spray cookie sheets.

There are two ways to roll these cookies. One method is to roll each quarter of dough on a lightly floured pastry cloth to an 18-inch circle. Cut into 12 wedges. Spoon about ¾ teaspoon of room-temperature poppy seed filling onto each wedge. Spread with the back of a spoon. The filling is stiff and does not spread easily. It is not necessary to cover entire surface of the dough. Sprinkle with raisins or currants. Roll cookies into crescent shapes and set seam side down on cookie sheets, about 1 inch apart.

The second method is to thinly roll out each quarter of dough and cut dough into 3-inch circles with a biscuit or cookie cutter. Spread about ¾ teaspoon of filling on each circle and sprinkle with a few raisins or currants. Roll up dough, jelly roll–style.

Brush cookies with beaten egg whites and sprinkle with sugar.

Bake cookies in the center of the oven for about 25 to 30 minutes, until cookies are golden. Let cool about 1 to 2 minutes on cookie sheets, then remove to wire racks to cool completely. These cookies are best served warm.

Tip: These are best eaten warm on the day they are baked.

Store: On a plate, wrapped with foil, for a day. For longer storage, put in an airtight tin.

Freeze: Yes

Mail: Yes

Easy Chocolate-Dipped Sandwich Cookies

Yield
24 cookies

4 ounces cream cheese, softened
½ cup confectioners' sugar
1 teaspoon Cointreau or Gran Marnier, or ½ teaspoon orange extract
48 small store-bought chocolate or vanilla wafer cookies
¼ teaspoon vanilla extract
2 tablespoons unsalted butter
6 ounces bittersweet chocolate, broken into pieces

To make filling, beat cream cheese with confectioners' sugar and orange liqueur or extract until smooth.

Spread about ½ teaspoon filling on the flat side of a wafer cookie. Top with another wafer cookie to make a sandwich. Repeat with remaining filling and cookies.

Place butter and chocolate in a microwave-proof bowl or in the top of a double boiler. Microwave on medium-high (80 percent) or heat over hot water, stirring occasionally, until melted and smooth.

Gently dip cookies into chocolate, spooning chocolate over to make sure they're coated. Lift from chocolate with a dipping fork or a two-pronged cooking fork, letting excess chocolate run off. Place cookies on a lightly oiled wire rack over waxed paper to catch drips. Let stand in a cool place until chocolate sets.

Store: In single layers on plates, in the refrigerator. Wrap loosely with foil. Let stand at room temperature 15 to 20 minutes before serving.

Freeze: No

Mail: No

Marzipan Strips

Yield
60 to 65
cookies

These delicacies walk the line between Danish pastries and cookies.

Pastry:

1¾ cups unbleached all-purpose flour
1 package (2¼ teaspoons) active dry yeast
¼ cup sugar
¼ teaspoon salt
½ cup warm milk
2 tablespoons (¼ stick) unsalted butter, softened
1 egg
½ teaspoon vanilla extract
½ cup (1 stick) cold unsalted butter

Filling:

1 cup almond paste
1 cup finely ground blanched almonds
1 egg
2 to 3 tablespoons freshly squeezed orange juice

Icing:

1½ cups confectioners' sugar
¼ cup freshly squeezed orange juice

To make the pastry: Stir flour, yeast, and sugar in the large bowl of an electric mixer fitted with a dough hook. Add salt, milk, 2 tablespoons butter, egg, and vanilla. Begin mixing on the lowest setting to blend ingredients, then adjust speed to high and knead for 3 minutes to make a smooth dough with the consistency of a soft bread dough, easily worked. If dough is too dry, add 1 tablespoon of milk. If dough is too sticky, knead in additional flour, a teaspoon at a time.

(To mix the dough by hand, beat with a wooden spoon, then turn out onto a lightly floured board and knead for 5 minutes.)

Refrigerate dough for 10 minutes.

Place dough on a lightly floured pastry cloth, turning to dust all sides with flour. Roll dough into an 8 × 15-inch rectangle, with one of the short sides nearest you. Slice the whole stick of chilled butter horizontally into 6 equal pieces. Place the sliced butter pieces on top half of pastry, breaking off pieces of butter and arranging to cover dough. Fold up the bottom half of the dough to cover the butter. Press dough together lightly with a rolling pin.

Roll dough out again to an 8 × 15-inch rectangle. Cover with plastic wrap or aluminum foil and refrigerate for 20 minutes.

Again, fold up bottom half of dough, then roll to an 8 × 15-inch rectangle. Cover and refrigerate for 20 minutes.

Meanwhile, prepare the filling: Combine all ingredients in a deep bowl and mix until smooth and spreadable. Set aside.

Preheat oven to 375 degrees. Place 2 nonstick cookie sheets or lightly greased or sprayed regular cookie sheets in the freezer or refrigerator while you roll and fill the dough.

Divide chilled dough in half. On a lightly floured board or pastry cloth, roll out each half to a rectangle 6 × 18 inches, then cut in half again to make 4 rectangles, each 3 × 18 inches. Spread a fourth of the filling on the lower half of one dough rectangle. Fold the top half of the dough over the filling. Repeat with remaining dough and filling. Press dough lightly with fingertips to seal.

Using a small, sharp knife, cut the dough into ½-inch-wide strips. Cut a horizontal slash in the center of each strip. Place cookies on cookie sheets, leaving an inch between them.

Bake in the center of the oven for 15 to 20 minutes or until cookies are a light golden color.

While cookies bake, prepare icing: Sift confectioners' sugar into a small bowl. Stir in the orange juice to make a smooth icing. Remove cookies from oven and let cool 3 minutes. Drizzle with icing while still warm.

Tips: The butter or margarine must stay cool while you roll the dough. Otherwise, it will seep out from between the layers of pastry. If at any point the butter begins to soften too much, return the dough to the refrigerator for 5 to 10 minutes.

These should be served warm. To reheat, place in a 300-degree oven for about 5 minutes, or 10 to 15 minutes if cookies are frozen. Or, reheat in the microwave at medium (50 percent) power until barely warm (start with 15 seconds; don't microwave too long, or the cookies will toughen).

Store: On a plate, wrapped with foil

Freeze: Yes; but don't ice until ready to serve

Mail: No

Cinnamon Horns

Yield
32 cookies

When Barbara was growing up in Massachusetts, she and her family loved the crescents that a local bakery called "frozen dough." The cookies were dark with cinnamon, and had crunchy, sugary bottoms. This recipe re-creates that childhood favorite. Unlike most cookies, it has no sugar in the dough. The currants and cinnamon sugar provide sweetness.

1 package (2¼ teaspoons) active dry yeast
3 cups unbleached all-purpose flour
1 cup (2 sticks) unsalted butter, at room temperature, cut into chunks
¼ teaspoon salt
3 egg yolks
1 cup sour cream
½ cup sugar
¼ cup ground cinnamon
1½ cups (loosely packed) dried currants
1 cup ground almonds

In the large bowl, sprinkle the yeast over the flour. Add butter and salt. On medium speed, mix for 3 to 5 minutes, until well blended. Mixture will be crumbly.

In a separate bowl, combine the egg yolks and the sour cream. Stir into flour-butter mixture to make a soft dough. Remove from bowl, scraping up all bits of the dough. With lightly floured hands, form dough into a ball.

Wrap in plastic wrap or foil and chill for at least 4 hours or up to overnight.

When ready to assemble cookies, remove dough from refrigerator. Preheat oven to 350 degrees. Combine sugar and cinnamon with a fork until cinnamon is evenly distributed. Sprinkle half of the cinnamon-sugar mixture evenly over a nonstick cookie sheet (or a regular one lined with baking parchment) that is 12 × 17 inches or larger. Set aside.

Sprinkle about 1½ tablespoons of the remaining sugar-cinnamon mixture evenly over the middle of a pastry cloth. Divide chilled dough into 4 equal-sized portions. Place 1 portion of dough on the pastry cloth. Pat the dough with the rolling pin to soften it slightly, then roll out to a circle about ⅛ inch thick. Sprinkle dough evenly with 6 tablespoons currants, pressing currants lightly into dough with the rolling pin. Sprinkle ¼ cup almonds evenly over dough. With a small, sharp knife or a pizza cutter, cut dough into 8 equal wedges.

Starting with the wide end, roll each wedge up toward the point, then twist into a crescent shape. Place cookies on cinnamon-sugar-sprinkled cookie sheet. They will not spread or rise much, and can be placed close together.

Roll and fill remaining portions of dough the same way.

Bake for 14 minutes, or until firm to the touch. Immediately slide a pastry knife under cookies to loosen them, then remove to racks to cool. (For crunchier bottoms, slide the hot cookies over the cinnamon-sugar-coated cookie sheet before placing on racks.)

Store: In an airtight container
Freeze: Yes
Mail: Yes

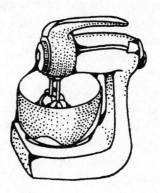

Cottage Cheese Strudel with Apricot Filling

Yield
65 slices

Crust:

¼ pound (1 stick) unsalted butter, at room temperature
¼ pound (1 stick) margarine, at room temperature
½ pound small-curd cottage cheese
2 cups all-purpose flour
¼ teaspoon salt

Filling:

1½ cups dried apricots, finely chopped
1½ cups golden raisins, chopped
2 cups chopped walnuts or pecans
1 cup chopped candied cherries, or flaked sweetened coconut
1 jar (13 ounces) apricot jam
1 cup fine bread crumbs
2 egg whites, slightly beaten

Cream butter and margarine on medium speed until light, about 2 minutes. Add cottage cheese and increase speed to high. Continue mixing until ingredients are combined. Add flour and salt; combine to make a soft dough. Shape dough into a ball and cover with plastic wrap or aluminum foil. Refrigerate for 1 hour, or until fairly firm.

Preheat oven to 375 degrees. Lightly grease or spray a large cookie sheet.

Divide dough into 2 equal parts. Roll each dough part on a lightly floured pastry cloth or board to about 12 inches. Do not roll too thin.

In a deep mixing bowl combine apricots, raisins, nuts, cherries or coconut, and apricot jam.

Sprinkle ½ of the bread crumbs over one half of pastry. Spread with ½ of the filling. Roll up the dough, jelly roll–style. Set roll, seam side down, on cookie sheet. Brush strudel with egg whites. Form the second roll the same way.

Bake in the center of the oven for 30 to 35 minutes, until golden brown.

Remove strudels from oven and cool on cookie sheets. Use a spatula to loosen bottom of strudels and then, with one or two spatulas, remove to a cutting board. Using a sharp knife, cut strips between ¼- and ½-inch slices. Arrange on serving dish.

Store: In an airtight container

Freeze: Yes

Mail: Yes

Sharon Sanders' Walnut Tartlets

Yield
48 cookies

Every Christmas, Sharon's friends, relatives, and colleagues look forward to a tin of wonderfully flaky and not-too-sweet nut tartlets that have become her holiday signature cookie. The recipe is inspired by an old American classic, Pecan Tassies, except that Sharon uses walnuts. Her unusual method of making them is easy and produces beautifully shaped cookies.

Crust:

1 cup (2 sticks) unsalted butter, at room temperature, cut into chunks
6 ounces cream cheese, at room temperature
2 cups unbleached all-purpose flour

Filling:

2 eggs
1½ cups packed light brown sugar
1½ teaspoons vanilla extract
1⅓ cups chopped walnuts, preferably toasted

To make the crust: Cream butter and cream cheese on medium speed until smooth. With a wooden spoon or your hands, work in flour to make a stiff but slightly sticky dough. Pinch off pieces of dough and roll between your palms to make 48 balls a bit larger than 1 inch in diameter. Roll them as smoothly as possible; cracks will make it harder to shape the cookies later. Place dough balls in two 24-cup miniature muffin tins or four 12-cup mini-muffin tins. (If you do not have that many tins, place the leftover dough balls on a plate and wrap loosely with plastic wrap.) Chill for about 30 minutes. Dough should be firm but not stiff. (The dough balls can also be refrigerated for up to several days. Let sit at room temperature for about 30 minutes, until pliable.)

To form cookies, use a wooden dowel about ¾ inch to 1 inch in diameter (see Tips). Press it into the center of a dough ball and rotate the dowel, lightly pressing it against the bottom and sides of the dough, to form a smooth, deep, even pastry shell. Repeat with remaining dough. If dough sticks to dowel, dip end of dowel in flour. Cover with plastic wrap and refrigerate for at least 30 minutes, until firm. (You can press the dough into the cups with your fingers, if you prefer, instead of using the dowel.)

To make the filling and assemble tarts: Preheat oven to 325 degrees.

In a mixing bowl, beat eggs and sugar with a fork, pressing with the back of the fork to dissolve lumps. Stir in vanilla, then walnuts. With a teaspoon, spoon filling into tart shells so that it comes just below top of pastry.

Bake in the center of the oven for about 25 minutes, or until crust is golden and top of filling is set. Remove pan to a wire rack for 4 to 5 minutes. To remove tarts, slide a butter knife carefully down side of each tart to lift it. Cool completely on wire racks.

Tips: Sharon insists on the best ingredients for these: really fresh walnuts (buy them in bulk from a nut store or good health food store), good cream cheese and unsalted butter, and an excellent vanilla extract. Wooden kitchen dowels are available at some cookware shops. You can use any short wooden dowel or handle ¾ to 1 inch in diameter—just make sure it's clean. We used the wooden handle of a large pizza wheel to shape the tart shells.

High-altitude: Bake at 300 degrees for about 30 minutes.

Store: In an airtight tin

Freeze: Yes

Mail: Yes

Chocolate Tarts

Yield
24 tarts

Crust:

1 cup all-purpose flour
¼ teaspoon baking powder
¼ teaspoon salt
½ cup cold vegetable shortening
1 egg, beaten

Filling:

6 ounces (about 1 cup) semisweet chocolate chips
1 tablespoon butter or margarine, softened
½ cup sugar
1 tablespoon milk
1 teaspoon instant espresso
1 tablespoon coffee liqueur or coffee cream liqueur
1 egg, beaten
24 small walnut pieces

In a large bowl sift flour, baking powder, and salt. Cut in shortening until mixture resembles coarse crumbs. A food processor works well. Stir in egg. Mix until dough clings together. Gather dough and shape into a ball. Cover dough with plastic wrap or aluminum foil and refrigerate for 30 minutes.

Preheat oven to 350 degrees. Lightly grease or spray two 12-cup miniature muffin tins or one 24-cup tin. Or, use nonstick tins.

Roll out dough on a lightly floured board to ⅛-inch thickness. Using a 2½-inch cookie cutter, cut out 24 circles. Press each dough circle into miniature muffin cups. Chill for 10 minutes.

While dough is chilling, prepare filling. Place chocolate in a microwave-proof bowl or in the top of a double boiler. Microwave on medium-high (80 percent) or heat over hot water, stirring occasionally, until melted and smooth. Stir in butter, then remaining filling ingredients except walnuts.

Spoon 1 scant tablespoon of the filling into each chilled pastry cup; top each with a walnut piece.

Bake in the center or the oven for 20 to 25 minutes, until crust is golden and filling is set. Cool. Remove tarts from pan. Serve at room temperature.

Storage: In single layers on plates, in the refrigerator. Cover loosely with foil.

Tips: Mix the filling butter in with the chocolate when it is warm. You can garnish the top of the tart with candied fruits or other nuts of your choice.

Freeze: No

Mail: No

Chocolate Peanut Butter Cups

Yield
24 cookies

1 cup plus 2 tablespoons all-purpose flour
⅓ cup unsweetened cocoa
⅔ cup confectioners' sugar
¼ teaspoon salt
½ cup cold butter, cut into small pieces
2 tablespoons cold vegetable shortening, cut into small pieces
1 egg, lightly beaten
1 to 2 tablespoons cold milk or cream, if needed

Filling:

1 cup creamy peanut butter
1 cup confectioners' sugar
1 teaspoon vanilla extract
1 egg yolk
4 to 6 tablespoons milk or cream, as needed

Sift together flour, cocoa, confectioners' sugar, and salt. Place in a mixing bowl or in the bowl of a food processor. Cut in butter and shortening until dough resembles coarse crumbs.

Stir in egg and, if necessary, milk or cream to make a soft, sticky dough. Wrap in plastic wrap or foil and refrigerate for 1 to 2 hours or longer, until dough firms up enough to roll easily.

Lightly grease or spray one 24-cup or two 12-cup mini-muffin pans.

On a floured board or cloth, roll dough out to ⅛ inch thick. Dough is soft; you may need to use a fair amount of flour. Brush off any excess flour from top of dough, then cut into 2½-inch rounds. Gently ease dough rounds into cups in muffin pan, and press gently against bottom and sides of pan. Gather up dough scraps and roll, then cut into rounds. If dough scraps have softened up, place in the refrigerator, along with the dough in the muffin tins, for 10 to 15 minutes, then roll. Discard any remaining scraps, or bake free-form.

Refrigerate dough cups for 20 to 30 minutes.

Meanwhile, preheat oven to 375 degrees. Make the filling: Beat peanut butter, confectioners' sugar, vanilla, egg yolk, and ¼ cup milk or cream until smooth. Add additional cream if necessary to make a pliable, but not sticky, dough.

Remove dough cups from the refrigerator. Roll peanut butter filling into balls slightly larger than 1 inch, and place in chocolate cups. Flatten filling slightly with your finger.

Bake in the center of the oven for 15 minutes. Filling should look puffy, and when you carefully insert a bread knife between a chocolate cup and the pan, the chocolate cup should slide easily.

Let cool in pans for 10 to 15 minutes, then gently pry cups out of pan with a bread knife. Finish cooling on wire racks.

Store: In an airtight container

Freeze: Yes

Mail: No

ETHNIC AND INTERNATIONAL COOKIES

Most American cookies, of course, originally came from other countries. In fact, many of the cookies we consider standard American holiday fare originated in the British Isles, Scandinavia, Germany, and central Europe.

We consider cookies "ethnic" or international if they still retain a strong imprint of their native countries, either in the choice of ingredients, when and where they are served, or how they are thought of by most cooks. Just about everyone thinks of those melt-in-the-mouth walnut tea cakes as Russian, most of the cookie bakers who make kolaches for Christmas are of eastern European descent, and cucidati remain a staple of St. Joseph's Day festivities in traditional Italian-American communities.

Some of these cookies will look and taste familiar; others may still seem a bit exotic. But we have no doubts that all deserve the widest recognition possible.

Viennese Marbled Hussar Cookies

Yield
24 to 25
cookies

½ cup (1 stick) unsalted butter, at room temperature
⅓ cup sugar
2 egg yolks
1¼ cups all-purpose flour
¼ cup semisweet chocolate chips
2 tablespoons all-purpose flour
1 egg white, lightly beaten
½ cup sliced almonds
About 2 tablespoons apricot or raspberry jam

Cream butter and sugar on medium speed until light, about 2 minutes. Blend in egg yolks. Add 1¼ cups flour and mix well. Dough will be soft. Gather dough in a ball and cover with plastic wrap or aluminum foil. Refrigerate for 1 hour.

Preheat oven to 350 degrees. Line cookie sheets with baking parchment.

Melt chocolate chips in a microwave or in the top of a double boiler over warm water, stirring occasionally. Remove from heat. Stir in 2 tablespoons flour.

Remove dough from refrigerator. If it is still sticky, sprinkle with flour and knead until it is incorporated. Divide dough in half. Mix half of the dough with the cooled chocolate mixture. Now knead the two doughs together lightly so that dough looks marbled.

Break off small pieces of dough and roll into ¾- to 1-inch balls. Press your thumb or a finger lightly into the top of each ball, making a depression in the cookie. Brush each cookie with egg white and roll in almonds, gently pressing almonds around the side of each cookie. Set cookies about 2 inches apart on cookie sheets.

Bake in the center of the oven for about 14 to 15 minutes, or until cookies look firm and are golden on the bottom. Fill each cookie with a small amount of jam. Cool cookies 2 minutes on cookie sheets, then remove to wire racks to cool completely.

Tip: You might want to slightly crush the almonds so that they will stick on to the cookie easily.

Store: In an airtight container. Cookies are fragile; layer carefully.

Freeze: Yes

Mail: No

Whole Wheat Viennese Vanilla Crescents

Yield
25 to 30
cookies

These famous melt-in-the-mouth German-Austrian cookies are usually made with white flour, so we were intrigued when we ran across a German recipe for whole wheat crescents. The whole wheat flour gives the cookies a deeper, nuttier flavor. If it matters, they're also higher in fiber than usual.

These cookies must sit for at least 10 days to allow the flavor of the vanilla to develop. They're worth the wait.

1 cup whole wheat pastry flour (see Tip)
¼ cup all-purpose flour
¼ cup confectioners' sugar
¼ teaspoon salt
1 cup (about 5 ounces) unshelled almonds, finely ground
2 vanilla beans, cut in half lengthwise and seeds scraped (reserve pods)
½ cup (1 stick) cold butter, cut into bits
2 egg yolks, lightly beaten
1 to 2 tablespoons ice water, as needed
½ cup confectioners' sugar mixed with 2 tablespoons
    granulated sugar, for dusting cookies

Place flours, ¼ cup sugar, salt, almonds, and scraped seeds from vanilla beans in the bowl of a food processor. Process until mixed. Add butter and pulse until mixture resembles coarse crumbs. (Dough can also be mixed by hand; place ingredients in a bowl, then work in butter with a pastry blender, two knives, or your fingertips.) Pulse or stir in egg yolks and enough water to make a dough that clings together.

Divide dough in half and roll into 2 logs about 1½ inches in diameter. Wrap tightly in waxed paper or plastic wrap and refrigerate for 30 minutes to 1 hour, until firm.

Preheat oven to 325 degrees.

Remove one log from the refrigerator and cut ½-inch slices from it. Roll each piece of dough into a rope about 3 inches long, then bend into a crescent shape, slightly tapering ends. Place crescents on ungreased baking sheets. Keep unbaked cookies and dough in the refrigerator while other cookies bake.

Bake in the center of the oven for 15 to 20 minutes, or until firm but not browned. Let cool on baking sheets for a minute, then dip warm cookies in confectioners'-granulated sugar mix. Place on wire racks. Handle cookies gently; they are fragile. Cover any leftover dusting sugar and set aside.

When all the cookies are baked and cooled, place the scraped vanilla pods in a cookie tin or other container with a tight-fitting lid. Gently lay cookies in container. Cover tightly and let stand for at least 10 days and preferably two to three weeks. Dust with additional sugar before serving.

Tip: Be sure to use whole wheat *pastry* flour, not regular whole wheat flour, in these. Whole wheat pastry flour, a finely ground flour made from soft wheat, is available in health food stores.

Store: In an airtight container

Freeze: Yes

Mail: No

German Strudel Cookies

Yield
60 cookies

1¼ cups bread flour
¼ teaspoon active dry yeast
⅛ teaspoon salt
1 egg yolk
¾ cup sour cream
½ cup (1 stick) cold butter, cut into small bits
1 tablespoon melted butter
3 tablespoons granulated sugar, plus some for dipping cookies

Mix flour, yeast, and salt. Work in egg yolk and sour cream with a fork; knead lightly to make a stiff, smooth dough. Roll out on a lightly floured board or pastry cloth to a rectangle a bit less than ¼ inch thick.

Scatter butter pieces evenly over dough. Fold one short side of dough over the center, then fold the other side over that, to make three layers. Roll out to about ¼ inch thick. Refrigerate for 15 to 20 minutes, until dough begins to firm up. Fold in thirds again, then roll out to between ⅛ and ¼ inch thick. Chill for 20 minutes. Roll into a rectangle about 14 by 17 inches; dough should be very thin, about 1/16 inch. Brush dough lightly with melted butter and sprinkle evenly with 3 tablespoons sugar. Starting with a long end, roll up jelly roll–fashion, as tightly as possible. Wrap in plastic wrap and chill for 2 hours, or until firm.

Preheat oven to 375 degrees. Butter baking sheets.

Cut strudel into ⅛-inch-thick slices, using a very sharp knife (a serrated knife works well). Dip one side of each cookie lightly in granulated sugar. Place on baking sheets, sugared sides up, and bake in the center of the oven for about 12 to 15 minutes, or until edges are turning golden. Carefully turn cookies over and return to oven for another 5 minutes, or until a rich golden brown.

Remove cookies immediately to wire racks to cool.

Store: In an airtight container
Freeze: Yes
Mail: Yes

*W*hite Pfeffernuesse (Peppernuts)

Yield
60 cookies

½ cup (1 stick) unsalted butter, at room temperature
2 cups sugar
2 eggs
½ cup heavy cream
2 tablespoons grated lemon zest
¼ teaspoon ground white pepper
1 teaspoon ground cardamom
1 teaspoon baking soda
6 cups all-purpose flour
½ cup finely chopped blanched almonds
½ cup finely chopped candied lemon peel
Sifted confectioners' sugar for dusting cookies

Preheat oven to 350 degrees. Lightly grease or spray cookie sheets.

Beat butter and sugar on medium speed until light, about 2 minutes. Add eggs, one at a time, beating well after each addition. Blend in cream, lemon zest, pepper, cardamom, and baking soda. Blend in flour, 1 cup at a time, to make a stiff dough. Mix in almonds and candied lemon peel.

Break off small pieces of dough and roll into 1-inch balls. Set on cookie sheets.

Bake cookies in the center of the oven for 12 to 15 minutes. Cookies should be firm to the touch but still pale.

Cool cookies for 2 minutes on cookie sheets. Sprinkle with sifted confectioners' sugar. Remove to wire racks to cool.

Tip: If you are having trouble rolling the cookies, dust your hands with flour.

Store: In an airtight container

Freeze: Yes

Mail: Yes

Lebkuchen Diamonds

Yield
40 to 44
cookies

Lebkuchen is a German honey cookie that is traditionally served at Christmas. But you can cut the dough in heart shapes for Valentine's Day, or use an oval cutter for Easter egg–shaped cookies.

1 cup clover or orange blossom honey
⅔ cup packed light brown sugar
1 egg, lightly beaten
1½ tablespoons orange juice
3 cups all-purpose flour
¾ teaspoon baking powder
¼ cup minced candied orange peel
1 teaspoon ground cinnamon
½ teaspoon ground cloves
½ teaspoon ground cardamom
½ cup pecans or walnuts, finely chopped
Orange Frosting (page 283)
½ cup chopped candied orange peel, for garnish (optional)

In a small, heavy saucepan over medium heat, bring honey to a boil. Remove from heat. Blend in sugar. If mixture is still hot, let cool to warm. Mix in beaten egg, orange juice, flour, baking powder, candied peel, spices, and nuts.

Scrape mixture into a deep mixing bowl and mix well. Dough will be soft and sticky. Cover and refrigerate 30 minutes, or until dough is stiff.

Preheat oven to 400 degrees. Lightly grease a cookie sheet.

Remove dough to a lightly floured board or pastry cloth and roll out to ½-inch thickness. Gently transfer dough to cookie sheet.

Bake in the center of the oven for 20 minutes, or until firm to the touch and golden. Let cool on the cookie sheet. Cut cooled lebkuchen into 1-inch diamonds.

While lebkuchen is cooling, prepare frosting. Frost cooled cookies, and decorate with orange peel if desired.

Tip: Instead of orange flavoring, you can substitute lemon juice and candied lemon peel.

Store: In an airtight container or wrapped in aluminum foil

Freeze: Yes

Mail: Yes

Teiglach (Jewish Honey New Year Cookies)

Yield
30 cookies

These cookies, which originated in central Europe, are set in a cone shape and served warm. Honey represents a sweet new year.

1 ¾ cups sifted all-purpose flour
1 teaspoon baking powder
¼ teaspoon salt
2 tablespoons peanut oil
3 eggs
½ teaspoon ground ginger
2 ½ cups clover honey
1 cup blanched slivered almonds
1 cup candied cherries

Sift flour and baking powder into a large mixing bowl. Add salt, oil, eggs, and ground ginger, beating on medium speed to incorporate ingredients. Then beat at high speed for 1 minute, until a soft and just slightly sticky dough is formed.

Gather dough together and knead until soft and smooth. Divide the dough in half and roll it on a pastry cloth to about ¾-inch thickness. Cut dough into ¾-inch pieces. Roll each piece into a ball.

Heat 1 ½ cups of the honey in a deep enameled saucepan over medium heat until it boils. Gently slide half of the cookies into the honey. Reduce heat to simmer and continue cooking for about 10 to 12 minutes or until the cookies are a dark golden brown. Stir once or twice while cooking. Set a piece of waxed paper on a serving dish. Remove cookies from the honey with a slotted spoon and stack them in a cone shape on the waxed paper. Add remaining honey to the pan. Bring to a boil, reduce heat to simmer, and cook the rest of the cookies. Stack them atop the first batch of cookies in a cone shape. Sprinkle the teiglach with almonds and set cherries decoratively in and around the cookies.

Serve as soon as possible, as the cookies will harden. They are best served warm. If the teiglach are cool, cut the cone with a knife as though you were cutting a cake.

Tip: These taste best served warm.

Store: Loosely covered with foil or waxed paper; serve the same day they are made.

Freeze: No

Mail: No

Mandelbrot

Yield
42 slices

The name of this cookie, alternately spelled as *mandelbrod,* translates to "almond bread" in German and Yiddish. It is a crisp, dry cookie, good for dunking into coffee or tea, and makes a nice breakfast biscuit.

4 eggs
1 cup sugar
½ cup vegetable shortening, melted and cooled
3 cups all-purpose flour, sifted
2 teaspoons baking powder
1 teaspoon vanilla extract
½ teaspoon almond extract
¼ teaspoon salt
¾ cup blanched slivered almonds
½ cup sliced candied cherries, or dried currants, or chocolate chips

Preheat oven to 350 degrees. Lightly grease or spray 2 cookie sheets.

Beat eggs and sugar until light, about 5 minutes. Stir in the cooled shortening, flour, baking powder, vanilla and almond extracts, and salt. Fold in almonds and cherries.

Shape the dough into three loaves, about 2 to 2½ inches wide. Set on cookie sheets. Bake in the center of the oven for 20 to 25 minutes, or until loaves are golden brown on top and a tester inserted into center of loaf comes out dry. Remove pans from oven. Cut loaves into ½-inch slices. Set slices, cut side up, on cookie sheet. Return pans to oven and reduce heat to 275 degrees. Bake for 5 minutes longer. Turn cookies over and bake for 3 to 4 minutes, until dry.

Cool cookies on wire rack.

Store: In an airtight container
Freeze: Yes
Mail: Yes

Rugelach with Strawberry Jam and Currants

Yield
36 cookies

Crust:

1 cup (2 sticks) unsalted butter, at room temperature
8 ounces cream cheese, at room temperature, cut into 2-inch pieces
2 egg yolks
½ cup sugar
2 teaspoons vanilla extract
¼ teaspoon salt
2 cups all-purpose flour

Filling:

2 jars (10 ounces each) strawberry jam
2 cups currants
2 eggs, lightly beaten with 2 teaspoons cold water

On medium speed, cream butter, cream cheese, egg yolks, sugar, vanilla, and salt. Add flour and continue mixing until dough comes together. Gather dough into a ball. Cover it with plastic wrap and refrigerate for 1 hour or longer.

Preheat oven to 350 degrees. Lightly grease or spray cookie sheets.

Divide dough into 3 equal pieces. On a lightly floured board or pastry cloth, roll one piece of dough at a time into a circle. Spread dough circle with strawberry jam and sprinkle with currants. Cut circle into 12 wedges and roll up each wedge into a crescent. Set cookies on cookie sheet. Brush cookies with beaten egg-water combination.

Bake in the center of the oven for 30 minutes or until cookies are golden brown on the bottom, and firm to the touch and golden on top. Cool 5 minutes. Remove cookies to a wire rack to cool completely.

Tips: Substitute raspberry or apricot jam if desired. Make a double batch and freeze cookies to have on hand for unexpected company.

Store: In an airtight container

Freeze: Yes

Mail: No

Dutch Spice Cookies (Speculaas)

Yield
About 30 to
40 cookies,
depending
on size

1 cup (2 sticks) unsalted butter, at room temperature
¾ cup packed light brown sugar
1 egg
2 tablespoons rum (optional)
2½ cups all-purpose flour (if omitting rum, use 2 cups)
1 teaspoon baking powder
½ teaspoon salt
1 teaspoon ground cinnamon
½ teaspoon ground nutmeg
½ teaspoon ground cloves
Sliced almonds (optional)

Cream butter with sugar on medium speed until well blended and creamy. Beat in egg and rum. Whisk together flour, baking powder, salt, and spices. Stir into butter mixture to make a medium stiff dough. Wrap dough in plastic wrap or foil and refrigerate for 30 to 40 minutes. Dough should be smooth and pliable, neither soft and sticky nor too firm.

Preheat oven to 350 degrees. Lightly grease or spray cookie sheets. If using cookie molds, lightly oil or spray them.

Press dough into cookie molds, and unmold onto cookie sheets. Or, roll dough out on a lightly floured board or pastry cloth to ⅛ inch thick, then cut into desired shapes with cookie cutters. Reroll scraps.

If desired, top each cookie with several almond slices, gently pressing almonds into dough.

Bake in the center of the oven for 9 to 11 minutes, or until edges of cookies are lightly browned. Let cool for a few seconds on cookie sheets, then transfer to wire racks to cool completely.

Tips: In Holland, this cookie traditionally is shaped into windmills and Santa Clauses. Variations of speculaas are popular in Belgium and Germany as well.

The rum is optional but recommended; it complements the spices and gives the cookies a mellow flavor.

Store: In an airtight container

Freeze: Yes

Mail: Yes

Pierre Pollin's Almond Tuiles

Yield
18 to 20
cookies

Tuiles, or "tiles," so named because of their resemblance to roof tiles, are a classic cookie of France. Pierre Pollin, chef-owner of Le Titi de Paris in Arlington Heights, Illinois, said these lacy, orange-scented tuiles are tempting on their own, but when he layers them with a passionfruit custard, raspberries, and caramelized bananas, it is "a dessert to die for."

¼ cup all-purpose flour
¾ cup confectioners' sugar
¼ cup (½ stick) unsalted butter, melted
3 ounces blanched almonds, toasted
   and finely chopped (a scant ⅔ cup)
3 tablespoons fresh orange juice
½ teaspoon finely grated orange zest
1 teaspoon Gran Marnier

Preheat oven to 375 degrees. Line heavy-duty cookie sheets with baking parchment.

Mix flour and sugar in a mixing bowl. Stir in remaining ingredients and mix well. Drop about 2 to 2½ teaspoons batter on parchment-lined cookie sheet. Drop batter for 2 more cookies on the parchment, leaving at least 2½ to 3 inches between them. Use the back of a spoon to spread batter into circles 2½ to 3 inches in diameter. Spread the batter very thinly; you should be able to see through it in places.

Bake in the center of the oven for 5 to 7 minutes, until golden brown and lacy. Let cool on cookie sheets for 4 to 5 minutes, until cookies have firmed up but are still warm and pliable. Gently remove cookies with a spatula and drape over a rolling pin or similar round object, using your fingers to gently press and mold them. Let cool another minute, then carefully remove to wire racks.

Tips: It is essential to use a heavy baking sheet and to line it with baking parchment. Do not make these cookies on a humid day, or they may be chewy instead of brittle.

These cookies are extremely fragile; handle them as little as possible.

Although the cookies taste great plain, they're even better as part of a dessert. For a simple dessert, place the cookies on plates, scatter raspberries in and around them, and pipe a dollop of whipped cream in the middle of the cookie. For a more elegant dessert, leave the cookies flat and layer them with custard (plain or flavored with passionfruit purée), raspberries, and caramelized bananas. (Cook the bananas in a skillet with a little butter and sugar until the sugar caramelizes.) Serve with a sauce of puréed, lightly sweetened raspberries.

Store: On wire racks; serve the same day. Or, place in single layers in large airtight tins.

Freeze: No

Mail: No

Chocolate Madeleines

Yield
22 to 24
cookies

Madeleine is a girl's name in France, but it is also the name of a small, delicate, shell-shaped sponge cake which is eaten like a cookie. Madeleines are baked in a special pan to give them the scalloped shape.

1 ounce bittersweet chocolate, coarsely chopped
10 tablespoons (1 stick plus 2 tablespoons)
    unsalted butter, cut into bits
4 eggs, room temperature
¾ cup sugar
1 cup all-purpose flour
2 tablespoons unsweetened cocoa
½ teaspoon salt
6 ounces white chocolate, roughly chopped

Preheat the oven to 350 degrees. Grease a madeleine pan.
Place chocolate and butter in a microwave-proof bowl or in the top of a double boiler. Microwave on medium-high (80 percent) or heat over hot water, stirring occasionally, until melted and smooth.

Beat eggs on high speed until thick and light, about 5 minutes. Sprinkle sugar over eggs and continue beating until sugar is absorbed.

Sift flour, cocoa, and salt together. Add flour-cocoa mixture to eggs alternately with the chocolate-butter mixture, beating until smooth. Spoon batter into the prepared pan, filling molds about two-thirds full. Bake in the center of the oven for 12 to 14 minutes, or until cookies spring back lightly when touched and a toothpick inserted in the center of a cookie comes out clean.

Cool cookies in pan for 10 minutes; they will begin to shrink from the edges of the molds. Remove from pan and cool completely on a wire rack. Repeat with remaining batter until all cookies are baked.

Place white chocolate in a microwave-proof bowl or in the top of a double boiler. Microwave on medium-high (80 percent) or heat over hot water, stirring occasionally, until melted and smooth.

Hold cooled madeleines by the larger end and dip them, one at a time, into the chocolate, covering about ½ to ¾ inch of the cookie. Let excess chocolate drip back into pan. Set cookies on a sheet of waxed paper until chocolate sets.

Tips: For an elegant presentation, arrange these cookies on a pretty tray and garnish with slivers of candied orange peel.

Madeleine pans are available at cookware shops.

Store: In a covered (not airtight) container, or wrapped on a plate. These are best served very fresh.

Mail: No

Lime Madeleines

Yield
40 to 42
cookies

4 eggs
⅔ cup sugar
¼ teaspoon salt
1 tablespoon freshly squeezed lime juice
2 teaspoons grated lime zest
1 cup sifted cake flour
½ cup (1 stick) unsalted butter, melted and cooled
Confectioners' sugar for garnish

Preheat oven to 350 degrees. Grease a madeleine pan, or use a non-stick pan.

Beat eggs, sugar, and salt on high speed until light, about 2 minutes. Blend in lime juice and zest.

Gently fold in flour and then the cooled butter, 2 tablespoons at a time. Batter should be loose, the consistency of sour cream.

Spoon batter into the madeleine pan, filling molds ⅔ full.

Bake in the center of the oven for 11 to 12 minutes, or until cookies are firm and begin to shrink from the sides of the pan. Press narrow ends of cookies to release them from the mold, or use the tip of a knife to help.

Cool cookies on a wire rack, pattern side up. When ready to serve, arrange on a serving dish and sprinkle with sifted confectioners' sugar.

Store: In a covered (not airtight) container, or wrapped on a plate. These are best served very fresh.

Freeze: No

Mail: No

Belgian Tea Biscuits

Yield
42 cookies

½ cup dried currants or raisins
2 tablespoons rum
½ cup (1 stick) unsalted butter, at room temperature
⅔ cup packed light brown sugar
3 eggs
1 cup cake flour
1½ teaspoons baking powder
½ teaspoon salt

Preheat oven to 350 degrees. Lightly grease or spray baking sheets.

Place currants and rum in a small, microwave-proof bowl. Heat on high (100 percent) for 30 seconds, or until hot. Stir, then let stand for 20 to 30 minutes. (Or, heat rum and raisins in a small saucepan on top of the stove.)

Beat butter until creamy, then add brown sugar and beat until fluffy. Beat in eggs, one at a time, beating well after each addition. Sift together flour, baking powder, and salt. Add to butter-egg mixture and beat on low speed just until mixed. Dough will be very soft and sticky. Stir in rum-soaked raisins.

Place dough in a large piping bag fitted with a ½-inch round or star tip. Pipe dough onto baking sheets, leaving at least 2 inches between cookies so they have room to spread. If you prefer, you can drop dough onto baking sheets by rounded teaspoonfuls; cookies will not be as uniformly round.

Bake in the center of the oven for about 15 minutes, until golden. Remove to wire racks to cool.

Tip: For crisper cookies, let these dry out at room temperature for a couple of hours before putting them in tins.

Store: In an airtight container
Freeze: Yes
Mail: Yes

Cherry-Flavored Scandinavian Stamp Cookies

Yield
40 cookies

1 cup (2 sticks) unsalted butter, at room temperature
¾ cup packed light brown sugar
2¼ cups all-purpose flour
2 teaspoons Cherry Heering or kirschwasser (see Tips)
3 tablespoons minced dried cherries
1 teaspoon vanilla extract

Cream butter on medium speed until light, about 2 minutes. Add sugar and beat for another 2 minutes. Add flour and mix well. Stir in cherry Heering or kirschwasser, minced dried cherries, and vanilla.

Gather dough into a ball and cover with plastic wrap or aluminum foil. Refrigerate for 30 minutes.

Preheat oven to 325 degrees. Lightly grease or spray cookie sheets.

Break off small pieces of dough and roll into 1-inch balls. Set 2 inches apart on cookie sheets. Oil a cookie stamp and press dough lightly on each cookie to make a design.

Bake cookies in the center of the oven for 10 to 12 minutes, or until firm. Let stand on cookie sheets for 2 to 3 minutes, then remove to wire racks to cool.

Tips: Be sure that the stamp is well oiled; oil it again after every few cookies have been stamped.

Cherry Heering is a Danish cherry liqueur; kirschwasser is a clear cherry brandy. You can substitute 1 teaspoon almond extract for the liqueur.

Store: In an airtight container
Freeze: Yes
Mail: Yes

Anise-Flavored Scandinavian Stamp Cookies

Yield
30 cookies

1 cup (2 sticks) unsalted butter, at room temperature
½ cup sugar
¾ teaspoon anise extract
¼ teaspoon salt
½ teaspoon anise seed
2 cups all-purpose flour

Cream butter until light, about 2 minutes. Add sugar and beat for another 2 minutes. Stir in anise extract, salt, and anise seed. Mix in flour until all ingredients are combined.

Gather dough into a ball and cover with plastic wrap or aluminum foil. Refrigerate for 30 minutes.

Preheat oven to 325 degrees. Lightly grease or spray cookie sheets.

Break off small pieces of dough and roll into 1-inch balls. Set 2 inches apart on cookie sheets. Oil a cookie stamp and press lightly into dough on each cookie to make a design.

Bake cookies in the center of the oven for 10 to 12 minutes, until firm. Let stand on cookie sheets for 2 to 3 minutes, then remove to wire racks to cool.

Tip: Be sure to oil stamp before starting to press the cookies, and oil it again after every few cookies, as necessary.

Store: In an airtight container

Freeze: Yes

Mail: Yes

Orange-Scented Scottish Shortbread

Yield
16 pieces

1 cup (2 sticks) unsalted butter, at room temperature
⅓ cup sugar
1¼ teaspoons vanilla extract
2¼ cups all-purpose flour, sifted
¼ cup white rice flour
¼ cup fresh orange juice

With an electric mixer beat butter and sugar until light, about 2 to 3 minutes. Mix in vanilla. By hand, using a wooden spoon, mix in all-purpose flour, rice flour, and orange juice.

Preheat oven to 300 degrees. Grease two 8-inch cake pans with removable bottoms, or lightly grease or spray a large (12 × 18-inch) cookie sheet.

Gather dough into a ball and set on a lightly floured pastry cloth. Knead dough for 2 minutes, until smooth and of medium consistency. Divide dough in half. Roll each half into an 8-inch round. Set dough in the cake pans or on the cookie sheet. Using a fork, then prick the dough in several places, as you would an unfilled pastry crust. Use a knife to lightly mark each shortbread in 8 wedges for easy cutting.

Bake in the center of the oven for 25 to 30 minutes or until the shortbread is pale golden, not brown. Remove it from the oven and cool on a wire rack without removing from the pan. When completely cool, remove cake pan sides or gently slide shortbreads from cookie sheet. Cut each into 8 wedges.

Tips: This shortbread is traditional in its use of rice flour, a very low-gluten flour that gives the shortbread more crunch and tenderness. White rice flour is available at Asian food stores, some specialty shops and health food stores, and some supermarkets.

If you happen to have a shortbread mold, by all means use it instead of a cake pan.

Store: In an airtight container

Freeze: Yes

Mail: Yes

Scottish Tea Biscuits with Great-Grandma Lucas's Lemon Butter

Yield
18 sandwich
cookies

¾ cup (1½ sticks) unsalted butter, at room temperature
Pinch of salt
1½ cups all-purpose flour
½ cup confectioners' sugar
1 tablespoon cold milk
Great-Grandma Lucas's Lemon Butter (page 290)
Confectioners' sugar for dusting

Cream butter until fluffy. Add ingredients through milk and beat on medium speed just until well mixed. Cover dough with plastic wrap or foil and refrigerate at least 1 hour, or until firm.

Preheat oven to 350 degrees. Roll dough out on a lightly floured board or pastry cloth to ⅛-inch thickness. Cut out 2-inch rounds with a biscuit cutter. If desired, cut out a small round, diamond, or other shape in the center of half the cookies.

Transfer to cookie sheets. Bake in the center of the oven for 12 to 15 minutes, or until just tinged golden around the edges. Remove immediately to racks to cool.

Shortly before serving, turn half the cookies bottom side up and spread each with ½ to ¾ teaspoon lemon butter. Top with remaining cookies. (If you have cut small shapes out of half of the cookies, those are the ones that should be on top.) Dust with confectioners' sugar.

Tips: To keep the cookies from softening, do not fill them until within an hour or two of serving. If you'd rather not bother with the lemon butter, you can fill these cookies with jam; black currant is nice.

Store: Unfilled cookies in an airtight container; filled cookies on a plate, loosely wrapped with foil

Freeze: Yes, unfilled

Mail: No

Oatcakes

Yield
16 large
cookies

Inhabitants of the British Isles often treat oatcakes as bread, serving them with jam for breakfast or with soup for dinner. These sturdy, slightly sweet cakes are delicious with a good marmalade, a dollop of lemon butter (page 290), or a fine, sharp cheese such as Cheddar or Gloucestershire.

1½ cups old-fashioned oats
1 cup all-purpose flour
6 tablespoons sugar
½ teaspoon baking powder
½ teaspoon salt
⅓ cup vegetable shortening
¼ teaspoon baking soda
½ cup cold water
Melted butter (optional)

Preheat oven to 375 degrees. Lightly grease or spray cookie sheets.

Place oats in a food processor or blender; grind on high speed for a few seconds to make a coarse meal. If using a large food processor, leave in the work bowl; otherwise, transfer to a mixing bowl.

Add flour, sugar, baking powder, and salt to oats and mix well. Cut in vegetable shortening to make a mealy mixture. Dissolve baking soda in cold water, then stir into oat mixture until mixture comes together in a medium, slightly sticky dough. If too dry, stir in a little additional water. If too wet, stir in a little additional flour.

On a heavily floured surface with a floured rolling pin, roll dough to between ⅛ and ¼ inch thick. Cut into rounds with 3-inch biscuit or cookie cutter. Place on cookie sheets and bake in the center of the oven for about 15 minutes, or until oatcakes are golden around the edges. If desired, brush with melted butter.

Remove immediately to wire racks to cool.

Store: In an airtight container
Freeze: Yes
Mail: Yes

Russian Walnut Tea Cakes

Yield
25 cookies

1 cup (2 sticks) unsalted butter, at room temperature
½ cup sifted confectioners' sugar
2¼ cups sifted all-purpose flour
¼ teaspoon salt
¾ cup finely chopped walnuts
1 cup confectioners' sugar, to roll warm baked cookies

Cream butter and ½ cup sugar until light. Mix in flour, salt, and walnuts. Gather dough together and form into a ball shape. Cover with plastic wrap or aluminum foil and refrigerate for 45 minutes.

Preheat oven to 400 degrees. Lightly grease or spray cookie sheets.

Roll small pieces of dough in your hands to form 1-inch balls. Set cookies on pan, 1½ inches apart. Bake in the center of the oven for 10 minutes or until lightly golden on the bottom and firm to the touch on the top.

Spread 1 cup confectioners' sugar on a plate. Roll hot cookies in sugar and set on a wire rack to cool. When the cookies are cool, roll in sugar again.

Store: In an airtight container
Freeze: Yes
Mail: Yes

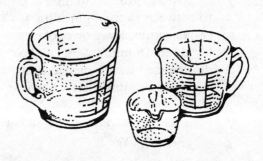

Chocolate-Dipped Hungarian Cookies

Yield
22 to 24
cookies

½ cup plus 2 tablespoons (1 stick plus 2 tablespoons)
   unsalted butter, at room temperature
⅓ cup sugar
1 cup finely ground almonds or walnuts
1 cup all-purpose flour
2 teaspoons ground cinnamon
1 to 2 tablespoons cold brewed coffee or water, if needed

Chocolate for dipping:

3 ounces bittersweet chocolate, chopped, or
   ½ cup semisweet chocolate chips
1 tablespoon butter

Cream butter and sugar on medium speed until light, about 2 minutes. Mix in nuts, flour, and cinnamon. If dough is too thick, add cold coffee or water by the tablespoonful to make a medium dough.

Gather dough into a ball and cover with plastic wrap or aluminum foil. Refrigerate for 30 minutes.

Preheat oven to 350 degrees. Lightly grease or spray cookie sheets.

Divide dough in half. Roll out one half of dough on a lightly floured board or pastry cloth to about ⅛-inch thickness. Cut in circles with a 1½-inch cookie cutter. Continue until all of the cookies have been prepared, rerolling dough. Set cookies on cookie sheets. Bake in the center of the oven for 10 to 12 minutes, or until cookies are golden on the bottom and firm to the touch on the top.

Remove cookies to wire racks to cool. While cookies are cooling, prepare the topping. Melt chocolate with butter in a microwave on 80 percent power, or in a double boiler over hot water, stirring occasionally.

Cool chocolate and dip tops of cooled cookies into the chocolate. Return cookies to rack and let stand in a cool place until chocolate sets. Wait until chocolate is firm before serving the cookies.

Tips: Instead of dipping them in chocolate, you could make these into sandwich cookies by spreading the chocolate thinly on the flat side of one cookie, then topping with another cookie. Or, sandwich a thin layer of raspberry or peach jam between cookies.

Store: In an airtight container

Freeze: Yes

Mail: Yes

Polish Honey Cookies (Piernik)

Yield
100 cookies;
recipe can
be halved.

These old Polish favorites are similar to lebkuchen. This version, inspired by a recipe we found in an old rosary society cookbook, gets an extra boost of flavor from browned honey and a bit of rye flour.

1 cup clover honey
2 eggs
1 cup sugar
1 teaspoon vanilla extract
¾ teaspoon almond extract
1 teaspoon baking soda
1 tablespoon hot water
¼ cup unsalted butter, melted and cooled
3 cups all-purpose flour
½ cup rye flour
Confectioners' sugar, Burnt Butter Icing (page 285),
    or Orange Frosting (page 283)

To brown the honey, pour it into a small, heavy saucepan. Bring to a simmer over medium heat. Reduce heat to low and cook about 8 to 10 minutes, or until honey just begins to give off a burnt-caramel aroma. Immediately pour into a heatproof glass measuring cup. There should be about ⅞ cup honey, and it should be a deep amber. Set aside to cool.

Beat eggs until thick and pale yellow. Add sugar and beat another minute. Add vanilla and almond extracts. Dissolve baking soda in hot water and stir into batter, then stir in melted butter. Stir in all-purpose and rye flours. Dough will be very soft and sticky, like a thick batter.

Chill dough for about 30 to 40 minutes, or just until you can work it. Preheat oven to 350 degrees. Lightly grease or spray cookie sheets.

With floured hands, pinch off small pieces of dough and roll into ¾- to 1-inch balls. Place on cookie sheets at least 2 inches apart (cookies will spread). Bake for 12 to 14 minutes, or until golden. Remove immediately to wire racks to cool.

Before serving, dust cookies with confectioners' sugar or spread with icing.

Tip: The browned honey gives these a nice flavor, but if you prefer to skip that step, you can substitute ¾ cup honey and 2 tablespoons molasses.

Store: In an airtight container

Freeze: Yes

Mail: Yes, without frosting

Prune-Filled Kolaches

Yield
62 to 65
cookies

Also called "kolachke" or "kolachky," variations of this pastry are popular among Czechs, Slovaks, Poles, Russians, and Bohemians. Most are made with yeast, as they are here, to produce light, fluffy cookies or small buns; other versions are made like a rich pastry.

Dough:

1 package (2¼ teaspoons) dry yeast
1 teaspoon sugar
¼ cup warm water
¾ cup unsalted butter, cut into bits
½ cup sugar
3 egg yolks, lightly beaten
1 cup sour cream
2 teaspoons salt
5 to 5½ cups unbleached all-purpose flour
Melted butter, if not using glaze

Filling:

16 ounces (about 2½ cups) pitted prunes
½ cup sugar
⅓ cup orange juice
2 teaspoons vanilla extract
⅛ teaspoon ground cinnamon

Glaze (optional):

¾ cup confectioners' sugar
2 tablespoons melted butter
¼ teaspoon vanilla extract
1 to 2 tablespoons water or milk, as needed

To make the dough: Dissolve yeast and 1 teaspoon sugar in warm water. Let stand 5 minutes or more, until foamy.

In a large mixing bowl, cream butter and ½ cup sugar at medium speed until fluffy. Beat in egg yolks, sour cream, yeast mixture, and salt just until well blended.

Stir in enough flour to make a pliable, slightly sticky dough. Cover bowl and refrigerate dough for several hours or overnight. Dough will not rise.

To make filling: Place prunes, sugar, orange juice, vanilla, and cinammon in a medium-sized, heavy saucepan. Cook over medium heat, stirring often, until the prunes are very tender and the liquid is thick and syrupy. Cool slightly, then purée in a food processor or blender. (If using a blender, purée the prune mixture in small batches.) Let cool. Use immediately, or cover and refrigerate for up to 1 week; bring to room temperature before using.

Preheat oven to 350 degrees. Lightly butter cookie sheets.

Divide dough into 3 or 4 portions. Roll out one portion on a lightly floured board or pastry cloth to a rectangle about ⅛ inch thick. Cut into squares about 2 inches. Place on cookie sheets. Repeat with remaining dough. Gather up scraps of dough, brushing excess flour from them, knead together briefly, roll out, and cut.

Place a generous teaspoon of filling in the center of each square and bring up the opposite corners of the square to meet in the middle. Kolaches should look like small "packages" with the filling showing in a cross shape.

Bake for about 10 to 12 minutes, until kolaches are golden on the bottom and corners are just beginning to be tinged with brown. Let sit on cookie sheets for 2 to 3 minutes, then drizzle glaze over warm kolaches. Remove to wire racks to cool.

While kolaches are baking, make the glaze: Whisk together confectioners' sugar, butter, vanilla, and water to make a thin, pourable icing.

Store: In single layers on plates, wrapped in foil

Freeze: Yes

Mail: Yes

Romanian Almond and Pine Nut Cookies

Yield
26 cookies

Similar to Italian amaretti, but with the delicious addition of toasted pine nuts, these crunchy macaroons are often served for Christmas.

8 ounces blanched slivered almonds (about 1¾ cups), toasted and cooled
¾ cup plus 2 tablespoons confectioners' sugar
2 egg whites, at room temperature
Pinch of salt or cream of tartar
1 teaspoon almond extract
4 ounces pine nuts (about ¾ cup)
Granulated sugar

Preheat oven to 325 degrees. Lightly grease or spray cookie sheets, then dust them lightly with confectioners' sugar. Rap bottoms of pans to shake off excess sugar.

Place the almonds in a food processor or blender with 2 tablespoons confectioners' sugar. Grind very finely. As soon as almonds show the first signs of clumping, stop grinding. (If you have a nut grinder or a clean coffee grinder, use that instead.)

Place egg whites and salt or cream of tartar in a very clean bowl. Beat until foamy. A tablespoon or two at a time, add the ¾ cup confectioners' sugar. Continue beating until egg whites stand in stiff, glossy peaks. Fold in extract and ground almonds.

Spread the pine nuts on a sheet of foil or waxed paper.

Using a teaspoon, scoop out about 2 teaspoons of the meringue mixture. Dip into the pine nuts, making sure at least 10 to 12 pine nuts are clinging to the meringue. Using another spoon or a mini-spatula, scrape the meringue mixture onto the cookie sheet, pine nut side down. Repeat with remaining meringue mixture. Gently press a pine nut into the center of each cookie, then sprinkle cookies with granulated sugar.

Bake in the center of the oven for 20 minutes, or until golden. Remove to wire racks to cool.

Tips: For the best flavor, it's essential to toast the almonds (see page 303) before making the cookies. Do not roast the pine nuts ahead of time; they turn golden while the cookies bake.

Store: In an airtight container

Freeze: Yes

Mail: Yes

Pistachio Biscotti

Yield
40 cookies

½ cup (1 stick) unsalted butter, at room temperature
1 cup sugar
3 eggs
¼ cup marsala, or dessert wine of your choice
2½ cups all-purpose flour
1½ teaspoons baking powder
3 tablespoons grated orange zest
1 cup chopped shelled pistachios

Preheat oven to 350 degrees. Lightly grease or spray a cookie sheet.

Cream butter and sugar until light, about 2 minutes. Add eggs, one at a time, beating well. Gradually stir in wine, flour, baking powder, orange zest, and pistachios, beating well. Dough will be stiff.

Divide dough into 4 equal portions. Mold each portion into a slightly flattened roll, about 1½ inches in diameter, on the cookie sheet. Bake in the center of the oven for 18 to 20 minutes, or until just firm to the touch and a golden color on the bottom.

Let cool, then slice on the diagonal with a serrated knife in ½- to ¾-inch pieces. Set slices, cut side up, on the cookie sheet. Reduce heat to 300 degrees. Return cookies to oven and continue baking for 6 minutes. Turn cookies over and bake another 4 minutes, or until golden and dry.

Cool biscotti on wire racks.

Tips: Pistachios add interesting color and flavor, but other nuts, especially sliced almonds, work well. Biscotti are good served with dessert wine, espresso, or regular coffee.

Store: Let biscotti stand out at room temperature for a day to dry out, then keep in an airtight container.

Freeze: Yes

Mail: Yes

Cucidati (Italian Fig Cookies)

Yield
26 to 30
cookies

This delicious Sicilian cookie is traditionally served on March 19, the feast day of St. Joseph.

Dough:

2 cups all-purpose flour
⅓ cup sugar
1 teaspoon baking powder
¼ cup cold butter, cut into small pieces
¼ cup cold vegetable shortening, in small lumps
1 egg
½ teaspoon vanilla extract
3 to 5 tablespoons cold cream or half-and-half

Filling:

6 ounces dried figs, stemmed and coarsely chopped
¼ cup seedless raisins
2 teaspoons grated orange zest
¼ cup sugar
¼ cup hot water
½ teaspoon ground cinnamon
1 tablespoon hazelnut or walnut liqueur, or rum
½ cup toasted, skinned hazelnuts (or walnuts), coarsely chopped

Glaze:

1½ cups confectioners' sugar
2 tablespoons freshly squeezed orange juice
¼ teaspoon vanilla extract

To make the dough: In a large bowl, whisk together flour, sugar, and baking powder. Cut in butter or shortening to make an evenly crumbly dough. In another bowl or measuring cup, whisk together egg, vanilla, and 3 tablespoons cream. Stir into dough until incorporated. Dough should be soft and slightly sticky; if necessary, add 1 to 2 additional tablespoons cream.

Cover and refrigerate for 30 minutes to an hour; dough should firm up slightly and lose some stickiness, but still be soft.

While dough is chilling, make the filling: Place all ingredients except liqueur and nuts in a small, heavy-bottomed saucepan. Cook over medium heat, stirring occasionally, just until fruits are warmed through and sugar dissolves.

Remove from heat and stir in liqueur and nuts. Place mixture in a food processor (or food grinder) and grind on high speed to make a thick paste. If mixture is too thick to purée, add a little water, a tablespoon at a time.

Preheat oven to 400 degrees.

On a floured board or pastry cloth, roll out dough very thinly, about 1/16 inch thick. Cut into rounds with a 2¼- to 2½-inch biscuit or cookie cutter. Reroll scraps once.

Arrange half the rounds on ungreased cookie sheets, leaving 1½ inches between cookies. Place about 1 tablespoon filling on top of each round; you want a fairly generous amount of filling in proportion to cookie size. Top with remaining dough rounds. Press each cookie gently with the palm of your hand, then press edges with the tines of a fork to seal. (If fork sticks to dough, flour the fork.)

Bake in the center of the oven for about 10 to 11 minutes, or until cookies are golden. Remove immediately to wire racks.

While cookies bake, make the glaze: Whisk together sugar, orange juice, and vanilla until smooth. Mixture should be runny. Spoon over warm cookies.

Store: In a covered (not airtight) container

Freeze: Yes, for up to two weeks

Mail: Yes

Italian Rope Cookies

Yield
15 cookies

These wreathlike cookies are excellent for dipping and enjoying with espresso, milk, or orange-flavored tea.

¼ cup vegetable shortening, at room temperature,
   in small pieces
1½ cups self-rising flour
1½ tablespoons milk or orange juice
⅓ cup sugar
1 teaspoon vanilla extract
1 egg, lightly beaten

Glaze:

1 cup confectioners' sugar
2 to 3 tablespoons orange juice
1 teaspoon grated orange zest

Preheat oven to 350 degrees. Lightly grease or spray cookie sheets.

Cream shortening. Beat in flour, scraping the sides of the bowl as necessary. Set aside.

In a small heavy saucepan over low heat, simmer milk and sugar for about 3 to 4 minutes, stirring occasionally, until sugar has dissolved. Remove from heat and stir in vanilla. In a slow stream, pour mixture into flour. Add egg and combine. Dough will be stiff.

Gather dough together and knead on a lightly floured pastry cloth or board until smooth and pliable.

Pinch off dough by teaspoonfuls and roll each piece into a very thin pencil shape, about 5 inches long. When all of the pencil shapes have been formed, form a rope by attaching two "pencils" together at the top and rolling and twisting them together for a braided look. Form into a circle and seal edges. Set on cookie sheets about 2 inches apart.

Bake in the center of the oven for 16 to 18 minutes, or until the cookies are a light golden color and firm.

While cookies are baking, prepare the glaze. Whisk or beat together sugar, orange juice, and zest. Add more juice if necessary, by the teaspoonful, until glaze is smooth and of spreading consistency.

Remove hot cookies to a wire rack. While cookies are still hot, spread glaze over the tops. Let stand on wire racks until completely cool.

Tip: You can substitute lemon juice and zest for the orange juice and zest.

Store: In an airtight container

Freeze: Yes

Mail: Yes

Kourabiedes from Salonika (Greek Nut Butter Cookies)

Yield
40 cookies

½ cup (1 stick) unsalted butter, at room temperature
½ cup vegetable shortening
6 tablespoons sifted confectioners' sugar
1 egg yolk
1¼ teaspoons vanilla extract
2 cups sifted all-purpose flour
¾ teaspoon baking powder
1 cup ground pecans
2 tablespoons Cognac
Confectioners' sugar for dusting cookies

With an electric mixer, beat the butter and shortening about 5 minutes. Sprinkle sifted sugar over butter and beat another 5 minutes. Beat in egg yolk and vanilla. Continue beating until ingredients are combined. Stir in flour and baking powder. Add ground pecans and Cognac. Dough will be stiff. Cover dough and chill for 30 minutes.

Preheat oven to 325 degrees. Lightly grease or spray cookie sheets.

Use your hands and shape dough into 1½-inch almond-shaped cookies. Set them on cookie sheet, about 1½-inches apart.

Bake cookies in the center of the oven for 25 to 30 minutes. Cookies will be firm to the touch.

Cool cookies on baking sheet. When cookies are cool, set on serving dish and sprinkle with sifted confectioners' sugar.

Tip: These cookies shatter on the first bite. The flavor is well worth the crumbs.

Store: In an airtight container

Freeze: Yes

Mail: Yes

Chocolate Kourabiedes

Yield
40 cookies

½ cup (1 stick) unsalted butter, at room temperature
½ cup vegetable shortening
½ cup sifted confectioners' sugar
½ cup sifted unsweetened cocoa
1 egg yolk
1 teaspoon vanilla extract
1¼ cups sifted all-purpose flour
¾ teaspoon baking powder
1 cup ground toasted almonds
Chocolate or white confectioners' sugar, sifted,
   for dusting cookies (see Tips)

Cream the butter and shortening on medium speed for about 5 minutes. Add sifted sugar and cocoa and beat another 5 minutes. Beat in egg yolk and vanilla, then flour and baking powder. Continue beating until ingredients are combined. Stir in ground nuts. Dough will be soft. Cover dough and chill for 30 minutes.

Preheat oven to 325 degrees. Lightly grease or spray cookie sheets.

Dust your hands with confectioners' sugar and shape dough into 1- to 1½-inch rounds. Set on cookie sheets, about 1½ inches apart. Bake cookies for 25 to 30 minutes. Cookies will be firm to the touch. Let cookies cool on cookie sheets. When ready to serve, sprinkle with sifted confectioners' sugar.

Tips: To intensify the chocolate flavor, you can add ½ teaspoon chocolate extract to the dough.

To dust these with chocolate-flavored confectioners' sugar, either buy it or make it by sifting 1 cup confectioners' sugar with 2 teaspoons unsweetened cocoa.

These cookies shatter easily when you take the first bite, but the flavor is worth the crumbs.

Store: In an airtight container

Freeze: Yes

Mail: Yes

Greek Easter Cookies

Yield
50 cookies

1 cup (2 sticks) unsalted butter, at room temperature
½ cup plus 2 tablespoons sugar
2 eggs
½ cup heavy cream
1 teaspoon vanilla extract
1½ teaspoons baking powder
4 cups all-purpose flour
1 egg white, lightly beaten with 1 tablespoon water
¾ cup sesame seeds

Preheat oven to 350 degrees. Lightly grease or spray cookie sheets.

Cream butter and sugar on medium speed until thick and light, about 5 minutes. Set aside.

In a separate bowl, beat eggs on high speed until light. Stir into butter mixture. Beat in heavy cream. Mix in vanilla and baking powder. Gradually beat in flour, 1 cup at a time, to make a soft and pliable dough.

Gather dough into a ball and knead on a lightly floured board or pastry cloth for about 3 minutes, or until dough is smooth.

Cover dough with a damp cloth to keep it soft while working on a section of the dough. With your hands, break off a walnut-sized piece of dough and roll into a pencil shape, about ½ inch to ¾ inch thick. Twist cookies as you set them on the cookie sheets, about 1 inch apart. They should look a bit like lengths of rope.

Bake in the center of the oven for 10 minutes. While cookies are baking, beat egg white with water.

Remove cookies from the oven. Brush with beaten egg white. Sprinkle with sesame seeds. Return to oven and continue baking 2 to 4 minutes, until egg white has set and cookies are a light golden color. Remove cookies to a wire rack to cool.

Tip: The dough must be smooth before rolling. If it cracks, it needs more kneading.

Store: In an airtight tin

Freeze: Yes

Mail: Yes

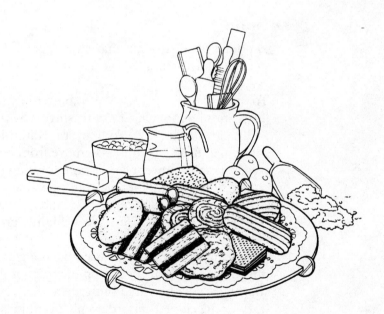

Greek Custard Pieces (Bougatsa)

Yield
36 pieces

Barbara's daughter Reba has moved to Thessolaniki, Greece, and we thank her for this and the other Greek recipes.

Filling:

½ cup (1 stick) unsalted butter
¾ cup semolina
4 cups milk, scalded and cooled
¾ cup sugar
2 eggs, beaten
2 egg yolks, beaten
1¼ teaspoons vanilla extract

Crust:

½ pound phyllo dough, thawed
½ cup (1 stick) unsalted butter, melted and cooled

To make the filling: Melt ½ cup butter in a saucepan over medium heat. Stir in semolina. Continue stirring as you carefully add the milk and sugar. Continue cooking over medium-low heat until the mixture thickens and coats a spoon. Remove from heat and let cool. Cover with plastic wrap to prevent a skin from forming on filling as it cools. The cooled filling should be thick but pourable.

Stir in beaten eggs, egg yolks, and vanilla.

Preheat oven to 375 degrees. Lightly grease or spray a 9 × 13-inch baking pan.

To make the crust and assemble bougatsa: Spread 12 sheets of phyllo over the bottom and up the sides of the pan, brushing each sheet lightly with melted butter before layering the next sheet on top of it. Pour the cooled custard evenly over phyllo, and fold any overhanging edges of dough over filling. Cover the custard with 6 phyllo sheets, again brushing each sheet lightly with butter. Tuck under or trim excess phyllo dough. Brush top of bougatsa with butter.

Bake the bougatsa 25 minutes, or until golden brown. Cool in pan. Custard firms up as it cools. Cut into pieces about 1 by 2 inches, and set on a serving dish. This is best served slightly warm.

Tips: Phyllo, paper-thin sheets of flour-and-water-pastry that crisp up as they bake, is available at Greek markets and in some larger supermarkets, usually in the freezer case. Semolina, finely ground durum wheat that is often labeled "pasta flour," is found in Greek, Middle Eastern, and Indian groceries, health food stores, and some supermarkets.

Store: In single layers on plates, in the refrigerator. Wrap loosely with foil.

Freeze: No

Mail: No

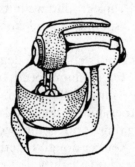

Greek Honey Cakes (Melomakarona)

Yield
76 cookies

¾ cup vegetable oil (olive oil is good)
¼ cup vegetable shortening
½ cup sugar
⅓ cup freshly squeezed orange juice
2 tablespoons Drambuie or Cognac
2 teaspoons grated orange zest
4 cups all-purpose flour
½ teaspoon baking soda
1 teaspoon baking powder
¼ teaspoon salt

Syrup:

1 cup honey
1 cup sugar
1 cup water
1 teaspoon freshly squeezed orange juice
1 tablespoon grated orange zest

Topping:

1¼ cups ground walnuts
2 teaspoons ground cinnamon

Preheat oven to 325 degrees. Lightly grease or spray cookie sheets.

On medium speed, beat oil, shortening, and sugar for about 2 minutes, until well blended. Add orange juice, liquor, and zest. Whisk together flour, baking soda, baking powder, and salt. Add to batter, 1 cup at a time, until combined.

Gather dough together. Dough should be stiff but easy to work. Knead on a lightly floured board or pastry cloth until soft and smooth, about 1 to 2 minutes.

Divide dough in half and roll out each half on a lightly floured board or pastry cloth to ¼ inch, or slightly thicker. Use an oval 1½-inch cookie cutter to cut cookies. Set the cookies on cookie sheets. Using a fork, draw lines down the length of the cookies in a decorative pattern. Bake them in the center of the oven for 22 to 25 minutes, or until they are a golden brown and firm to the touch.

While cookies are baking, prepare the syrup: In a medium heavy pan, combine the honey, sugar, water, orange juice, and zest. Bring mixture to a boil over medium heat. Reduce heat to a simmer and cook for 6 to 8 minutes.

Working quickly, remove hot cookies to a wire rack with a sheet of waxed paper underneath to catch extra syrup. Brush cookies on both sides with syrup. Wait until syrup is absorbed and apply syrup again, 2 or 3 more times. Let cool. Mix walnuts and cinnamon, then sprinkle over cookies.

Store: In single layers on plates, wrapped with foil.
Freeze: No
Mail: No

Moroccan Phyllo Nut Rolls

Yield
About 48 rolls

1½ cups ground blanched almonds, walnuts, and/or pistachios
½ cup sugar
½ cup whipping cream
¼ cup unsalted butter, melted and cooled
1 egg
3 egg yolks
1 teaspoon almond extract
¼ teaspoon vanilla extract
1 tablespoon semolina
¼ pound phyllo pastry
¾ cup unsalted butter or margarine, melted

Syrup:

1 cup sugar
¾ cup water
¼ cup light corn syrup
1½ tablespoons fresh squeezed lemon juice
2 tablespoons grated lemon zest

Preheat oven to 375 degrees. Lightly grease or spray cookie sheets.

To make the filling, use a mixing bowl and combine the almonds, sugar, cream, butter, egg, egg yolks, almond and vanilla extracts, and semolina.

Use 8 sheets of dough. Cut the fresh, defrosted phyllo in thirds lengthwise and then cut each sheet in half. Use 1 strip at a time. Brush it lightly with butter. Place 1 tablespoon of the filling at the beginning of a sheet.

Tightly roll up the phyllo wrappings and filling, jelly roll–style. Place on the cookie sheet about 1½ inches apart, seam side down. Brush tops of the rolls with any remaining butter.

Bake in the center of the oven for about 10 minutes, or until crisp and golden brown. Using a spatula, remove rolls to a buttered sheet of aluminum foil or waxed paper.

While rolls are baking, prepare the syrup. Combine sugar, water, and corn syrup in a heavy saucepan. Bring mixture to a boil over medium heat. Stir in lemon juice and zest. Reduce heat to simmer and continue cooking about 7 minutes. Drizzle rolls with syrup or brush with syrup. When syrup is absorbed, brush them again. Then brush them a third time.

Tips: Keep unused portion of phyllo dough covered with a damp cloth until ready to use. This will help prevent it from drying and cracking. When brushing rolls with syrup, set a sheet of waxed paper underneath to catch drips.

Store: On waxed paper–lined plates, lightly covered with waxed paper and refrigerated

Freeze: No

Mail: No

Arabian-Style Sesame Seed Cookies

Yield
54 cookies

1 tablespoon honey mixed with 2 teaspoons hot water
½ cup sesame seeds, toasted
1 cup unsalted butter, at room temperature
⅔ cup sugar
2 tablespoons honey
2¼ cups all-purpose flour
½ teaspoon baking powder
¼ teaspoon salt

Preheat oven to 350 degrees. Lightly grease or spray cookie sheets.

Stir honey-water mixture into sesame seeds, stirring well to coat. Set aside.

Cream butter with sugar and honey until light and fluffy. Mix flour with baking powder and salt. Stir into butter-sugar mixture to make a smooth dough.

Pinch off pieces of dough and roll into 1-inch balls. Dip one side of balls in sesame seeds. Place on cookie sheets, sesame seed side up. Flatten slightly with the bottom of a drinking glass. Bake in the center of the oven for 13 to 15 minutes, until golden. Let stand on cookie sheets for a minute, then remove to wire racks to cool.

Store: In an airtight container
Freeze: Yes
Mail: Yes

Nanaimo Bars

Yield
24 bars

Residents of the United States and Canada share many cookies in common. But one famous bar cookie is strictly Canadian—Nanaimo bars (pronounced nuh-NYE-mo), named for a city on Vancouver Island. Although Canadians aren't sure exactly who first created these candy-like bars, they all agree they taste great.

Crust:

½ cup unsalted butter
¼ cup granulated sugar
¼ cup unsweetened cocoa
1 egg, lightly beaten
1 teaspoon vanilla extract
1½ cups fine graham cracker crumbs
¾ cup sweetened shredded or flaked coconut
¾ cup finely chopped walnuts

Filling:

½ cup unsalted butter, softened
2 cups confectioners' sugar
1 teaspoon vanilla extract
1 tablespoon rum or amaretto (optional)
1 to 2 tablespoons milk, as needed

Chocolate glaze:

4 ounces semisweet or bittersweet chocolate
1 tablespoon unsalted butter
Toasted coconut or chopped walnuts, for garnish (optional)

Lightly butter a 9-inch square cake pan, or use an unbuttered nonstick pan.

To make the crust: In a heavy saucepan, melt the butter. Stir in sugar, cocoa, egg, and vanilla until smooth. Cook over medium-low heat, stirring frequently, until mixture is steaming hot and thickened.

Stir in the crumbs, coconut, and walnuts. Press mixture evenly over bottom of prepared pan. Set aside.

To make the filling: Beat the butter, confectioners' sugar, vanilla, and rum or amaretto (if desired) to make a smooth and thick but spreadable buttercream. Add a little milk if necessary to make buttercream spread easily. Spread evenly over crust. Refrigerate for about 15 minutes, or until buttercream has begun to firm up but is not hard.

To make the glaze: Melt chocolate and butter or shortening together over hot water or in a microwave at 80 percent power, stirring until melted and smooth. Spread evenly over buttercream filling. If desired, sprinkle top of bars with coconut or walnuts.

Chill at least 2 hours, or until firm. Cut into squares with a sharp knife; the bars will cut better if you clean off knife between cuttings.

Store: In single layers on plates, in the refrigerator. Cover loosely with foil.

Freeze: No

Mail: No

Mexican Sugar Cookies (Biscochitos)

Yield
24 to 25
cookies

½ cup unsalted butter, at room temperature
½ cup vegetable shortening
1 cup sugar
2 tablespoons sherry (sweet or dry)
1 egg
½ teaspoon vanilla extract
2 teaspoons anise seed, finely crushed or ground,
   or 1 teaspoon anise extract
2½ cups flour
1½ teaspoons baking powder
½ teaspoon salt
¼ cup sugar mixed with 1½ teaspoons cinnamon

Preheat oven to 350 degrees.

Cream butter, shortening, and sugar on medium speed until light. Beat in sherry, egg, and vanilla. Beat in anise. Whisk together flour, baking powder, and salt; stir into butter-egg mixture to make a medium dough.

Divide dough in half. Wrap in plastic wrap and chill for 30 minutes to 1 hour, or until dough has firmed up a little and is not sticky, but is still quite pliable.

On a lightly floured board or pastry cloth, roll each half of dough out ⅛ inch thick. Cut into desired shapes with cookie cutters, rerolling scraps once. Place on ungreased cookie sheets and sprinkle with cinnamon sugar.

Bake in the center of the oven for 10 to 12 minutes, or until golden. Remove to wire racks to cool.

Store: In an airtight container
Freeze: Yes
Mail: Yes

Fried Mexican Cookies (Buñuelos)

Yield
24 cookies

½ cup milk
2½ cups all-purpose flour
¼ cup (½ stick) unsalted butter, melted and cooled
¼ teaspoon salt
¾ teaspoon baking powder
1 extra large egg
Vegetable oil for frying
½ cup sugar
1 teaspoon ground cinnamon

In a large mixing bowl, combine milk, flour, butter, salt, baking powder, and egg to make a soft dough. Place dough on a lightly floured board and knead for 2 minutes or until smooth.

Divide dough into 24 equal balls and place on a cookie sheet. Cover lightly and refrigerate for 20 minutes.

On a lightly floured board, roll each ball to a 3-inch circle.

Pour oil into a 7- or 9-inch frying pan with deep sides to a depth of at least 1 inch. Heat to 375 degrees. Add one cookie to the oil and fry for about 20 seconds on each side, or until golden brown. Use 2 forks to turn the cookie over, and watch carefully so it does not burn.

Combine sugar and cinnamon. Sprinkle over cookies. Serve immediately.

Tip: These cookies, which are like fritters, are large. It is easiest to fry them one at a time.

Store: Eat immediately; as with all fried foods, these do not store well.

Freeze: No

Mail: No

Peruvian Sandwich Cookies with White Caramel

Yield
20 to 22
sandwich
cookies

We've also seen these cookies described as an Argentine treat. Some South American cooks make their caramel with fresh milk and sugar, but using condensed milk is much more convenient.

Filling:

1 can (14 ounces) sweetened condensed milk
1½ teaspoons vanilla extract

Cookies:

2½ cups flour
3 tablespoons confectioners' sugar
¼ teaspoon salt
½ cup cold vegetable shortening, in small chunks
½ cup cold unsalted butter, in small chunks
1 egg yolk
1 tablespoon cold milk or cream, plus more as needed
Confectioners' sugar

Make the filling first: Pour condensed milk into a heavy-bottomed saucepan. Cook over medium heat until milk is hot. Turn heat to low and continue cooking, stirring almost constantly, until milk turns into a pale golden, thick caramel; this may take up to 20 minutes. When you drag the spoon over the bottom of the pan, you should see the pan bottom for 2 to 3 seconds before the milk closes back over the gap. And when you lift the spoon and let the caramel run off, it should form threads as it cools. Remove from heat and stir in vanilla. Scrape into a shallow bowl and place buttered waxed paper directly on surface of caramel, buttered side down. Set aside to cool.

Preheat oven to 350 degrees.

In a food processor or a mixing bowl, combine flour, 3 tablespoons confectioners' sugar, and salt. Add shortening and butter; cut into flour until mixture resembles coarse crumbs. Beat egg yolk into 1 tablespoon milk; add to dough. Stir in enough additional milk so that mixture comes together in a dough. If using a food processor, add milk with motor running; stop the machine as soon as the dough begins to form a ball.

Roll dough on a lightly floured board or pastry cloth to ⅛ inch thick. (If dough is too soft to roll, refrigerate for 15 to 30 minutes.) Cut into rounds with a 2½-inch biscuit or cookie cutter. Reroll scraps once. Place rounds on ungreased cookie sheets. Prick each in 2 or 3 places with a fork.

Bake in the center of the oven for 12 to 15 minutes, or until edges of cookies are beginning to turn a pale gold; tops of cookies should still be white. Let cool on cookie sheets for a minute, then remove to wire racks to cool completely.

Shortly before serving, spread the cooled custard on the bottom side of one cookie round, then top with another cookie. Press together very gently; cookies are fragile and shatter easily. If custard is too thick, rewarm gently over low heat until it loosens just enough to spread on cookies without breaking them. Dust cookies with confectioners' sugar.

Tips: Some South American recipes for *manjar blanco* (the white caramel) call for simmering an unopened can of condensed milk in water for several hours. This practice, which used to show up in old U.S. recipes as well, is extremely dangerous, since the heat may make the can explode. If you run across such a recipe, do not use the closed-can method. Instead, safely caramelize the condensed milk by pouring it into the pan before cooking it.

Store: In an airtight container

Freeze: Yes

Mail: No

Chinese Almond Cookies

Yield
48 cookies

¼ cup unsalted butter, at room temperature
¾ cup solid vegetable shortening, at room temperature
1½ cups sugar
1 egg
2 egg yolks
2 teaspoons almond extract
2½ cups all-purpose flour
1 teaspoon cream of tartar
1 teaspoon baking soda
½ teaspoon salt
2 to 3 tablespoons finely chopped blanched almonds (optional)

Preheat oven to 375 degrees. Spray or lightly grease baking sheets.

Cream butter and shortening with sugar until light and fluffy. Beat in egg and egg yolks, one at a time, then beat in almond extract. Whisk together flour, cream of tartar, baking soda, and salt. Stir into egg mixture until well blended.

Pinch off pieces of dough and roll into 1-inch balls. (If dough is too soft to handle, refrigerate for 15 to 30 minutes.) If desired, roll tops of balls in chopped almonds. Place on prepared baking sheets, leaving at least 1½ inches between cookies.

Bake in the center of the oven for 10 to 12 minutes, until cookies are golden, flattened, and crackled on top. Remove to wire racks to cool.

Store: In an airtight container
Freeze: Yes
Mail: Yes

Fortune Cookies

Yield
30 cookies

2 egg whites
¼ cup vegetable oil
½ teaspoon coconut flavoring or extract
½ cup all-purpose flour
¼ cup sugar
1 tablespoon cornstarch
⅛ teaspoon salt
2 to 4 tablespoons water
30 fortunes, typed or written on ½ × 2½-inch strips of paper

With electric mixer, beat egg whites until they begin to foam. Mix in oil, coconut flavoring, flour, sugar, cornstarch, and salt. Add 2 tablespoons of water. Cover bowl and refrigerate for 30 minutes.

To prepare the cookies, use a nonstick griddle. It might be necessary to grease it just lightly. Heat pan over medium-high heat. Stir batter. It should be of medium consistency; if necessary, add water by the tablespoon. Spoon the batter by heaping teaspoonfuls onto the hot griddle, making about 3 cookies at a time. Using the back of the spoon, smooth batter into circles 2½ inches to 3 inches in diameter. When the cookies are golden brown on the underside—this will take only about 10 seconds or so—turn them over and brown the other side.

Moving fast, remove one cookie at a time. Set a fortune in the center. Fold cookie in half and set it on the edge of a glass, pulling down the sides to make a fortune cookie shape. Continue until all of the cookies have been formed. The cookies will be soft. Let them cool completely on a wire rack overnight.

Tips: For extra silliness, make your fortunes very specific to the people who will be eating these, and "code" the cookies so you know which cookie to give to each person. Some examples: "You will enjoy dinner in the company of good friends," for anyone at the table. "Happy Birthday," for the guest of honor. "Blue becomes you," for the friend who just bought a new dress in that color. "You will marry a woman named Anne in June," for the lucky husband-to-be. "You are about to embark on a vertical journey," for a mountain climber. "There's a matched set in your future," for the mom-to-be of twins. Or, "College is around the corner," for the dad who's been tussling with his teenager.

Store: Covered loosely, at room temperature

Freeze: No

Mail: No; cookies may soften

Korean Fried Honey Cakes

Yield
36 to 40
cookies

These sticky-sweet, hard-crunchy cookies are popular throughout Korea, especially at teatime. Sometimes the dough is rolled thicker and cut into chrysanthemum shapes, but we like these little "bows" best.

1 cup honey
2 tablespoons water
1 cup all-purpose flour
2½ tablespoons sugar
3 tablespoons rice wine, sake, or dry sherry
½ teaspoon dark (Asian-style) sesame oil (optional)
1 to 4 teaspoons water, as needed
Corn or peanut oil for deep-frying
Toasted sesame seeds

Combine the honey and water in a shallow saucepan. Cook over low heat until it comes to a boil; stir. Remove from heat and set aside.

Mix flour and sugar. Stir in rice wine and sesame oil, adding water as necessary to make a fairly soft, workable dough. Knead for 2 or 3 minutes, until smooth and pliable. Dough will be slightly sticky.

On a lightly floured board or pastry cloth, roll dough out to a rectangle between 1/16 and 1/8 inch thick. Trim edges, then with a sharp knife or pizza cutter, cut dough into rectangles about ¾ to 1 inch wide and 2½ to 3 inches long. Cut a lengthwise slit ¾ to 1 inch long in the center of each rectangle. Pull one end of the dough through the slit to make a kind of keyhole or bow shape.

In a heavy skillet or saucepan, heat about 1 inch of oil to 375 degrees. Deep-fry the cookies, a few at a time, turning once, until they are a nice golden brown. Remove to paper towels with a slotted spoon. After a brief draining—cookies should still be warm—drop the hot cookies into the honey mixture, turning to coat. Let them stand in the honey for at least 5 minutes. Remove from the honey with a fork and place on a waxed paper–lined plate. Sprinkle with toasted sesame seeds.

Tips: Be sure the oil is nice and hot, so that the honey cakes fry without getting greasy. Instead of sesame seeds, you can sprinkle the cookies with finely ground toasted pine nuts.

Store: On a plate, loosely wrapped with foil. They should be eaten as soon as possible.

Freeze: No

Mail: No

COOKIES FOR SPECIAL OCCASIONS

When making large batches of cookies for Christmas or any other special occasion, it's convenient to have one basic dough you can turn into different cookies. Pat the dough into a pan, and it's a crust. Roll it into balls, and it's the makings of angel faces or snowpeople. Roll it out thinly and sprinkle with colored sugar, and it's a basic Christmas cookie. Form it into a log and slice, and you have icebox cookies.

This chapter opens with three multipurpose doughs—butter, sugar, and peanut butter. After each dough, we've listed several recipes that use it. But let your imagination roam freely—we're sure you can think of many other ways to put these doughs to good use.

Every complete cookie book needs a gingerbread house or its equivalent, for those who think big for Christmas. Ours is a good old-fashioned red barn, complete with farmyard, all decked out for the holiday.

Although Christmas and cookies go together like butter and sugar—and certainly, most of the cookies in this book can easily adorn a Christmas tray—other occasions certainly call for nibbling on a cookie or two. That's why we're serving up cookies for St. Patrick's Day, Passover, a wedding shower, and even Mardi Gras.

Basic Butter Cookies

Butter cookies, as the name implies, have a high percentage of butter, making them tender-crisp and not too sweet. Here's a basic butter dough, followed by ideas for four different festive cookies.

The yields given for each cookie assume you are using the whole batch of dough. You can, of course, divide the dough in portions and make two or more different cookies from one batch. You can also easily double the dough recipe.

1 cup (2 sticks) unsalted butter, at room temperature
1 cup sugar
1 teaspoon vanilla extract
¼ teaspoon salt
2 cups flour

Cream butter and sugar on medium speed until light. Beat in vanilla and salt. Stir in flour to make a medium-stiff dough. Refrigerate, shape, and bake as directed.

Tropical Sandwich Cookies

Yield
24 sandwich
cookies

Chill dough for at least 45 minutes to 1 hour, until firm. Preheat oven to 350 degrees.

Roll out dough to ⅛ inch thick. Cut into 2-inch rounds. Brush tops of half the cookies with 1 egg white beaten with 1 teaspoon water. Sprinkle lightly with a little shredded sweetened coconut. Transfer cookies to ungreased cookie sheets. Bake in center of oven for 8 to 10 minutes, until faintly golden. When cookies are cool, spread bottoms of half the cookies with guava paste that has been warmed with a little water or rum to thin it. Guava paste is available at Hispanic markets. You can use any tropical-flavor jam instead, such as mango, kiwifruit, passionfruit, or pineapple. Top with the coconut-topped cookies to make sandwiches.

Store: Unfilled cookies in an airtight container; filled cookies on a plate, wrapped with foil
Freeze: Yes
Mail: No

Little Feet

Yield
48 to 50
cookies

These are great for a baby shower.

Preheat oven to 350 degrees.

Roll chilled dough on a floured board or pastry cloth to ⅛ inch thick. Cut out with 3-inch foot-shaped cookie cutters. Transfer to cookie sheets. Bake in the center of the oven for 8 to 10 minutes, until faintly golden.

If desired, ice cooled cookies with thinned Royal Icing (page 286) that has been tinted blue, pink, and yellow. Otherwise, just dust them with confectioners' sugar after baking. Serve cookies in a pastel basket with pink, blue, and yellow napkins (or napkins with baby designs). Tie a big yellow, pink, or blue bow on the basket handle.

Store: In an airtight tin
Freeze: Yes
Mail: Yes

Chocolate Glazed Walnut Bars

Yield
48 bars

1 recipe basic butter cookie dough

3 eggs
¾ cup packed light brown sugar
¼ cup corn syrup
1 tablespoon vanilla
2 cups chopped walnuts
9 ounces (about 1½ cups) semisweet chocolate chips, or chopped
    bittersweet chocolate

Preheat oven to 350 degrees. Press dough evenly over bottom of a 9 × 13-inch pan. Bake in the center of the oven for 15 minutes, until golden. Mix together eggs, sugar, corn syrup, and vanilla until smooth. Stir in walnuts. Pour over hot crust, picking up pan with pot holders and rocking gently back and forth to distribute filling. Bake another 20 to 25 minutes, until topping is set and golden. Sprinkle chocolate chips evenly over walnut filling and return to oven for another minute, until chips begin to melt. Spread melted chips evenly over walnut filling. Let cool in pan, then cut into small bars.

Store: In a covered (not airtight) container; keep cool.

Freeze: Yes

Mail: No

Cranberry Orange Slice-and-Bake Cookies

Yield
55 to 60
cookies

Add 1 cup finely chopped dried cranberries and 1 tablespoon grated orange zest to basic butter dough. Form into a log about 1½ inches in diameter. Refrigerate several hours or overnight, until very firm. Cut into slices a bit thicker than ⅛ inch, using a serrated knife, and place on ungreased cookie sheets. Bake in the center of the oven for 10 to 12 minutes, until pale golden around the edges. Remove to wire racks to cool.

Store: In an airtight container

Freeze: Yes

Mail: Yes

*B*asic Sugar Cookies

Sugar cookies have a higher percentage of sugar to butter and contain eggs and leavening. This makes them sweeter, sturdier, and more three-dimensional than butter cookies.

The yields given for each cookie assume you are using the whole batch of dough. You can, of course, divide the dough into portions and make two or more different cookies from one batch. The dough recipe can also be doubled.

½ cup (1 stick) unsalted butter, at room temperature
1 cup sugar
2 eggs
1 teaspoon vanilla extract
2¼ cups all-purpose flour
1½ teaspoons baking powder
¼ teaspoon salt

Cream butter and sugar on medium speed until light and fluffy, about 2 minutes. Add eggs, one at a time, and vanilla. Continue beating until combined. Mix in flour, baking powder, and salt. Continue mixing, stopping to scrape down sides of the bowl as necessary. Dough will be soft. Gather dough in a ball, wrap in plastic wrap or aluminum foil, and refrigerate for 1 hour or longer, until firm.

*C*andied Violet Valentines

Yield
22 to 26
three-inch
cookies

You'll need extra sugar for sprinkling on the cookies, and ½ cup of candied violets. Crush the violets in a food processor or between 2 sheets of waxed paper using a rolling pin.

Preheat oven to 375 degrees. Lightly grease or spray cookie sheets. Cut the dough in half, and work with one half at a time. Roll out one half of the dough on a pastry cloth that has been sprinkled with sugar to between ¼ and ½ inch thick. Sprinkle top of dough lightly with sugar. Using a 3-inch heart cookie cutter, cut cookies and transfer to cookie sheets, leaving at least 1 inch between cookies. Sprinkle with ground candied violets.

Bake in the center of the oven for 10 to 12 minutes, until cookies are firm to the touch and beginning to turn faintly golden around the

edges. Let cookies stand for 1 to 2 minutes on cookie sheets, then remove to wire racks to cool completely.

Tip: The candied violets are a romantic touch, but could be re-
placed by colored sugar.

Store: In an airtight container

Mail: Yes

Angels

Yield
10 angels,
about
6 inches tall

You can, of course, simply cut the dough with angel-shaped cookie cutters, but we think these large, whimsical angels have infinitely more
charm.

You'll need 1 recipe of sugar cookie dough and 1 egg white, lightly
beaten. You'll also need Egg Yolk Tempura (page 288), or colored decorating sugars, tinted Royal Icing (page 286) or Paint Glaze (page 289).
For eyes, use small decors or mini-chocolate chips.

Preheat oven to 350 degrees. Lightly grease or spray cookie sheets.

Make sure dough is cold and firm. Roll dough out on a lightly
floured board or pastry cloth into a large rectangle about ⅛ inch thick.
Cut 2 rectangles from dough, 2½ inches wide by 15 inches long. With
a sharp knife, cut each rectangle at 3-inch intervals to make 5 rectangles
2 ½ inches by 3 inches (see fig. 7.1). Cut through each rectangle on
the diagonal to make 2 triangles.

Gather up dough scraps. Roll ⅛ inch thick. Cut 10 rectangles 1
inch wide by 4 inches long. Gather up the remaining dough. Pinch
off pieces of dough and roll into 10 one-inch balls.

Place 2 triangles, short sides touching at one point and triangles
tilted upward on a slight angle, on a cookie sheet (fig. 7.2). These are
the "wings." Repeat with remaining triangles.

Using your finger or a small brush, paint the facing edges of the triangles with egg white. Place a 1 × 4-inch rectangle in the center of the
wings; the top of the rectangle should be even with the point where the
triangles meet.

Brush the top of the rectangle lightly with egg white. Place a ball of
dough at the top of the rectangle, overlapping slightly. Press lightly to
flatten into a thick circle. (See fig. 7.3 for what a completed angel looks
like.)

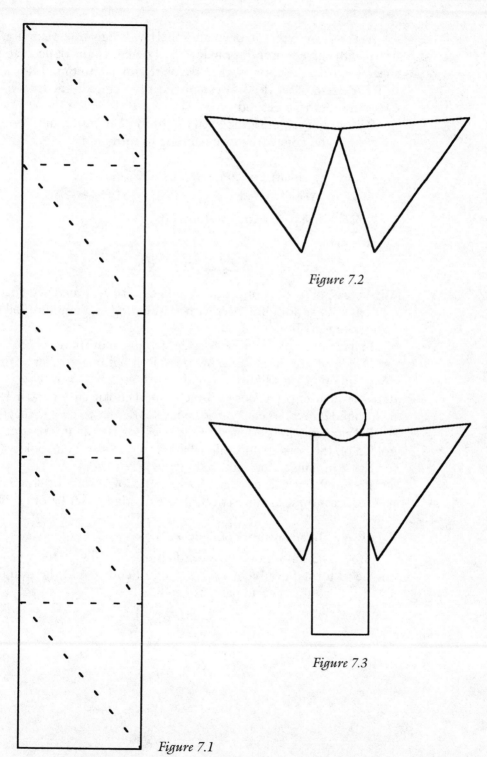

Figure 7.2

Figure 7.3

Figure 7.1

At this point, you can decorate angels with Egg Yolk Tempura. Or, brush with egg white and sprinkle with different colors of decorating sugar. Or, bake the cookies, then decorate either with tinted Royal Icing or Paint Glaze. Place decors or mini-chocolate chips in the faces to make eyes and mouths, if desired.

Bake in the center of the oven for 10 to 11 minutes, until bottoms are golden and edges are just beginning to turn gold.

Store: In an airtight container; handle carefully

Freeze: Yes

Mail: Yes; pack extra carefully.

Painted Rings

Yield
48 cookies

Mix ½ teaspoon coconut extract and ¼ cup flaked sweetened coconut into basic sugar dough. Cover with plastic wrap or aluminum foil and refrigerate for 1 hour.

Preheat oven to 350 degrees. Lightly grease or spray cookie sheets.

Divide chilled dough into quarters. Roll out one quarter of the dough at a time on a lightly floured board or pastry cloth. Use a doughnut cutter (or a 2½- to 3-inch round cookie cutter and a 1-inch round cutter) to cut "ring" cookies. Transfer to cookie sheets.

Bake cookies in the center of the oven for 10 minutes or until golden on the bottom and still pale on top. Let stand on cookie sheets for 1 to 2 minutes, then remove to wire racks to cool.

Prepare Paint Glaze (page 289). Paint cookies, leaving some unpainted areas for a shading effect. Allow frosting to set before serving.

Store: In an airtight container

Tip: You can set one uncooked cookie partially on top of a second cookie to form a double ring. You can, of course, cut the dough into any shapes you want, and paint as you like.

Mail: Yes

Basic Soft Peanut Butter Cookies

If you're planning a party for kids—young or old—peanut butter cookies are hard to beat.

The yields given for each cookie assume you are using the whole batch of dough. You can divide the dough into portions and make two or more different cookies from one batch. The dough recipe can also be doubled.

½ cup (1 stick) unsalted butter or margarine, at room temperature
¾ cup granulated sugar
¾ cup packed light brown sugar
1 cup smooth peanut butter, at room temperature
2 eggs
1 teaspoon vanilla extract
2 ½ cups all-purpose flour
1 teaspoon baking soda
¼ teaspoon salt

Preheat oven to 350 degrees. Lightly grease or spray cookie sheets.

Cream butter and sugars on medium speed until light, about 2 to 3 minutes. Add peanut butter. Mix well. Add eggs, one at a time, beating well after each addition. Blend in vanilla. Whisk together flour, baking soda, and salt. Stir into batter to make a soft dough. Form into shape of your choice, and bake as directed.

Cookies with a Kiss

Yield
45 cookies

Roll dough into 1-inch balls. Place a Hershey's Kiss (or similar candy) in the center of each cookie. Place on cookie sheets 1½ inches apart. Bake in the center of the oven for 10 to 12 minutes, until cookies are set and golden on the bottom. Let cookies stand on cookie sheets for 3 minutes, then remove to wire racks to cool.

Store: In an airtight container
Freeze: Yes
Mail: Yes

Peanut Butter Cookies with Rum Raisin Centers

Yield
45 cookies

Put ½ cup raisins in a cup or small bowl. Stir in ½ cup dark rum. Let raisins stand for 30 minutes before mixing up the cookie dough.

Roll dough into 1-inch balls, then flatten each ball into a disk. Put a few drained raisins in the center of each cookie, then remold the dough into a ball, with raisins in the center. Set cookies on cookie sheets.

Bake in the center of the oven for 10 to 12 minutes, until cookies are set on top and golden brown on the bottom. Let cookies stand for 2 to 3 minutes, then remove to wire racks to cool.

Tips: You could use chocolate-covered raisins (skip the rum).
Store: In a covered (not airtight) container
Freeze: Yes
Mail: Yes

Old-Fashioned Chunky Peanut Butter Cookies

Yield
45 cookies

Substitute chunky peanut butter for creamy peanut butter. Stir ½ cup chopped peanuts and ½ cup chopped walnuts or pecans into the dough.

Shape dough into 1-inch balls. Set cookies on pan. Continue until all of the cookies are formed.

Bake in the center of the oven for 10 to 12 minutes, until cookies are set on top and golden brown on the bottom. Let stand on cookie sheets for 2 to 3 minutes, then remove to wire racks to cool.

Store: In an airtight container
Freeze: Yes
Mail: No

Peanut Butter and Jelly Sandwich Cookies

Yield
30 to 35
cookies

You'll need about ⅔ cup best-quality strawberry jam. Prepare dough. Gather it into a ball. Knead it on floured surface for 1 to 2 minutes. Shape dough into a 1½-inch roll. Press ends of the roll with a spatula to flatten the ends. Cover dough with aluminum foil or plastic wrap. Refrigerate for at least 1 hour, or until firm.

Preheat oven to 350 degrees. Lightly grease or spray cookie sheets.

On a cutting board, slice the cookies with a sharp knife or serrated knife into ¼-inch or thinner slices. Transfer slices to cookie sheets. Bake in the center of the oven for 10 to 12 minutes, until cookies are set and golden on the bottom. Let stand on cookie sheets for about 3 minutes, then remove to wire racks to cool.

When cookies are cooled completely, spread a little jam on the bottom of half of the cookies. Secure remaining cookies on top of the jam. If you like, you could set a peanut on top of half of the cookies before baking them. Use the cookies with the peanut for the top cookie.

Store: On a plate, wrapped with foil. Use waxed paper between layers.

Freeze: Yes, unfilled

Mail: Yes

Peanut Butter Cookies with Candied Peanuts

Yield
40 to 45
cookies

½ to ¾ cup candied peanuts, chopped
1 egg white, slightly beaten

Prepare dough. Gather it into a ball. Knead dough on a floured surface for 1 to 2 minutes. Shape into a roll about 1½ inches in diameter. Tap ends of the roll with a spatula to shape ends. Cover dough with aluminum foil or plastic wrap. Refrigerate dough for at least 1 hour, or until firm.

Preheat oven to 350 degrees. Lightly grease or spray cookie sheets.

On a cutting board, slice the cookies with a sharp knife or serrated knife into ¼ inch or thinner slices. Transfer slices to cookie sheets. Brush cookies with egg white. Sprinkle chopped nuts on top and press slightly into the cookies.

Bake in the center of the oven for 10 to 12 minutes. Cookies will be set and golden on the bottom. Let stand on cookie sheets for 2 to 3 minutes, then remove wire racks to cool completely.

Store: In an airtight container
Freeze: Yes
Mail: Yes

Peanut Butter Peppermint Cookies

Yield
**40 to 45
cookies**

1 egg white, slightly beaten
1 cup crushed red-and-white peppermint candies (crush them, un-
    wrapped, in a food processor or between 2 pieces of waxed paper
    using a rolling pin)

Prepare dough. Gather it into a ball. Knead it on a floured surface for 1 to 2 minutes. Shape into a roll about 1½ inches in diameter. Tap ends of the roll with a spatula to shape ends. Cover dough with aluminum foil or plastic wrap. Refrigerate dough for at least 1 hour, or until firm.

Preheat oven to 350 degrees. Lightly grease or spray cookie sheets.

On a cutting board, slice the cookies with a sharp knife or serrated knife into ¼-inch or thinner slices. Transfer slices to cookie sheets. Bake in the center of the oven for 5 minutes. Brush lightly with egg white. Sprinkle crushed peppermint on top and return to oven for another 5 to 7 minutes. Cookies will be set and golden on the bottom. Let stand on cookie sheets for about 3 minutes, then remove to wire racks to cool completely.

Store: In an airtight container
Freeze: Yes
Mail: Yes

Peanut Butter Cutouts

Yield
About 50 cookies, but depends on size of cutter

Icing to decorate cookies (optional)
1½ cups chocolate or strawberry-flavored confectioners' sugar, sifted
2 to 3 tablespoons milk or cream

Prepare dough. Gather it into a ball. Knead dough on floured surface for 1 to 2 minutes. Again gather it into a ball. Cover with plastic wrap. Refrigerate it for 1 hour or until ready to make the cookies.
Preheat oven to 350 degrees. Use 2 or 3 nonstick cookie sheets.

Discard wrapping. Divide dough into four equal parts. Roll each part on a lightly floured pastry cloth to ⅛- to ¼-inch thickness. Use your favorite cookie cutters. Shape cookies and set on pan.

Bake cookies in the center of the oven for 10 to 12 minutes. Cookies will be set and just beginning to turn a golden color. Remove from the oven and let cookies stand for 2 minutes. Using a spatula remove cookies to a wire rack.

If you want to decorate cookies, prepare icing while cookies are baking. Put one flavor of the sifted confectioners' sugar in a bowl. Stir in the milk. Stir until the icing is firm. If icing is too firm add milk, by the teaspoon, until it is of spreading consistency. Decorate cookies if desired. Let cookies set before enjoying them.

Store: In an airtight container
Freeze: Yes
Mail: Yes

Gingerbread

Yield
Enough dough
for 18 to 20
(4-inch)
gingerbread
people, or half
the amount
necessary to
construct
Barnyard at
Christmas

1 cup vegetable shortening
1 cup sugar
1 egg
1 cup unsulphured molasses
2 tablespoons cider vinegar or lemon juice
5 to 5½ cups all-purpose flour
1½ teaspoons baking soda
½ teaspoon salt
2 teaspoons ground ginger
1½ teaspoons ground cinnamon
½ teaspoon ground allspice

Cream shortening and sugar until fluffy. Beat in egg, then beat in molasses and vinegar. Dough will curdle. Whisk 2 cups of the flour with baking soda, salt, ginger, cinnamon, and allspice. Stir into shortening mixture. Add 3 to 3½ cups additional flour, enough to make a dough that is fairly stiff but pliable and holds together. (If you're mixing in the flour with a heavy-duty mixer, the dough is ready when it cleans the side of the bowl.) Turn dough out of bowl and knead briefly to completely incorporate flour.

Divide dough in half. Pat into thick disks, wrap well in plastic wrap, and refrigerate for at least 1 hour, and up to 2 days. Let stand at room temperature for 15 to 20 minutes before rolling.

Roll dough out on a floured board or pastry cloth to ⅛ to ¼ inch thick, then cut into gingerbread people shapes. Or, roll and cut as directed in Barnyard at Christmas (page 269). Reroll scraps once. Use a large, flexible spatula to gently transfer cutout cookies to baking sheets.

If making gingerbread people, bake in the center of the oven for 10 to 15 minutes, depending on size of cookies, until firm and just turning golden on the edges. Let cool on baking sheets for 1 to 2 minutes, then transfer to wire racks. Decorate immediately with Royal Icing (page 286) and candy decorations of your choice. Or, store to be decorated later.

Tip: This dough is fairly stiff and tends to crack. Roll it out with firm, even strokes; it should smooth out. If not, let it soften a little longer at room temperature.

Store: In an airtight container

Freeze: Yes

Mail: Yes

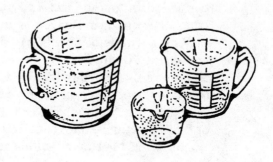

Cherry Christmas Slices

Yield
72 cookies

1 cup maraschino or candied cherries, coarsely chopped
2 tablespoons cherry brandy (kirschwasser) or liqueur
1 cup (2 sticks) unsalted butter, at room temperature
3 ounces cream cheese, at room temperature
1 cup sugar
½ teaspoon almond extract
2⅓ cups all-purpose flour
Plenty of green decorating sugar

Place chopped cherries in a glass bowl. Add cherry brandy or liqueur and toss to coat cherries. Let stand 15 minutes.

In a large mixing bowl, cream butter and cream cheese on medium speed. Add sugar and cream until light. Add cherries and brandy, and almond extract. Beat just until mixed. Stir in flour to make a soft dough.

Divide dough in half. Place each half of dough on a sheet of waxed paper. With your hands and the waxed paper, roll dough into a log about 1½ inches in diameter. If dough is too sticky to handle, refrigerate for 15 to 30 minutes.

Sprinkle a band of green sugar alongside log on both sides. Roll log back and forth, and sprinkle with additional sugar, until log is completely coated in green sugar. Roll log up in waxed paper, tucking in ends.

Repeat with remaining half of dough. Refrigerate dough for at least 4 to 6 hours, or until very firm.

Preheat oven to 350 degrees. Cut slices a bit thinner than ¼ inch from dough and place on ungreased baking sheets. If desired, sprinkle very lightly with additional green sugar. Bake in the center of the oven for 8 to 10 minutes, until cookies are set and bottoms are golden. Let cool on sheets for 1 minute, then remove to racks.

Tips: You can make all or half of the dough with green cherries, and roll the logs in red sugar.

For a tastier but less colorful cookie, replace the maraschino cherries with ½ cup dried, coarsely chopped cherries. Heat the liqueur before adding it to the cherries.

Store: In an airtight container

Freeze: Yes

Mail: Yes

Mrs. Swentko's Christmas Trees

Yield
78 small
cookies

Every neighborhood needs a good cookie baker, the one who stands at the oven in December and turns out unforgettable treats for neighbors, friends, and relatives. When Virginia was a kid, the most beloved cookie baker in the neighborhood was Ann Swentko, a gentle soul who won the hearts of children near and far by supplying them with ample amounts of cookies and candy.

1 cup margarine
½ cup sugar
1 teaspoon vanilla extract
2½ cups all-purpose flour
1½ tablespoons cream or milk, or as needed
Green and red sugar

Preheat oven to 350 degrees. Lightly grease or spray cookie sheets.

Cream margarine and sugar until light. Gradually work in vanilla, flour, and cream. Dough will be fairly soft but should not be sticky. You might have to add a speck more flour. It's just about the right consistency when you can roll a smooth ball of it in your hand.

Put dough through a cookie press to make trees (or other shapes of your choice). Place cookies on cookie sheets and sprinkle with red and green sugar. Bake in the center of the oven for about 10 to 12 minutes, or just until a soft golden color—not too dark. Remove to wire racks to cool.

Tips: The right consistency of dough is important. This recipe was designed for margarine; it does not work as well with butter. If you like, you can tint the dough with a couple of drops of green food coloring, and decorate the trees with red sugar.

Store: In an airtight container
Freeze: Yes
Mail: Yes

Olivia Wu's Spiced Meringues

Yield
36 to 40
cookies

Olivia says these unusual, spicy meringues are her antidote to the overdose of rich butter cookies during the holidays. "The cayenne is the cornerstone," she says. Shaped like pretty stars and fragrant with spices, they keep forever, she adds—or would, if her son Erling didn't eat them all. Sometimes she sandwiches a buttercream between them, but they taste wonderful alone.

5 egg whites, at room temperature
1¼ cups sugar
1 teaspoon five-spice powder
⅛ to ¼ teaspoon cayenne, to taste
¼ teaspoon ground ginger
⅛ to ¼ teaspoon freshly grated nutmeg

Preheat oven to 250 degrees. Line cookie sheets with foil or spray, then dust with flour.

Beat eggs on high speed until foamy. Gradually beat in sugar, and continue beating until meringue holds stiff, glossy peaks. Sprinkle five-spice, cayenne, ginger, and nutmeg over meringue, then gently fold into egg whites.

Using a pastry bag fitted with a ½-inch star tip, pipe meringue onto baking sheets, making cookies about 1½ inches in diameter. Cookies won't spread, and you can space them close together. Bake in the center of the oven for 30 minutes. Turn off the oven, but do not open the oven door. Let meringues stay in the closed oven for at least 4 to 5 hours, or until dry and crisp.

Tip: Do not make meringues on a humid day; they will absorb moisture and become gummy.

Store: In an airtight container

Freeze: Yes

Mail: No

Chocolate Ice Cream Sandwiches

Yield
14 sandwiches

1½ ounces (1½ squares) unsweetened chocolate
1 cup all-purpose flour
¼ teaspoon salt
1 cup uncooked instant oatmeal
1 cup sugar
1 egg
½ teaspoon vanilla
½ cup vegetable shortening, room temperature
14 slices of firm frozen chocolate, vanilla, or cookies-and-cream ice
    cream; cut in 2¼ × 2¾ × ¾-inch pieces

Preheat oven to 350 degrees. Lightly grease or spray cookie sheets.

Put flour and salt in a mixing bowl.

Place chocolate in a microwave-proof bowl or in the top of a double boiler. Microwave on medium-high (80 percent) or heat over hot water, stirring occasionally, until melted and smooth.

Stir oatmeal and sugar into flour and add cooled chocolate. Stir in egg and vanilla. Beat in shortening. Batter will be slightly firm.

Roll out dough on a lightly floured pastry cloth to ¼ inch thick. Cut dough into 2½ × 3-inch pieces. Reroll scraps and cut remaining cookies.

Transfer cookies to cookie sheets. Bake in the center of the oven for 10 to 12 minutes, or until firm. Remove to wire racks to cool. When cookies are cool, fill each with a rectangle of ice cream. Serve immediately. Or wrap well and freeze.

Store: Unfilled cookies in a covered container. Filled cookies, wrapped well, in the freezer.

Freeze: Yes, plain or filled

Mail: No

Brownie Pizza with All the Trimmings

Yield
6 servings

Crust:

2 ounces semisweet chocolate
2 ounces unsweetened chocolate
¾ cup (1½ sticks) unsalted butter, at room temperature
1 cup sugar
4 eggs
¾ teaspoon vanilla extract
½ teaspoon coconut flavoring or extract
1 cup all-purpose flour
¼ teaspoon baking powder
⅛ teaspoon salt

Toppings:

½ cup white chocolate chips
1 cup semisweet chocolate chips
½ cup grated sweetened coconut
½ cup sliced almonds, or to taste
½ cup maraschino cherries, drained
1½ tablespoons butter

Preheat oven to 350 degrees. Use an 11- to 12-inch pizza pan or round baking pan. Line the pan with a double thickness of aluminum foil, letting foil extend over sides of pan for easy removal of brownie pizza. Lightly grease foil.

Place semisweet and unsweetened chocolates and butter in a microwave-proof bowl or in the top of a double boiler. Microwave on medium-high (80 percent) or heat over hot water, stirring occasionally, until melted and smooth. Let cool.

Beat sugar and eggs on high speed until light. Add vanilla and coconut flavoring. Spoon in cooled chocolate mixture and blend well. Stir in flour, baking powder, and salt to make a soft, smooth batter.

Carefully spoon batter into the prepared pan. Smooth with the back of a spoon. Set in the center of the oven. Bake for 20 minutes or until a toothpick inserted into the center of the brownie comes out dry.

Remove brownie crust from the oven and set on a wire rack. Sprinkle hot crust with white chocolate chips, ½ cup semisweet chocolate chips, coconut, and almonds; scatter cherries decoratively over top of pizza.

Place remaining ½ cup chocolate chips and butter in a microwave-proof bowl or in the top of a double boiler. Microwave on medium-high (80 percent) or heat over hot water, stirring occasionally, until melted and smooth.

Drizzle melted chocolate from a teaspoon over the top of the pizza. Cool pizza.

To serve, set brownie pizza on a serving dish. Cut into wedges.

Tip: You can decorate the pizza according to individual taste. For example, you can melt white chocolate to drizzle over top of the pizza, or use walnuts instead of almonds.

Store: Wrapped loosely in foil

Freeze: No

Mail: No

Jumbo Chocolate Chip Message Cookie

Yield
1 cookie,
about 9 inches
in diameter

¼ cup (½ stick) unsalted butter, at room temperature
2 tablespoons vegetable shortening
¼ cup granulated sugar
¼ cup packed dark brown sugar
1 egg
⅔ cup all-purpose flour
¼ teaspoon baking powder
¼ teaspoon baking soda
¼ teaspoon salt
¾ teaspoon vanilla extract
1 scant teaspoon dry instant coffee crystals
½ cup semisweet chocolate chips
¼ cup dark raisins

Icing:

2 cups confectioners' sugar
¼ cup (½ stick) unsalted butter
1 ounce semisweet chocolate
3 tablespoons milk
1 teaspoon vanilla extract
½ teaspoon chocolate extract

Preheat oven to 350 degrees. Remove the bottom from a 9-inch springform pan and set the bottom aside; you will need only the ring (sides) of the pan for this recipe. Grease the pan and a cookie sheet.

Cream the butter and vegetable shortening on medium speed until light, about 2 minutes. Add sugars and mix well. Add egg and beat to incorporate. Whisk together flour, baking powder, baking soda, and salt; add to batter. Mix in vanilla, instant coffee, chocolate chips, and raisins. Dough will be somewhat stiff.

Set greased springform pan on greased cookie sheet. Spoon batter into the pan. Smooth out the dough with the back of the spoon. Set cookie in the middle of the oven and bake for 25 minutes, until golden brown but still soft to the touch.

Cool cookie in pan. Remove pan sides carefully, then use 1 or 2 spatulas or a pizza peel to gently lift cookie from cookie sheet onto a serving plate.

To make icing for writing the message, sift sugar into a bowl. Place butter and chocolate in a microwave-proof bowl or in the top of a double boiler. Microwave on medium-high (80 percent) or heat over hot water, stirring occasionally, until melted and smooth.

Stir chocolate mixture into sugar. Blend in milk, and vanilla and chocolate extracts. The icing should be stiff; add more sugar if necessary.

Spoon icing into a pastry bag fitted with a fairly fine round tip. Write message on the cookie.

Tip: Instead of making icing, you can use the packaged chocolate decorating gel available in supermarkets.

Store: On a plate, loosely covered so as not to smudge the icing

Freeze: Yes, before icing

Mail: No

*D*ominos

Yield
36 cookies

1 cup all-purpose flour, sifted
½ teaspoon salt
1½ ounces unsweetened chocolate
1 cup uncooked instant oatmeal
1 cup sugar
1 egg
½ teaspoon vanilla extract
½ cup vegetable shortening, at room temperature

Frosting:

2 cups confectioners' sugar, sifted
¼ cup (½ stick) unsalted butter, melted
¼ cup unsweetened cocoa
1 teaspoon instant espresso or regular coffee crystals
½ teaspoon vanilla extract
1 to 3 tablespoons milk
Royal Icing (page 286)

Preheat oven to 350 degrees. Lightly grease a cookie sheet.

Put flour and salt together in a mixing bowl.

Place chocolate in a microwave-proof bowl or in the top of a double boiler. Microwave on medium-high (80 percent) or heat over hot water, stirring occasionally, until melted and smooth. Let cool.

Stir oatmeal and sugar into flour and add cooled chocolate. Stir in egg and vanilla. Beat in shortening to make a fairly firm dough.

Roll out dough on a lightly floured board or pastry cloth to ¼ inch thick.

Cut dough into rectangles about 1 inch wide by 2 to 3 inches long.

Transfer to cookie sheets. Bake in the center of the oven for 10 to 12 minutes, until firm. Remove cookies to wire racks to cool.

To prepare frosting: Put sugar in a bowl. Mix in butter, cocoa, coffee, vanilla, and enough milk to make a somewhat stiff frosting.

To assemble, frost cooled cookies and let frosting set. Prepare Royal Icing just before you are ready to use it. Spoon icing into a pastry bag with a fine round tip. Decorate dominos, making a line across the center and the appropriate number of dots on each side of the domino. Let cookies dry on rack.

Store: In a covered (not airtight) container
Freeze: Yes
Mail: Yes

Chocolate Tangerine Moons for Halloween

Yield
30 cookies

1½ cups vegetable shortening, at room temperature
1 cup sugar
½ cup instant nonfat dry milk
1 teaspoon light corn syrup
3 eggs
4 cups cake flour
1½ teaspoons baking powder
¼ teaspoon salt
¾ cup water
2 tablespoons grated tangerine zest
1¼ teaspoons vanilla extract

Chocolate Frosting:

2 tablespoons unsalted butter, at room temperature
2½ tablespoons unsweetened cocoa
2 teaspoons light corn syrup
½ teaspoon vanilla extract
⅔ cup confectioners' sugar
1½ tablespoons milk, or as needed

Tangerine Frosting:

¼ cup cream cheese, softened
2½ tablespoons unsalted butter, at room temperature
2 tablespoons tangerine juice
1 tablespoon grated tangerine zest
1⅓ cups confectioners' sugar

Preheat oven to 350 degrees. Lightly grease or spray cookie sheets.

Cream shortening and sugar on medium to high speed for 2 to 3 minutes. Beat in dry milk, corn syrup, and eggs, one at a time, until combined. At medium speed, mix in flour, baking powder, salt, water, tangerine zest, and vanilla. Batter will be firm but pliable.

Using a ¼-cup measure, scoop out scant cup (about 3 tablespoon-fuls) of batter and set on prepared cookie sheets, about 2 inches apart. Use a butter knife to smooth cookies into 2½-inch circles.

Bake cookies for 14 to 16 minutes, or until cookies are firm to the touch and a toothpick inserted in the center comes out dry. Remove cookies to wire racks and let cool completely.

Meanwhile, prepare the frostings. To prepare the Chocolate Frosting, cream butter on medium speed until light, about 2 minutes. Mix in remaining ingredients. At high speed, mix frosting until it is smooth and creamy. Add milk as necessary to make frosting soft and spreadable but not too loose. Set aside.

To prepare the Tangerine Frosting, beat all ingredients together on medium speed. Increase speed to high and continue beating to make a creamy, spreadable frosting. Add more juice if necessary to make frosting soft and spreadable but not too loose.

To frost cookies, spread half of each cookie with Chocolate Frosting and half of each cookie with Tangerine Frosting in a curved pattern, so the cookies look like half moons.

Store: In single layers on plates, in the refrigerator. Wrap loosely with foil.

Freeze: Unfrosted; frost before serving

Mail: No

Gingerbread Stained Glass Valentines

Yield
30 cookies

3 tablespoons unsalted butter or margarine, at room temperature
½ cup firmly packed dark brown sugar
¾ cup dark molasses
⅓ cup water
3 cups all-purpose flour
1 teaspoon baking soda
¼ teaspoon salt
½ teaspoon ground cinnamon
½ teaspoon ground ginger
⅛ teaspoon ground allspice
⅛ teaspoon ground nutmeg
5 to 6 ounces red and white hard peppermint candies

Cream butter on medium speed until light. Add sugar and molasses and beat at high speed. Blend in water. Add flour, baking soda, salt, and spices. Shape dough into a ball, and cover with plastic wrap or aluminum foil. Refrigerate for 45 minutes, or until firm but pliable.

Preheat oven to 350 degrees. Cover 2 cookie sheets with aluminum foil.

Trace heart designs gently onto the foil. Divide dough in thirds, then divide each portion of dough into 10 pieces. Roll each piece of dough into a rope between ¼ and ½ inch thick. Outline designs with ropes of dough, sealing edges tightly.

Crush and coarsely chop candies between two sheets of waxed paper with a rolling pin or in a food processor. Fill in the insides of the hearts with the crushed candies.

Bake in the center of the oven for 4 to 5 minutes or until the cookie dough is set and the candy melts. Cool cookies on cookie sheets, then remove to wire racks.

Tip: To make yellow stained glass (for Christmas or another occasion), crush hard lemon drops instead of the peppermint candies. If you can find them, Sour Balls make excellent stained glass in assorted colors.

Store: On a plate, wrapped with foil

Freeze: Yes

Mail: No

Letter Cookies

Yield
20 letters,
about
1 ½ inches high

½ cup (1 stick) unsalted butter or margarine, at room temperature
¼ cup confectioners' sugar
1 cup all-purpose flour
½ cup old-fashioned oats
¼ teaspoon salt
1 teaspoon vanilla extract
1 cup confectioners' sugar, for rolling cookies
1 teaspoon ground cinnamon

Preheat oven to 325 degrees. Lightly grease or spray cookie sheets.

Cream butter or margarine at medium speed until light. Beat in confectioners' sugar and combine. Mix in flour and oats at high speed. Add salt and vanilla. Dough will be slightly stiff. Remove it from the mixer and knead a minute, or until pliable.

Break off walnut-sized pieces of dough and roll with your hands into ropes. Form into desired letters. It is always fun to make the guest of honor's name or spell out "Happy Birthday," "Congratulations," or some other appropriate message. Set the letters on cookie sheets. Bake in the center of the oven for 15 minutes or until firm to the touch and lightly golden on the bottom. Let cookies stand for a few minutes to cool.

Stir together the confectioners' sugar and the ground cinnamon, and place on a plate. While cookies are still warm, gently roll them in the cinnamon sugar. Set on wire racks to cool completely.

Store: In an airtight container
Freeze: Yes
Mail: No

Saint Patrick's Day Cookies

Yield
50 cookies

1 cup (2 sticks) unsalted butter or a combination of butter
    and margarine, at room temperature
1½ cups sugar
1 egg
1½ teaspoons vanilla extract
2½ cups all-purpose flour
1½ teaspoons baking powder
¼ teaspoon salt
3 ounces candied green cherries, chopped
1 ounce unsweetened baking chocolate, melted and cooled
⅓ cup chopped pecans or walnuts
Lightly beaten egg white

Cream butter and sugar on medium speed until light, about 2 minutes. Add egg and vanilla; mix well. Whisk together flour, baking powder, and salt. Blend into batter. Gather dough together and knead into a workable ball. Divide it into 3 equal pieces.

Stir cherries into ⅓ of the dough. Blend melted chocolate and nuts into remaining portions of dough.

On a lightly floured board or pastry cloth, shape the green cherry dough into a narrow rectangle about 18 inches long. Shape each half of the chocolate dough into a similar-sized piece. Brush the cherry dough on both sides with the egg white. Place cherry dough atop one of the chocolate pieces, then layer the other chocolate portion on top of the cherry dough. Press together gently. You should have a log of dough with chocolate on the top and bottom and cherry dough in the middle. Wrap dough in aluminum foil or plastic wrap and shape into an even, squared log. Refrigerate for at least 2 to 4 hours, until very firm.

Preheat oven to 350 degrees. Lightly grease or spray cookie sheets. Remove dough from refrigerator. Cut into ¼-inch slices with a serrated knife or a sharp knife.

Transfer to cookie sheets. Bake in the center of the oven for about 10 minutes or until cookies are set and beginning to turn golden on the bottom.

Let stand on cookie sheets for 2 to 3 minutes, then remove to wire racks to cool.

Store: In an airtight container
Freeze: Yes
Mail: No

Gumdrop Cookies

Yield
14 cookies

½ cup shortening
½ cup firmly packed light brown sugar
1 egg
½ teaspoon vanilla extract
¾ cup all-purpose flour
¼ teaspoon baking soda
¼ teaspoon salt
¾ cup gumdrops, cut in half
¾ cup old-fashioned oats

Preheat oven to 350 degrees. Lightly grease or spray cookie sheets.

Using an electric mixer, beat shortening and sugar until light, about 2 minutes. Mix in egg and vanilla. Whisk together flour, baking soda, and salt; stir into batter. Gently mix in gumdrops and oats.

Drop dough by tablespoonfuls onto cookie sheets. Bake cookies in the center of the oven for 10 to 12 minutes, until firm on top and golden on the bottom. Let stand on cookie sheets for 2 minutes, then remove to wire racks to cool completely.

Store: In an airtight container
Freeze: Yes
Mail: Yes

Buttermilk Party Triangles with Color Shots

Yield
32 cookies

¾ cup (1½ sticks) unsalted butter or margarine, at room temperature
¾ cup sugar
1 egg
¾ teaspoon vanilla
1½ cups all-purpose flour
½ cup cake flour
½ teaspoon baking soda
¼ teaspoon salt
¼ cup buttermilk
1 egg white, slightly beaten
1 bottle (1.75 ounces) color shots (sprinkles)

Cream butter or margarine and sugar on medium speed until light, about 2 to 3 minutes. Beat in egg and vanilla. Whisk together flours, baking soda, and salt. Stir into batter. Blend in buttermilk to make a soft dough. If dough is too sticky to handle, knead in a little more flour, a tablespoon at a time, to make a smooth but soft dough.

Gather dough and shape into a triangular log, using a dough scraper or a spatula to shape the sides. Cover dough with plastic wrap or aluminum foil and refrigerate for several hours or overnight, until very firm.

Preheat oven to 350 degrees. Lightly grease or spray cookie sheets.

When ready to bake cookies, cut ⅛- to ¼-inch slices from dough using a sharp or serrated knife. Cut these large triangles in half to make skinny triangles. Transfer to cookie sheets. Brush cookies with beaten egg white. Sprinkle with color shots, covering the entire cookie.

Bake in the center of the oven for 12 to 14 minutes, until cookies are golden on the bottom. Let stand on cookie sheets for 2 to 3 minutes, then remove to wire racks to cool.

Tips: Cut the cookies when they are very cold; this will help to keep the shape. Use your fingers to reform any misshapen unbaked cookies.

Use plenty of color shots in various colors for a festive look.

You can leave the cookies whole if you prefer, but they are rather large.

Store: In an airtight container
Freeze: Yes
Mail: No

Flourless Cinnamon Balls

Yield
22 to 25
cookies

This is a good cookie for Passover, when Jewish cooks use no flour or leavening. Make sure all ingredients are kosher for Passover.

2 egg whites, at room temperature
½ cup sugar
2½ cups ground almonds
1 tablespoon ground cinnamon
⅛ teaspoon ground nutmeg
½ cup sugar to roll uncooked cookies

Preheat oven to 400 degrees. Oil the cookie sheets.

Beat the egg whites until soft peaks form. Sprinkle half of the sugar over egg whites and beat to incorporate. Sprinkle remaining sugar over egg whites and continue beating until stiff, glossy peaks form. Gently fold in almonds, cinnamon, and nutmeg. Dough will be soft.

Pinch off pieces of dough and shape into ¾-inch balls. Sprinkle sugar over cookies or roll each cookie in sugar before setting it on the cookie sheet.

Bake in the center of the oven for 10 to 12 minutes, until cookies are golden on the bottom and firm on the top.

Let cookies stand on cookie sheets for 2 to 3 minutes, then remove to wire racks to cool completely.

Store: In an airtight container
Freeze: Yes
Mail: Yes

Flourless Coconut Cookies

Yield
22 cookies

These are good packed into lunch boxes during Passover—or any other time of the year.

½ cup (1 stick) unsalted butter or margarine, at room temperature
½ cup sugar
1 egg
¾ cup matzo cake meal
2¼ cups grated coconut
½ to ¾ cup sugar for rolling uncooked cookies

Preheat oven to 350 degrees. Oil 2 cookie sheets.

Beat butter or margarine and sugar on medium speed until light, about 2 minutes. Add egg; beat well. Blend in the cake meal. Stir in the coconut.

Break off pieces of dough and shape into ¾- to 1-inch balls. Roll in sugar and set on cookie sheets. Lightly press cookies with back of spoon or the tines of a fork. Cookies will flatten out during baking.

Bake cookies in the center of the oven for 10 to 12 minutes, until golden on the bottom. Let stand on cookie sheets for 2 to 3 minutes, then remove to wire racks to cool.

Store: In an airtight container
Freeze: Yes
Mail: No

Lemon Tulipes with Pecan Praline Cream

Yield
22 to 24
cookies

These cookies require some time and effort, but make an excellent dessert for a dinner party. The pecan praline–scented cream puts us in mind of New Orleans, and we really like these cookies for a Mardi Gras bash.

⅓ cup flour
⅔ cup confectioners' sugar
2 egg whites, lightly beaten
¼ cup unsalted butter, melted
2 teaspoons finely grated lemon zest
1 tablespoon fresh lemon juice
1 to 2 tablespoons water, as needed

Filling:

½ teaspoon gelatin (optional)
1 tablespoon cold water (optional)
1 cup heavy whipping cream
2 tablespoons brown sugar
½ teaspoon vanilla
1 teaspoon hazelnut or almond liqueur (optional)
½ cup pecan praline powder (page 293), plus some for sprinkling
Toasted pecan halves for garnish (optional)

Preheat oven to 450 degrees. Butter heavy-duty cookie sheets without nonstick coatings. Have ready a paper towel and 3 or 4 small shot glasses or spice bottles.

In a medium bowl, whisk together flour and sugar. Beat in egg whites, butter, lemon zest, and juice. Whisk until smooth. Add water as necessary to make a thin, crepelike batter.

Drop ½ tablespoon batter onto one of the cookie sheets; smooth out batter with the back of a spoon to make a circle about 3 inches in diameter. Batter should be very thin; add a teaspoon or two of water if necessary. Drop 2 or 3 more spoonfuls of batter onto cookie sheet. Form only 3 or 4 cookies per baking sheet.

Bake in the center of the oven for 3 to 5 minutes, or just until cookies are golden around the edges. Keep an eye on them; they burn quickly. Remove from oven. With a wide spatula, remove a hot cookie and drape it over the inverted shot glass or the spice bottle. Placing a paper towel between your hand and the cookie to keep from burning your fingers, gently but firmly press the cookie around the glass or spice bottle to make a cup shape. Repeat with remaining cookies, leaving them on the bottles or glasses until they firm up and are crisp. Place cookie cup on a wire rack. Repeat with remaining cookies, working as quickly as possible so cookies do not have a chance to harden before you shape them. (If they do harden, return to the oven for 30 seconds to soften them.)

To prepare the filling: If you wish to beat the cream several hours before you use it, you can stabilize it with gelatin. Otherwise, the cream should be beaten no longer than 1 hour before you plan to serve it.

To make stabilized cream, soften the gelatin on the cold water in a small pan or a microwave-proof cup. Heat over low heat, or in the microwave on medium-high (70 percent), stirring once or twice, just until gelatin completely dissolves. This will take only 30 seconds to a minute. Let cool. The gelatin must cool completely before you add it to the cream, but must not set or it will form lumps.

To beat the cream, chill the cream, bowl, and beaters. Beat cream on high speed until it begins to grow thicker and you can see traces in the cream when you lift up the beaters. Beat in the brown sugar, then beat in gelatin in a steady stream. Add vanilla and liqueur. Beat just until cream forms stiff peaks when beaters are lifted; do not overbeat. Cover and chill until needed; cream should hold for up to 24 hours.

Just before serving, fold ½ cup praline into the cream. Pipe or spoon a dollop of cream in each cookie cup. Sprinkle lightly with additional praline. Garnish with a pecan if desired.

Serve cookies individually, or in groups of two or three for a dinner party dessert.

Tips: This yield allows for some waste, since cookies are fragile and break easily.

For all-lemon cookies, fill these with a 50-50 mixture of Lemon Butter (page 290) and whipped cream.

Store: Unfilled, in a single layer on plates, covered loosely with plastic wrap.

Freeze: Yes, unfilled. Place each cookie in a small plastic sandwich bag, then arrange carefully in tins.

Mail: No

Golden Rings

Yield
50 cookies

With more couples living longer, fiftieth anniversary parties are no longer rare. If a cake seems like a bit too much, we suggest these cookies. They're small and will be appreciated by a crowd that takes its sweets in small doses.

1 cup (2 sticks) unsalted butter, at room temperature
1 cup confectioners' sugar
1 tablespoon fresh orange juice
1½ to 2 tablespoons finely grated orange zest
1 teaspoon vanilla extract
¼ teaspoon almond extract
4 egg yolks
½ teaspoon salt
2¼ cups all-purpose flour
1 egg white, lightly beaten with 1 teaspoon water
Yellow-gold decorating sugar

Cream butter and sugar together until light. Beat in orange juice, zest, vanilla and almond extracts, egg yolks, and salt. Stir in flour to make a medium-soft, sticky dough.

Wrap dough in plastic wrap and refrigerate for 30 minutes to 1 hour, or until dough is firm and no longer sticky, but pliable. (Dough can be refrigerated for up to two days; remove from refrigerator and let stand at room temperature about 30 minutes, until pliable.)

Preheat oven to 350 degrees.

Divide dough in half and work with one half at a time; leave the other half in the refrigerator. Break off a piece of dough about 1 inch in diameter. Using your palms, roll dough on a lightly floured board or pastry cloth into a "rope" about 5 inches long. Place dough on an ungreased cookie sheet, arranging into a circle and gently pressing ends of dough together. Repeat with remaining dough.

(If you prefer, you can make a fancier rope by dividing the dough for each cookie in half, and rolling each piece into a skinny rope. Twist the two ropes together, then form into a circle.)

Lightly brush tops of cookies with egg white–water mixture. Sprinkle with decorating sugar.

Bake in the center of the oven for about 10 minutes, or until cookies are set but not browned. Let cool on cookie sheets for 1 minute, then carefully remove to wire racks to finish cooling.

Tips: To make an attractive arrangement for a fiftieth anniversary party, place a low floral arrangement—we like shaggy white mums—in the center of a gold-tone platter. Arrange the cookies in a ring around the edges of the platter. If desired, sprinkle additional decorating sugar over the cookies.

If you're feeling flush and want a truly elegant look, omit the gold decorating sugar. Drizzle the baked, cooled cookies lightly with melted white chocolate. Let the chocolate set, then dust cookies with gold leaf (see page 309 for a mail-order source).

Store: In an airtight container

Freeze: Yes

Mail: No

White on White Chocolate Sandwiches

Yield
15 to 16
sandwich
cookies

These beautiful, rich cookies would be ideal for a wedding shower or rehearsal luncheon, or any elegant occasion.

White Chocolate Rounds (page 130)
About 3 tablespoons best-quality raspberry jam
12 ounces white chocolate, broken or chopped into small bits
2 teaspoons vegetable shortening

Shape, bake, and cool cookies as directed in the White Chocolate Rounds recipe, using a pastry bag to make them evenly round.

When cookies are cool, turn one cookie upside down and spread about ½ teaspoon raspberry jam evenly over cookie. Do not use too much jam; you want just a smear of jam between cookies. Top with another cookie, right side up. Brush crumbs from cookies. Repeat with remaining cookies.

Lightly oil a wire rack and set atop a sheet of waxed paper. Place chocolate and shortening in a microwave-proof bowl or in the top of a double boiler. Microwave on medium-high (80 percent) or heat over hot water, stirring occasionally, until melted and smooth. Place a cookie in the white chocolate and spoon white chocolate over cookie to completely cover it. Lift cookie from chocolate with a dipping fork or 2-pronged cooking fork, gently tapping fork against bowl or pan to shake off excess chocolate. Set cookie on oiled rack. With a narrow spoon or the tines of a fork, drizzle a little white chocolate on top of cookie to make a swirly design.

Repeat with remaining cookies, reheating chocolate briefly if it begins to firm up too much. Refrigerate cookies.

Store: In single layers on waxed paper–lined plates, wrapped with foil. Refrigerate; let stand at room temperature 10 to 15 minutes before serving.

Freeze: No
Mail: No

Barnyard at Christmas

We're not the first to create a barnyard Christmas, but in all immodesty, we like our barn best. It's unusual among gingerbread projects in that it uses a combination of decorating techniques, with an emphasis on painting, rather than piping. An egg yolk tempura gives the barn a beautiful, glossy "old red" color that looks remarkably realistic. The animals are coated with a thin layer of Royal Icing and painted as well to give their faces more expression.

We figured that more people feel comfortable with a paintbrush—even if their last painting project was in seventh grade—than a pastry bag. Of course, you're free to do whatever you like with the barn and its inhabitants, and you can use whatever decorations you like. You can skip the pretzel fence or other details. If you are used to decorating cakes and cookies with frosting, you might prefer to pipe, rather than paint, decorations on the animals. If you're ambitious, you can use a small paring knife to cut the animals more to scale. If you prefer a barn that can be moved (carefully) independently, you can make a floor. You'll need to make another half recipe of gingerbread and roll it ¼ inch thick. Cut a rectangle 8½ inches wide by 10½ inches long.

You can even outfit the barn so that it can be lit up from inside. You'll need to cut a hole in the back of the barn so that you can insert a small corded or battery-operated light. Make sure the switch is accessible from the back; you won't be able to reach inside the barn once the roof is on.

This project is not difficult, but it is time-consuming. Allow a weekend to complete it. Or, do the project in stages: Bake the gingerbread one weekend, assemble the barn a second weekend, and decorate it when you get the chance.

The supplies for this project can be found at craft or art supply stores.

Please note: The barn and animals are theoretically edible, but the hard gingerbread and frosting and the metallic-flavored food colorings would appeal to only the most determined child. Think of this as a decoration, not food.

Also, it's tempting to save the barn display for the following year, but success is highly unlikely. The gingerbread will eventually shrink—if it doesn't mold or become dinner for the mice in your garage or attic first—and cause the barn to collapse or the decorations to come off. If you feel compelled to try, spray the barn with a fixative (found at art or craft supply stores), keep it in a cool, dry place, and hope for the best.

Ingredients:

2 recipes gingerbread (page 242; do not double the recipe,
   but make two batches)

Triple recipe of Royal Icing (page 286)

Nonstick cooking spray

Egg Yolk Tempura (page 288); tint about 2 teaspoons of it green
   and the rest red

Red, yellow, and green food colors

Black paste food color, or blue liquid food color

Granulated sugar (at least 2 cups)

Various edible decorations; we used small round fruit-flavored decors,
   M&Ms, and red cinnamon candies

Shredded Wheat (optional; regular, not spoon-size)

12 to 16 thin pretzels (optional)

Edible white glitter (gum acacia; optional)

Equipment and supplies:

Stiff, thin cardboard for making templates

Carbon paper (optional, but helpful)

X-acto knife or scissors

Cookie cutters: we used star, tree, and small candy cane cutters,
   and farm animals that included a pig, cow, cat, sheep, duck, and
   a small lamb

At least two or three cookie sheets, the heavier the better

Ruler or other sturdy straightedge

Sharp paring knife

Pizza cutting wheel (optional, but very helpful)

20 × 24-inch sheet of white foam board or heavy poster board

Canned goods (to prop up barn while it dries)

One or two 10- or 12-inch pastry bags (two disposable bags make
   cleanup easier)

2 round metal decorating tips, one small (No. 4 or 5) and one
   medium (No. 9 or 10); similar-size star tips can be used instead

Fine artist's watercolor brush (No. 1 or 2), or food color pens (see
   Mail-Order Sources in Appendix B, pages 309–310)

Larger, flatter artist's paintbrush, not too stiff (No. 10 or 12)

Small icing spatula or butter knife for icing animals

Tweezers (optional; can make picking up small candies easier)

3 toothpicks, black paint or food coloring, white glue, and a small
   gold paper star (optional; for weathervane)

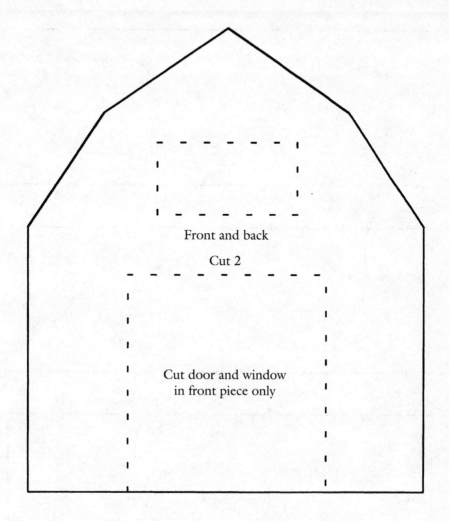

Front and back

Cut 2

Cut door and window
in front piece only

Cupola (optional)

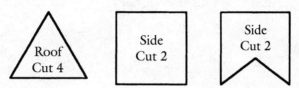

Roof
Cut 4

Side
Cut 2

Side
Cut 2

BARN TEMPLATES
Enlarge all patterns to 200%

Figure 7.4

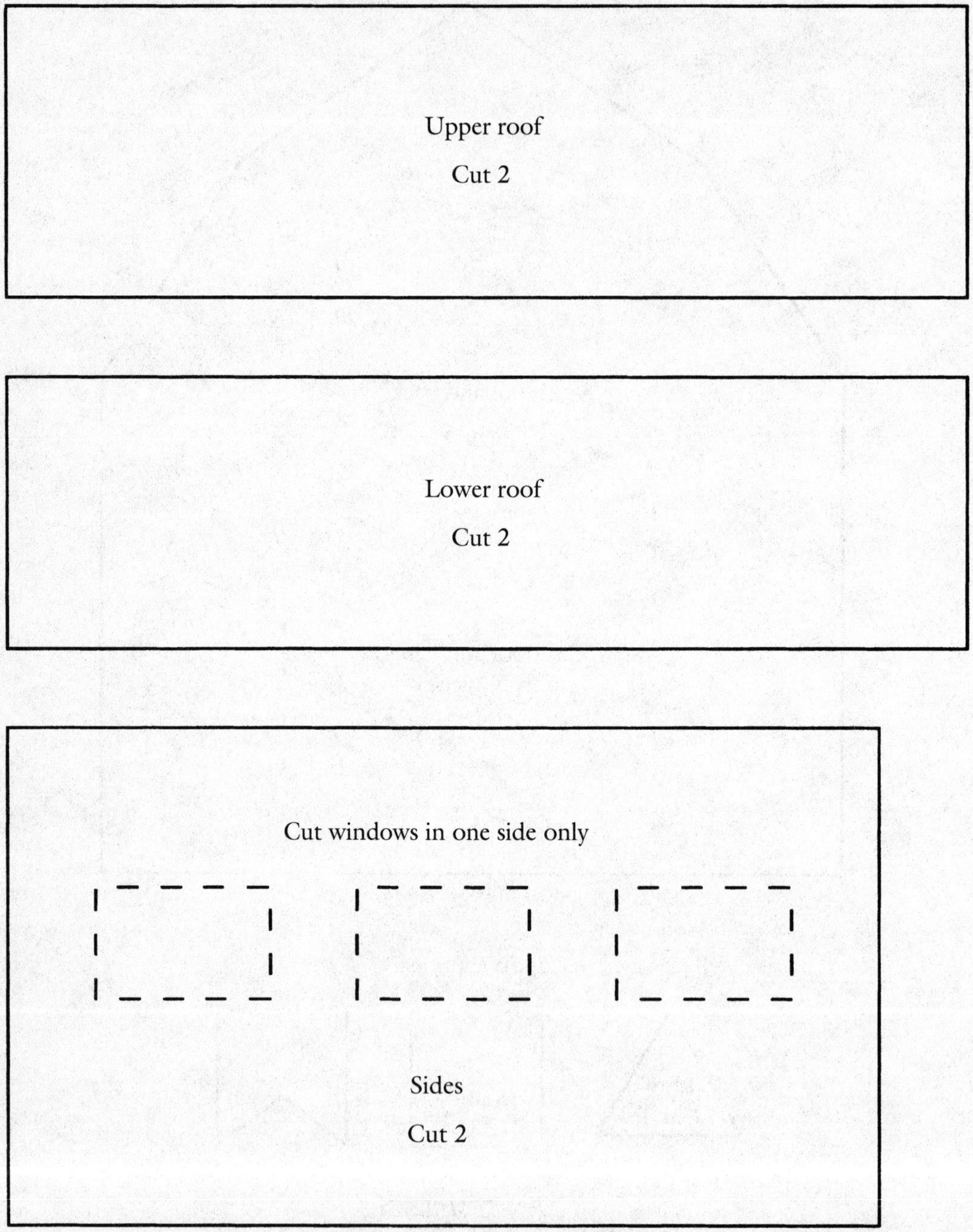

Upper roof

Cut 2

Lower roof

Cut 2

Cut windows in one side only

Sides

Cut 2

BARN TEMPLATES
Enlarge all patterns to 200%

Figure 7.5

Directions for baking and assembly:

1. Enlarge the patterns in figs. 7.4 and 7.5 by 200 percent. (Not all copying machines have the capacity to enlarge that much; check with the photocopy shop ahead of time.) Or, skip the copying machine and enlarge by hand to the dimensions shown.

2. Trace the templates onto thin cardboard, using carbon paper if you have it. Cut out the cardboard templates using the X-acto knife or scissors. Spray one side of each template with nonstick cooking spray. (This will help keep dough from sticking to the templates.)

3. Preheat oven to 350 degrees. Prepare 2 or 3 cookie sheets. If your cookie sheets have sides, turn them upside down. Spray lightly with nonstick cooking spray, then dust lightly with flour. Set aside.

4. Place about 2 teaspoons of the egg yolk–water mixture in a small cup or bowl. Add two or three drops of green food coloring, plus a drop of blue if you like, and whisk with a fork until color is evenly mixed. To remaining egg yolk–water mixture, add ¼ teaspoon red food coloring and whisk until mixed. Set aside, with the large, flat artist's brush nearby. Whisk these egg yolk tempuras again before you brush them on the cookies.

5. Divide the chilled gingerbread dough into 4 equal portions. Place one portion of the chilled gingerbread dough directly on one of the prepared cookie sheets (without sides, or upside down). Roll to a long rectangle slightly more than ⅛ inch thick. (Placing a towel under the cookie sheet will help keep it from slipping as you roll.) Place the upper roof template on the dough, sprayed side down, and cut around the template using a sharp paring knife or pizza cutter. Repeat so that you have 2 upper roof pieces. Gather up the remaining dough, roll out on a lightly floured board or cloth to slightly more than ⅛ inch thick, and use the cookie cutters to cut out a star, 2 trees, and farm animals of your choice. It's best to cut at least two of each shape, so that you have spares in case a cookie breaks or you make a mistake in painting it. Reroll scraps. Cut some of the leftover dough into small rectangles to be used as stands for the animals. Use a large flexible spatula to gently transfer the cookies to cookie sheets, leaving at least 1 inch between cookies.

   Gather up any leftover dough, wrap in plastic wrap, and set aside.

Bake in the center of the oven for 10 to 15 minutes, depending on size, or until cookies are firm and just beginning to turn golden on the edges. (You will probably have to remove the smaller cookies from the oven before the roof piece is completely done.) When the Christmas trees are just firm but not turning golden, brush lightly with the green tempura; return to the oven for at least 1 minute to set the color. Do not brush any of the other pieces with tempura.

Let cool on cookie sheets before transferring to wire racks. It's very important to let the roof piece (and all other large pieces) cool and firm up completely before moving them; otherwise, they'll crack. While roof pieces are still warm, trim bumpy or uneven edges on the long sides with a sharp knife or pizza cutter, using the ruler or straightedge as a guide.

6. Roll out another portion of chilled dough directly on a prepared cookie sheet to ¼ inch thick. Cut out the back of the barn, using the front/back template. Using a sharp paring knife or pizza wheel and the ruler or straightedge, score the dough vertically at ½-inch intervals to make "siding." Cut about ⅔ of the way through the dough. Do not cut out window or door.

If you plan to make the cupola, roll out dough to slightly more than ⅛ inch thick and cut the 4 side pieces and 4 roof pieces.

Gather any dough scraps, add to previous dough scraps, wrap in plastic wrap, and set aside.

Bake pieces in the center of the oven for 10 minutes, or until back of barn is fairly firm. Using the large, flat artist's brush, gently brush red tempura evenly over back of barn and sides (but not roof) of cupola. Brush tempura onto sides of cookies, being careful not to get too much on the cookie sheet. Return to oven for another minute for cupola sides, and 5 to 10 minutes for back of barn, until gingerbread is firm and beginning to turn golden around the edges.

7. Roll out the third portion of the dough to slightly more than ⅛ inch thick. Cut out the 2 lower roof pieces. Gather up dough scraps, add to previously saved scraps, wrap in plastic wrap, and set aside.

Bake and trim the lower roof pieces as you did the upper roof pieces in Step 5.

8. Roll out the last portion of the dough directly on a prepared cookie sheet to ¼ inch thick. Cut out barn front. Cut out the window and door, but do not remove the window and door pieces; leave them in place. (This keeps the openings from distorting too much during baking.) Using a pizza wheel or sharp knife, score the dough at ½-inch intervals, as you did the back. Then score the door vertically at ¼-inch intervals, cutting completely through, but leaving pieces in place.

9. Gather up scraps and add them to the scraps of dough you reserved earlier. Knead briefly until smooth. If dough has softened too much, refrigerate it for 15 minutes. Roll out directly on a cookie sheet to ¼ inch thick. Cut out 2 sides of barn. On 1 side piece only, cut out 3 windows as shown, leaving cutout sections in place. Score the dough at ½-inch intervals to make "siding." Bake, paint, and cool sides of barn as you did the front and back. While still warm, trim uneven or bumpy spots along the edges, using a sharp knife or pizza cutter and a ruler or straightedge.

10. Using a sharp paring knife, cut or pry out the cutout window and door pieces on cooled barn pieces. Save the door pieces; the window pieces can be discarded or used as stands for the animals.

11. Let cooled barn pieces stand on wire racks for at least 12 hours before constructing barn; this will let them dry out slightly so they are sturdier. If you want to store them beyond that, wrap in plastic wrap, then foil, and store for up to a week. Store the animals in an airtight tin.

12. Construct and decorate the barn on a cool, dry day. First, make a triple recipe of royal icing (or a single recipe, if not decorating the barn until later). Icing dries out quickly; be sure to keep it completely covered when not in use. You can keep royal icing up to two days; rebeat before using.

13. Lay the foam board on a flat surface. Decide where you want the barn to go (we think it looks nice in a rear corner, facing diagonally). Fit a pastry bag with the No. 9 or 10 tip and fill with royal icing. Pipe a thick, straight line of icing on the board where the back of the barn will go. Stand the back of the barn (the piece without the door and window) upright in the icing, painted side to the outside. Brace it with canned goods on either side to keep it upright.

14. To erect one side of the barn, pipe another line of icing on the board, at a right angle to the back and to your left as you face what will be the front of the barn. Stand the windowless side of the barn in the icing, painted side facing out, and join the side piece to the back piece with royal icing. Brace the side with canned goods to hold it upright.

15. Repeat this procedure with the right side of the barn—the side with windows.

16. Pipe a line of icing where the front of the barn (the piece with the door and window) will go. Stand the front piece in the icing, and attach it to the two sides with royal icing. Brace with canned goods.

    Fill in any small gaps in the barn with royal icing.

17. Pipe 2 lines of icing on the board coming out from the doorway, where the doors will go. (We like to have them swinging open; if you prefer them closed, you may have to trim them to refit the opening.) Affix doors to sides of doorway with royal icing, then stand upright in the icing on board. Brace if necessary.

18. Using a moistened paper towel, wipe off any excess royal icing from the outsides of the barn. Let the barn stand for at least 30 minutes to 1 hour, or until the icing has set enough so that barn pieces stay in place without bracing.

19. Remove the canned goods bracing the barn. If you like, crumble up Shredded Wheat and scatter over the floor of the barn for "hay." Pipe royal icing all along the barn's rooflines (back, front, and sides). Fit one upper roof piece on top of the barn. Press it gently onto the barn. Repeat with the other upper roof piece. Attach the sides of the cupola, if using, to the upper roof and to each other with royal icing. The notches in 2 of the cupola sides should fit against the peak of the barn roof. Do not put the cupola roof in place at this time. Pipe a line of icing along the seam in the barn roof.

20. Attach the lower roof pieces, gently pressing into place. With a moistened paper towel, wipe off any excess royal icing that has dripped onto the barn.

21. Let barn sit for at least 1 hour, and up to one week, before decorating it. While the barn stands, you can decorate the animals and star. Place 1 to 2 tablespoons of royal icing in each of several small bowls; the number depends on how many different colors you need. Thin the royal icing in the bowls with water to

*P*ecan Praline

Yield
1 heaping cup

1 cup pecan halves, toasted and very coarsely chopped
½ cup sugar
2 tablespoons water

Measure out the pecans and have handy by the stove. Butter a cookie sheet.

In a small, heavy saucepan or skillet, heat sugar and water, swirling pan gently from time to time, until they come to a boil. Reduce heat to medium-high, cover pan, and continue boiling for 3 minutes. Uncover pan and boil for another 2 to 4 minutes, without stirring, until sugar turns a deep golden color and begins to smell like burnt caramel. Immediately remove from heat—syrup burns quickly—and stir in pecans. Turn mixture out onto buttered baking sheet and spread as thinly as possible with a spatula or wooden spoon. Let cool until hardened.

To make chunky praline (good for adding to butter cookie doughs or sprinkling on top of cookies before baking), place cooled praline in a heavy-duty plastic bag and pound the bag with a heavy spoon or rolling pin to break the praline into small chunks.

To make praline powder, use the above method and keep pounding until the praline is the consistency of a coarse powder. Or, put the cooled praline in a food processor and grind until powdered.

Tip: For a European style praline, substitute roasted, skinned hazelnuts for the pecans.

Store: In an airtight container

Freeze: Yes

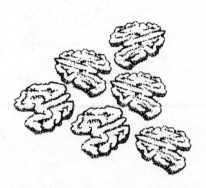

Real Vanilla Sugar

Yield
2 cups

You can buy "vanilla" sugar in many supermarkets, but it's artificially flavored, which to us seems to miss the whole point of using vanilla sugar. It takes a couple of weeks to produce a real vanilla sugar, but it's worth every minute of the wait. You can use this in place of regular sugar in just about any cookie where you want an extra boost of vanilla.

2 cups granulated sugar
1 vanilla bean

Pour sugar into a canister or airtight jar. Prick the vanilla bean in several places along its length with a needle or the tip of a small, sharp knife. Bury it in the sugar.

Cover tightly and let stand at least 2 weeks, shaking occasionally. The moisture from the vanilla bean will make the sugar clump up; shaking the jar vigorously should loosen it.

After 2 weeks, remove the vanilla bean. The sugar should give off a definite vanilla aroma; if it does not, return the vanilla to the jar and let stand another week.

Use vanilla sugar in recipes in place of regular sugar. Reserve the vanilla bean for another use, or use it to make a new batch of vanilla sugar.

EQUIPMENT AND INGREDIENTS

Equipment

Cookie Sheets

To bake most cookies you need at least two good cookie or baking sheets. You need two for efficiency's sake. You bake one sheetful, then when those cookies are done, you can pop in another sheetful without waiting for the first baking sheet to cool.

Don't use flimsy cookie sheets. They warp and do not heat evenly, and they can actually cause cookies to crack and/or burn. They also quickly discolor, meaning the cookie dough is touching baked-on grease instead of the pan. Some recipes for thin, wafer-type cookies simply will not work on flimsy cookie sheets. Buy thick, sturdy cookie sheets, available at cookware shops.

Baking sheets come with low sides and without sides. The ones without sides allow the air to circulate more evenly around the cookies. That said, we still prefer pans with sides—commonly referred to as jelly roll pans—because they can be used for baking drop cookies, pan and bar cookies, and sponge cakes.

For most cookies, we prefer to use a shiny, heavy aluminum cookie sheet. A good nonstick baking sheet can come in handy for wafers, meringues, and other cookies that tend to stick to the pan, but its dark surface tends to burn most cookies around the edges and bottoms before they're really cooked through the center. If you're using nonstick pans, count on shorter baking times.

We like **insulated baking sheets** for cookies. They consist of two layers of metal with a layer of air sandwiched between them. The air layer moderates the oven temperature, making the cookies bake slowly and evenly. Cookies take a minute or two longer to bake on insulated sheets. In fact, if your oven tends to run a bit hot, an insulated baking sheet can help offset the temperature.

Baking sheets come in many different sizes. We've found that the sheets that measure about 12 × 17 inches are ideal. They're large enough to hold 15 average drop cookies, but small enough to fit in most home ovens.

For pan cookies, you'll want a 10 × 15-inch pan with sides as well. Many bars are baked in cake pans: choose a 9 × 13-inch pan, and an 8-inch and/or 9-inch square pan. (Cookies will tolerate a little "fudging" on pan sizes; if a recipe calls for an 8-inch pan, you often can make it work in a 9-inch pan, or vice versa.)

You'll also want to buy **baking parchment**, a coated paper for lining baking sheets when you make cookies such as tuiles. Baking parchment is available in cookware shops and some supermarkets. Permanent non-stick liners (for lining cookie sheets when you bake meringues or other sticky cookies) are optional, but great to have on hand.

Electric Mixer

Although you can beat cookies by hand, an electric mixer makes life much easier. A good stand mixer kneads even heavy doughs and frees you to do other tasks while the butter is creaming. But unless you do a lot of baking, a good-quality hand mixer will suffice.

Food Processor

A food processor is handy for such chores as grinding nuts, grating citrus zests with sugar, and grinding oats. A food processor works wonders with pastry-type cookies that require cutting in of butter or other fat. It allows you to quickly and evenly cut in the fat without overheating the dough.

If you don't have a food processor, use a good pastry blender, a hand tool that consists of blades or wires curved into a semicircle and attached to a handle. You use it to work the fat into the flour in a chopping motion. The blade-style blenders work much better than those with wires.

Rolling Pin

Walk into any cookware shop—not to mention any antique store—and you'll see that rolling pins come in a mind-boggling array of sizes, weights, and materials. Fancy stuff aside, a rolling pin should be well-constructed and heavy for its size. Marble is great, but a nice, heavy wooden pin works fine.

Miscellaneous Utensils

A good **rubber spatula**, for scraping down the sides of bowls and folding in ingredients, is indispensable. You'll also need a thin, flexible **metal spatula**—a pancake turner—for transferring dough to cookie sheets and baked cookies to wire racks.

Ingredients

Almond Paste

Most supermarkets carry canned almond paste, a thick blend of almonds, sugar, and flavorings. Some stores also carry almond paste in tubes. Almond paste has the consistency of children's modeling dough, and needs to be broken up or smashed into small pieces.

Butter

It's best to use Grade AA unsalted, or "sweet," butter, which we believe has the cleanest cream flavor. If you have only salted butter on hand, subtract ¼ teaspoon salt from the recipe for each stick (½ cup) of butter used.

Butter may be frozen for up to six months, although it's best if you use it within four to six weeks. If possible, leave the butter in its box; otherwise, seal the wrapped sticks in additional foil. This helps keep out freezer flavors. Even if the butter does absorb flavors, they tend to disappear during baking.

Most cookie recipes call for butter at room temperature, meaning it is not hard but still holds its shape. Softened butter is butter that can be easily mashed with a spoon.

If you buy it in sticks, butter is easy to measure—just follow the lines on the package. If you buy it in pounds rather than sticks, measure it by weighing it or by packing it solidly into a dry-measure cup.

Candied Fruits, Peel, and Ginger

These are boiled in a sugar syrup until they turn into candy. Candied cherries and similar fruits taste like sugar, not fruit, and are used mainly to add color and texture to baked goods. Candied peel is mostly sweet, with traces of bitterness; it has a slightly perfumed flavor. Candied peels vary widely in quality; some can be unpleasantly bitter. You can get top-quality peel from some cookware and specialty shops (see Mail-Order Sources).

Unlike candied fruits, ginger retains most of its sweet-hot character when candied. It's a delicious addition to cookies. You can buy it sliced or diced, or you can make your own (page 291).

Chocolate and Cocoa

All chocolate begins with chocolate liquor, a bitter paste extracted from roasted cocoa beans. Unsweetened powdered cocoa is chocolate liquor from which nearly all of the fat (cocoa butter) has been removed. Unsweetened (baking) chocolate is chocolate liquor and cocoa butter.

To make bittersweet, semisweet, and sweet chocolates, processors add sugar, cocoa butter and/or lecithin, and flavorings such as vanilla to the chocolate liquor. **Bittersweet chocolate** contains at least 35 percent chocolate liquor by weight, and semisweet and sweet chocolates between 15 and 35 percent. Most bittersweet chocolate sold in this country comes from Europe, and you'll be more likely to find it in the candy aisle than the baking aisle in the supermarket (Lindt Excellence and Tobler Extra are two popular bittersweet chocolates).

Milk chocolate is sweet chocolate that also contains milk powder. It may contain as little as 10 percent chocolate liquor.

White chocolate contains no chocolate liquor and thus is not true chocolate. It does have cocoa butter, along with sugar, milk solids, lecithin, and vanilla. Confectionery or summer coating contains vegetable oil instead of cocoa butter. To further confuse matters, real white chocolate bars are often labeled "confectionery." To see if the package contains real white chocolate, check the ingredients list for cocoa butter.

To melt chocolate, chop or break the chocolate into small pieces. Use a microwave-proof bowl and make sure it's clean and absolutely dry; a drop or two of liquid can make chocolate "seize" (turn into a thick, gummy mess).

Microwave on 80 percent power (medium-high) for 1 minute, then give the chocolate a stir. Continue microwaving in 15-second increments, stirring occasionally, until melted and smooth.

You also can melt chocolate by placing the broken or chopped chocolate in the top of a double boiler over hot (not boiling) water. Chocolate burns easily, so do not melt it over direct heat.

Dark chocolate melts more smoothly than milk and white chocolates. Because they contain milk solids, they tend to stay fairly thick, like mayonnaise, when melted. You can thin them with a little vegetable oil or shortening. The same holds true for melted chocolate chips, which are formulated to keep their shape during baking.

Coconut

Although you can buy unsweetened coconut, cookies are almost always made with sweetened coconut. Flaked, shredded, or grated sweetened coconut is readily available in supermarkets. Toasting brings out its flavor. Spread the coconut out on a baking sheet and toast in a 350-degree oven for 5 to 8 minutes, until it is tinged with gold.

Cookie Crumbs

To crush graham crackers or cookies for crumbs, break them into pieces and toss them into the food processor, then grind away. Or, put the cookie pieces on a sheet of waxed paper, cover with another sheet of waxed paper, and pound and roll into crumbs with a rolling pin.

Dairy Products

Use whole sour cream and cream cheese in recipes; their low-fat counterparts contain binders that can change the texture of the cookie. Don't even think about using nonfat sour cream and cream cheese in cookies.

   If a cookie calls for a small amount of milk or cream, it doesn't matter what kind you use—anything from skim milk to heavy cream will do the trick.

   Buttermilk and yogurt give cookies a pleasant tang and, in partnership with baking soda, make them rise. If you do not have one or the other on hand, you can often substitute; see Equivalents and Substitutions on page 307.

Dried Fruits

Dried apricots, figs, prunes, currants, raisins, cherries, blueberries, apples, cranberries—all are readily available in large supermarkets these days. We're also listing dates here because many people may not realize they are fresh fruits. (They are so loaded with natural sugars that they seem dried.)

   After chopping dates or other sticky fruits to be added to dough, sprinkle them with a little sugar or flour so the pieces don't clump together.

   To plump dried fruits, soak them in liquor (such as rum) or hot water for 15 to 30 minutes. Drain and pat dry.

Eggs

Unless otherwise noted, by *eggs* we mean those labeled large. You may notice, by the way, that eggs vary quite a bit in size, even within the *large* category. That's because egg sizes are determined by weight; a dozen medium eggs weighs at least 21 ounces; a dozen large eggs 24 ounces; a dozen extra-large 27 ounces; a dozen jumbo 30 ounces.

In most cookie recipes, which call for only one or two eggs, it makes little difference which size of egg you use. For recipes that require three or more whole eggs, yolks, or whites, you might have to make adjustments if you use a different size; see Equivalents and Substitutions on page 307.

Flours

The vast majority of recipes in this book call for all-purpose flour. It is a medium-protein flour that is suitable for all-around baking. Bread flour is rarely used for cookies. Some cookies call for cake flour, which is lower in protein and creates a softer crumb.

All-purpose flour is bleached or unbleached. Bleached flour is whitened by chemical agents; unbleached flour grows whiter through natural aging and has a slightly higher protein content. For most cookies, all-purpose (bleached) flour works fine. You can use unbleached flour if you prefer. The reverse does not necessarily hold true—in recipes that specifically call for unbleached flour, that is the kind you should use.

Whole wheat flour, which is used in a few of the cookies, contains germ and bran and thus more natural oils, than regular flour. Cookies made with whole wheat flour tend to be more fragile and crunchy.

Note that flours can vary quite a bit from brand to brand, batch to batch, and year to year. The flour is the most variable ingredient in a recipe. The recipes were tested with national brands, but you could wind up using just a bit more or less flour than we call for, depending on the kind you're using. Fortunately, cookies are fairly forgiving. If the dough is a bit stiffer or stickier than it should be, it probably won't matter much.

Because flour is so variable, it's especially important to measure it accurately. First stir up the flour in the bag or canister. Dip a dry-measure cup into the flour to scoop up a heaping cupful. Then use a butter knife or the back of a scoop or spoon to level off the flour even with the top of the cup.

Honey, Molasses, Maple Syrup

Most supermarket **honey** is clover honey. Other honeys, with the exception of buckwheat, which has a strong flavor, will work fine in most cookies. Do not substitute liquid syrups such as honey or molasses for sugar in baked goods.

Warming honey or molasses briefly in the microwave makes it easier to pour. To measure sticky syrups, lightly oil the measuring cup first. The oil will keep them from sticking.

Maple syrup may carry a grade or not, depending on where it's produced. For baking, a dark syrup is best. In maple syrup country, you often can find Grade B syrup, a very dark, deeply flavored syrup ideal for baking. Otherwise, use dark or medium amber. A little maple extract helps boost the flavor.

Molasses is what's left over when sugar processors extract the sugar crystals from the boiled beet or cane liquid. Light molasses comes from the first boiling, and dark molasses from the second. Sulphur may or may not be used during processing, and unsulphured molasses tends to be sweeter and milder.

The kind of molasses you use depends on your taste as much as anything else. Dark molasses is slightly more bitter than light molasses—but its deeper flavor comes through better in cookies. Blackstrap molasses, from the third boiling of the syrup, has a harsh, burnt-bitter flavor that makes it a no-no for baking.

Honey and molasses are acidic. For best results, they should be paired with baking soda as a leavening.

Leavenings

All dry leavenings work the same way—they release carbon dioxide when they're mixed with liquid, forming gas bubbles that make baked goods rise.

Baking soda, or bicarbonate of soda, works in the presence of acid, which is why it's often the chief leavening in doughs that contain acidic ingredients such as honey, molasses, or buttermilk. Baking soda starts working as soon as it gets wet, so you should bake baking soda–leavened doughs as soon as possible.

Double-acting baking powder, the only kind you're likely to find on store shelves, contains baking soda, an acid ingredient (sometimes cream of tartar), and ingredients to keep it from caking. It acts in two stages, releasing some carbon dioxide when it gets wet, and more during baking.

Old-fashioned cookie recipes often call for **cream of tartar**, an acid that comes from crystals deposited on wine barrels. This practice dates back to the days when home bakers made their own baking powder with cream of tartar and baking soda. Cooks still routinely add cream of tartar to egg whites; its acid changes the egg proteins, making the whites easier to beat.

Lemon, Orange, and Lime Juice

Use fresh lemon and lime juices whenever possible. The bottled juices contain preservatives that give them an "off" flavor. In recipes that call for orange juice, fresh or pasteurized juice is best.

Liqueurs

Some recipes call for liqueurs or rum. Like fat, alcohol helps carry the flavors of the other ingredients. If you don't drink liqueurs or spirits but want to use them in baking, buy miniature bottles. Most liquor stores stock mini-bottles near the cash register.

Margarine

We prefer butter to margarine in most cookies because of its full, creamy flavor. In recipes that call for margarine, use hard stick margarine, not tub margarine.

You can try substituting margarine for butter in some of the recipes if you like. Be sure to use hard stick margarine; tub margarine contains too much liquid oil and air. We won't guarantee the results; in some cookies, using butter instead of margarine, or vice versa, can noticeably change not only the flavor, but the texture or shape. It's safest to substitute in cookies with a small amount of fat relative to the other ingredients.

Nonstick Cooking Spray

For our money, this is one of the cookie baker's best friends. It makes greasing cookie sheets a breeze. Baker's Joy, a combination of flour and nonstick cooking spray, is great for coating pans when you're baking sticky cookies such as meringues.

Nuts and Seeds

Nearly all nuts taste better toasted, but pecans, hazelnuts, pine nuts, and almonds especially perk up after a brief stay in the oven. Toasting also brings out the nutty flavor of sesame seeds.

To toast nuts, spread them in a single layer on a baking sheet with sides. Roast in a preheated 350-degree oven for 10 to 15 minutes, stirring once, until the nuts just begin to turn golden and smell toasted.

If you're toasting a small amount of **sesame seeds**, it's easier to use a small skillet. Put the seeds in a dry skillet and heat over medium heat, shaking the pan constantly, just until they begin to turn golden. Immediately pour them into a bowl.

Toasting **hazelnuts** is usually the recommended method for removing their thick, slightly bitter skins. You can roast them as directed above, or use lower heat—275 to 300 degrees, and roast them for anywhere from 30 minutes to an hour. They're ready to take out of the oven when the skins start splitting.

Remove them from the oven, let them cool briefly, then rub them between a clean, dry kitchen towel to remove the skins. Note that it's impossible to remove all of the skins this way; you just want most of the skins off.

If you encounter an especially stubborn batch of hazelnuts where the skins just refuse to come off easily, here's another trick we read about: Simmer the nuts for 2 minutes in 1 quart water to which you've added 3 tablespoons baking soda. Drain the nuts, dry them off with paper towels, then roast them at 350 degrees for about 10 minutes. The skins will slip right off. Because this method does have a tendency to soften the nuts, we recommend it only if roasting alone isn't working well, or if you want completely skin-free hazelnuts.

You can also use this method—minus the baking soda—if you need blanched almonds and have only whole almonds in the house.

To finely grind nuts in a food processor, grind them with a bit of the sugar or flour from the recipe to keep them from turning into a paste. If you grind nuts or spices frequently, you may want to buy a nut grinder or a coffee grinder (which will NOT be used for coffee) for the purpose. The sharper, faster blades mince the nuts without smashing them.

Nearly all kinds of nuts are available year-round these days. An exception is hazelnuts. In the spring and summer, we sometimes have trouble finding them in stores. For a mail-order source, see page 309. Also, supermarkets generally carry pistachios in the shell, but not necessarily the shelled nuts. Middle Eastern and Indian groceries as well as many health food stores carry shelled pistachios.

Oats

Rolled oats come in three varieties: Old-fashioned, the biggest flakes; quick-cooking, slightly smaller flakes; and instant, very fine flakes with added flavorings and, usually, sugar. Old-fashioned and quick-cooking oats work best in cookies. Although they absorb liquid differently, you can usually get by with substituting one for the other. Unless the recipe specifically calls for them, do not use instant oats.

Oat flour can add textural interest to chewy-style cookies such as chocolate chip or oatmeal. To make it, grind oats to a coarse powder in a blender or food processor. You can replace up to a fourth of the all-purpose flour with oat flour.

Spices

It's amazing what a difference good, fresh spices can make to baked goods. We follow one rule of thumb: Your nose knows. When you open the cinnamon jar, it should shout, "Cinnamon!" If your nose can barely distinguish between the allspice and the nutmeg, it's time to dump the spices and start over.

Sugar

Granulated sugar is made from sugar cane or sugar beets. The juice is clarified, cooked down to concentrate it, then crystallized. The resulting brown crystals are raw sugar. The molasses is removed and the crystals are further refined to produce white sugar. To measure granulated sugar, you can either spoon it into the cup or dip the cup into the sugar.

Brown sugar is white sugar with the addition of molasses and natural flavors and colors. One type of brown sugar is made by boiling the flavored molasses syrup until crystals form; another is made by adding the syrup to white sugar crystals. Brown sugar is higher in moisture than granulated sugar, and it makes cookies more chewy or crisp. **Dark brown sugar** has a stronger molasses flavor than light brown, but generally speaking, they're interchangeable in most cookies.

To measure brown sugar, spoon it into the cup and pack it down firmly.

Confectioners' or powdered sugar is white sugar that is ground to a powder and has cornstarch added to prevent clumping. It gives cookies a dry, melt-in-the-mouth quality. To measure confectioners' sugar, spoon it lightly into the cup.

If you use an electric mixer, you usually do not have to sift confectioners' sugar before adding it to doughs or icings. To sift it over cookies before serving, put about ¼ cup of confectioners' sugar in a small strainer and tap gently with your finger or a knife to dust it over the cookies.

Coarse granulated sugar is for decorations. Supermarkets carry coarse colored sugars; plain coarse sugar is available from some stores that carry cake-decorating supplies. If you're out of decorating sugar or can't find the color you want, you can work a dab of paste food color (not liquid color) into regular sugar with your fingers until the color is evenly distributed.

As a rule you cannot substitute one sugar for another. An exception is brown sugar—if you run out, you can make a close approximation with granulated sugar and molasses (see Equivalents and Substitutions, page 307).

Vanilla and Other Extracts

Extracts cost more than artificial flavorings—for good reason. Vanillin, for example, has an unpleasant chemical flavor that cannot compete with real vanilla.

Even real extracts vary widely. The best vanilla extracts contain only vanilla and alcohol. Most extracts also contain corn syrup or other sweeteners. This is acceptable as long as the sweetener is not predominant.

Vanilla is also available in its natural form, as beans—or to be more accurate, long seed pods. Vanilla beans have an intense aroma and flavor. To remove the seeds, slit the bean lengthwise, then scrape the black pulpy seeds out with a small paring knife. To keep vanilla beans for a long time, wrap them well in foil and freeze them.

A variety of other extracts are available: almond, anise, chocolate, coconut, lemon, maple, orange, peppermint, and rum. You should be able to find real almond and peppermint extracts in the supermarket, and usually lemon and orange. For other extracts, you might have to try a cookware shop, specialty food shop, or a mail-order source (see pages 309–310). If you cannot find a pure extract in the flavor you're looking for, use the flavoring.

Extracts enhance the flavors of similar ingredients. We often add a little chocolate extract to chocolate cookies, or a drop or two of lemon or orange extract to doughs that contain lemon or orange zest.

Vegetable Shortening

While butter makes cookies tender or crisp, vegetable shortening makes them flaky. It's the modern, less expensive stand-in for lard, or rendered pork fat, which once was widely used in flaky pastries. Unlike lard, shortening has no flavor, which is why we often pair it with butter.

For recipes in which you cut the shortening into the flour, pie crust–style, it helps if the shortening is cold. To chill it quickly, measure it out onto a small plate and stick it in the freezer for 10 minutes.

To measure shortening, use a rubber spatula to pack it tightly into a dry measure and level it off. Rinsing the measuring cup with cold water before you put in the shortening makes it easier to scoop it out.

Zest

This refers to the outermost, colored part of a citrus peel, minus the bitter white pith. The easiest way to get grated zest is to use a citrus zester, a small tool that has sharp-edged holes that you drag along the outside of the rind. It produces fine, long shreds; you can further mince them with a knife.

Another way is to use a vegetable peeler to peel off long strips of zest. You can then finely mince these strips, or better yet, chop them, then toss them into a food processor or blender with some or all of the sugar from the recipe. Process on high until the zest is finely flecked through the sugar. To estimate how much zest you'll get this way, see Equivalents and Substitutions on page 307.

The third way is to rub the orange or lemon over the fine holes of a grater, being careful to grate only the outermost skin.

To keep zest on hand for baking, grate the peel from several oranges or lemons. Put the zest in a small self-sealing freezer bag and store it in the freezer. It will keep for up to six months.

EQUIVALENTS AND SUBSTITUTIONS

Baking powder

1 teaspoon = ⅝ teaspoon cream of tartar + ¼ teaspoon baking soda

Butter

1 pound = 4 sticks = 2 cups

1 stick = 1 stick hard margarine or ½ cup vegetable shortening

1 stick salted = 1 stick unsalted plus ¼ teaspoon salt

Buttermilk

1 cup = ½ cup skim or 1% milk + ½ cup nonfat or low-fat plain yogurt

1 cup = 1 tablespoon lemon juice or white vinegar, plus enough skim or 1% milk to make 1 cup (use in doughs, but not icings)

1 cup yogurt = ¾ cup buttermilk

Chocolate

1 ounce unsweetened = 3 tablespoons unsweetened cocoa + 1 tablespoon melted shortening

2 ounces bittersweet = 1 ½ ounces semisweet + ½ ounce unsweetened

1 cup chocolate chips = approx. 6 ounces

Citrus juice

2 tablespoons = juice from 1 medium lemon, 1 large lime, or ½ medium orange

Citrus zest

1 tablespoon = grated zest from 2 medium lemons, 3 medium limes, or 1 large orange

1 tablespoon = 1 teaspoon lemon or orange extract

Eggs

1 or 2 large = same number of medium, extra-large or jumbo eggs

3 large = 2 jumbo, 3 medium, or 3 extra-large

4 large = 3 jumbo, 5 medium, or 4 extra-large

1 large egg white = 2 tablespoons

1 cup egg whites = 8 medium, 7 large, 6 extra-large, or 5 jumbo

Flour

1 cup cake flour = 1 cup minus 2 tablespoons all-purpose

1 cup whole wheat = ¾ cup all-purpose plus ¼ cup wheat bran or germ

Sugar

1 cup brown sugar = ⅞ cup granulated sugar plus 2 tablespoons molasses

MAIL-ORDER SOURCES

Sweet Celebrations
P.O. Box 39426
Edina, MN 55439
(800) 328-6722 or (612) 943-1508

Formerly Maid of Scandinavia. Huge assortment of cookie cutters, presses, and molds; decorating sugars; flavorings, including Cook's vanilla; chocolate including Callebaut and Nestle's Peter; gold leaf; baking equipment; food color pens. Catalog $2.

Williams-Sonoma
P.O. Box 7456
San Francisco, CA 94120-7456
(800) 541-2233

Fine European baking chocolate, cocoa, top-quality candied peel and crystallized ginger, baking equipment. Retail stores in many cities. Mail-order catalog available.

King Arthur Flour
P.O. Box 876
Norwich, VT 05055
(800) 827-6836

High-quality flours. Unbleached all-purpose, cake and pastry flours; professional-quality bread flours; whole-grain flours and whole grains; whole white wheat flour; Oatrim, an oat-derived fat substitute; and baking equipment.

Kitchen Krafts
P.O. Box 442
Waukon, Iowa 52170
(800) 776-0575
Fax: (800) 850-3093

Cookie cutters and scoops, parchment paper, coarse sugar, and other baking supplies. Catalog $1.

American Spoon Foods
P.O. Box 566
Petoskey, MI 49770
(800) 222-5886

Dried cherries (tart and sweet), blueberries, and cranberries; nuts, including wild nuts such as hickory and butternuts; high-quality and unusual preserves, jams, butters, and jellies.

Penzey's, Ltd.
P.O. Box 1448
Waukesha, WI 53187
(414) 574-0277
Fax: (414) 574-0278

Outstanding spices, spice blends, and extracts. Cinnamon is a specialty.

Dundee Hazelnuts
P.O. Box 185
Dundee, OR 97115
(503) 537-2959 (voice and fax)

Oregon hazelnuts in gift packs; also available in bulk.

Cook's Flavoring Company
P.O. Box 890
Tacoma, WA 98401
(800) 735-0545

Top-quality vanilla, maple, and other extracts. Products available in many gourmet shops; also by mail.

Index

A

After-dinner mints, 117
All-purpose flour, about, 300
Almond
   crescents, chocolate tipped, 132–133
   and pine nut cookies, Romanian, 201–202
   squares, 76
   tuiles, Pierre Pollin's, 183–184
   wafers, 50
Almond cookies
   Chinese, 225
   curried, 128
Almond paste
   about, 297
   macaroons, 55
Altitude, 5–6
Amaretto cream cheese, chocolate cherry bars
      with, 63
Angels, 234–235
Anise
   flavored Scandinavian stamp cookies, 190
   lemon thins, 108
Apple
   black walnut bars with, 66
   fig bars, whole wheat, 152–153
   oatmeal cinnamon bar cookies filled with,
      90–91
Applesauce bars, 67
Apricot
   bars, 84
   filling, cottage cheese strudel with,
      162–163
Arabian-style sesame seed cookies, 218
Autumn leaves, 110

B

Backpacker's bars, 98
Baking parchment, 296
Baking powder, about, 301–302
Baking sheets, insulated, 295–297
Baking soda, about, 301
Banana
   chip cookies, 36
   and coconut bars, 72–73
Bar cookies, about, 57–58
Barnyard at Christmas, 269–279
Basic butter cookies, 230
   chocolate glazed walnut bar, 231–232
Basic soft peanut butter cookies, 237
Basic sugar cookies, 233
Basic vanilla buttercream frosting, 282
Basil lemon refrigerator cookies, 123
Belgian tea biscuits, 188
Berry–cherry, cream cheese triangles
      and, 115
Bev Bennett's Parmesan sticks, 124
Biscochitos, 221
Biscotti, pistachio, 203
Bittersweet chocolate, about, 298
Black walnut
   apple bars, 66
   sandwich cookies, 148
Blond brownies, 64
Blueberry cheesecake squares, 75
Blue cheese, walnut crackers, 127
Bougatsa, 212–213
Brownies
   blond, 64
   classic chocolate lover's, 59
   marbled chocolate–peanut butter,
      60–61
   pizza with all the trimmings, 248–249
   toffee, 62
Brown sugar
   about, 304
   cookies, with burnt butter icing, 14
Buñuelos, 222
Burnt butter, 292
   icing, 285
Busia Kwiecien's coffee nuggets, 131